STATES OF INJUSTICE

States of Injustice

A Guide to Human Rights and Civil Liberties in the European Union

Michael Spencer

Pluto Press

First published 1995 by Pluto Press
345 Archway Road, London N6 5AA

British Library Cataloguing in Publication Data
A catalogue record for this book is available from the British Library

ISBN 0 7453 0979 8 hbk

Library of Congress Cataloging in Publication Data
Available from the Library of Congress

Designed and produced for Pluto Press by
Chase Production Services, Chipping Norton, OX7 5QR
Typeset from disk by Stanford DTP Services, Milton Keynes
Printed in the EC by TJ Press, Padstow, England

Contents

Acknowledgements

The research for this book could not have been done without grants to cover travel and other expenses from the Nuffield Foundation and the Lyndhurst Settlement. This made it possible to visit first Brussels and then 20 other cities in France, Germany, the Netherlands, Italy, Spain and Sweden. While there I was able to talk with more than a hundred experts in various fields, all of whom provided essential insights into the problems facing both their own countries and the European Union as a whole. They were also generous in supplying published and unpublished material for later analysis and citation. Without these personal contacts I would not have felt able to tackle with any confidence the range of subjects covered here.

It would be invidious to mention individuals by name out of so large a number, but I would like to thank all those I met for giving up their time so readily. When it came later to writing the various chapters, those I approached again with a request to check what I had written were equally helpful in agreeing immediately to help and in offering comments at short notice. A number of friends and associates in the UK were also invaluable in this respect. Many others from NGOs and institutions responded readily to requests for specific items of information. The custodians of the European Parliament and Commission libraries in London were exceptionally helpful in keeping me up to date with relevant documents. Any mistakes or omissions in the book remain, of course, my own. Finally I would like to thank the Civil Liberties Trust for administering the grants and making its library and other facilities available.

Michael Spencer
March 1995

Introduction

This is a book with two main purposes. On the one hand, as its title indicates, it is a general and comparative study of current problems in human rights and civil liberties in the countries of the European Union (EU). At a more basic level it is a handbook on how the whole system works: how laws are made at the European level, what the defects of the system are, and what might be done to improve things.

It used to be assumed that the former European Economic Community had little cause for concern about human rights within its own boundaries. We shall see that this complacency is far from justified. A number of factors have conspired to undermine the consensus that led to the universal signing of international treaties like the Convention Relating to the Status of Refugees (the Geneva Convention) and the European Convention on Human Rights, not to mention the various treaties and declarations drawn up by the United Nations. Although politicians still pay lip service to the standards set by these agreements, their actions when in government increasingly belie their words. Other problems have arisen which were not anticipated when the Community was founded: racism, for instance, has emerged as an endemic disease of Europe that can break out unexpectedly in new and ugly forms, and no effective action to counteract it has been agreed.

This abandonment of principles arises from governments being faced with problems that have been either ignored for too long or simply not foreseen. Some of the problems are a logical outcome of the drive to establish a common market without internal frontiers. The purpose of the Single European Act of 1987 was to establish a single market in which free movement of 'goods, persons, services and capital' was guaranteed. The initial motivation was purely economic.

Now it is possible for goods to be transported back and forth across the Union without hindrance, leading to such an increase in traffic that environmentalists express alarm about the pollution and energy costs involved. International capital flows freely between countries of the Union so that profits can be maximised. Clearly businesses have

1

benefited, with multinationals taking full advantage of the opening up of the vast new internal market. However, the idea of abolishing internal frontier controls led early on to expressions of alarm from some police and customs officers who feared that Europe would be swamped by an uncontrollable tide of international crime and terrorism.

The pressure thus grew to establish a 'fortress Europe' with tight external borders on the UK model, together with increased internal checks on the activities of individuals. National governments were eager to be seen to be doing something about the supposed threats to public order and security. They agreed with each other on restrictive measures that took scant account of the need to safeguard individual rights. Cooperation between police forces and other state agencies was allowed to develop without ensuring proper lines of accountability for their activities.

Other problems have been external in origin, though the countries of Western Europe can be accused of helping to create them in the first place. The desperate poverty and political instability of much of the Third World have generated enormous numbers of would-be immigrants and refugees at the very time when the gates of the fortress are clanging shut. With rising unemployment within the Union, popular prejudice (fuelled by some politicians and by the media) has led to calls for their exclusion. Applicants for asylum or for immigration to work in Europe now find themselves lumped with terrorists and drug smugglers as 'undesirables' to be kept out.

With honourable exceptions, now becoming fewer, the Member States of the Union have used the wording of the Geneva Convention to label as less deserving or even 'bogus' all asylum-seekers who are not subject to individual persecution. Their journeys are categorised as 'disorderly movements' or 'irregular migration'. A new class of euphemisms has been coined to make the actions of governments more acceptable: 'accelerated procedures' to speed up expulsion and 're-admission agreements' enabling unwanted immigrants and rejected asylum seekers to be forcibly returned to neighbouring countries such as Poland and Romania. These states, as aspiring members of the Union, are in turn negotiating similar agreements with an outer ring of more distant states. The root causes of the influx include poverty arising from worsening terms of trade and conflicts incited by the former combatants in the Cold War. They are well known but apparently beyond the capacity of the Union to tackle in any but a token manner.

Apart from the question of whether this response to human need is worthy of a Union of advanced and prosperous countries, or even sensible in the longer term, it is becoming clear that for everyone inside the fortress there could well be negative consequences. These are likely to be most pronounced for those who lack citizenship of the Union, which at present is synonymous with nationality of a Member State. The number of legally resident 'third-country nationals' (also called 'non-EU nationals) not having this citizenship is about 10 million. In addition, an unknown number of illegal residents extract a precarious living in the 'black economy' of underpaid workers who enjoy none of the protection of the Union's social policy.

The contribution of both groups to the economy of the Union must be considerable, but their only reward when unemployment increases is to be stigmatised as taking jobs away from honest Europeans. Worse still, the well-publicised efforts of governments to keep out illegal immigrants and 'bogus' asylum seekers result in public suspicion and hostility directed at all those whose appearance implies a non-European origin. New arrivals and non-white citizens of long standing are equally affected. Racist attitudes and violent attacks have increased all over the Union, yet the governments of the Member States have refused to accept that such problems arise from Union policy or come within the legal competence of the Union institutions. Mainstream politicians anxious to achieve re-election have tended to adopt the agenda of the far right and invoke a nationalistic prejudice against foreigners.

The 'compensatory measures' of internal control that follow border abolition bear unequally on different groups in society. It is the non-white resident who stands to suffer most from random interrogation and harassment – not only by the police, but increasingly by the officials administering state benefits, health services and local authority housing. In a further effort to hunt down 'illegals', employers are likely in future to be visited by inspectors charged with seeking them out. Increased alienation from the authorities and mistrust between white and non-white groups will be difficult to avoid or counteract, and some governments seem to have given it little thought. Furthermore, an increased emphasis on identity checks – whether directed against international criminals or illegal immigrants – is also likely to affect other groups such as young people, and anyone whose appearance is unconventional. The 'chilling effect' associated with a feeling of being perpetually watched and checked up on by the authorities should not be underestimated.

SOCIAL POLICY AND INDIVIDUAL RIGHTS

Various individual rights exist under Community law which come under the general heading of economic and social rights – equal pay for equal work by women and men is an example – and here again the Union is facing some new problems. There is an ongoing and sometimes acrimonious dialogue between institutions of the Union (the Council, the Commission and the European Parliament) about how rapidly and how vigorously particular areas of social policy should be developed. A major unresolved question is the extent to which third-country nationals should benefit, especially where voting rights and the freedom to move in search of work are concerned; the more civil and political rights are offered to citizens, the greater the gap between citizens and non-citizens. Another area of debate is privacy and data protection, where the interests of the individual may conflict with those of governments and business. Other issues arise from major differences between the laws of Member States affecting particular groups such as lesbians and gay men.

In all of this, social policy and the guaranteeing of individual rights have really been no more than means to the end of establishing an internal market in labour as well as in goods. It has always been clear that if fair competition between Member States is to operate, then there is a need for minimum standards of working conditions and social policy affecting workers. Without such standards, competition can be distorted when a Member State encourages exploitation of its workers as a means of reducing export prices and attracting investment from abroad. Recognition of the need to guarantee specific workers' rights in labour relations has taken longer to achieve, and even now this topic is relegated to a Social Protocol of the Maastricht treaty which the UK refused to endorse.

The Treaty of Rome established two areas where legislation was essential: equal treatment at work of men and women, and health and safety requirements. Other areas were proposed in the non-binding Social Charter of 1989 and incorporated into the Social Protocol mentioned above. Apart from workers, other categories such as students and pensioners have benefited from rules allowing them free access to other Member States.

Many people feel, however, that piecemeal adoption of particular rights for utilitarian reasons is not enough; they argue (as will be done here) that social policy should be a driving force for the Union on at least an equal footing with the economic imperative. Although this principle did not find its way into the wording of the Maastricht treaty, it was in fact espoused as an aim by 'summit' meetings of government leaders in 1988 and 1989 and repeated in the Social Charter.

As the publicity material from the Commission so often reminds us, we are supposed to be living in a 'people's Europe'. For this to be fully achieved it will probably be necessary to establish a legally binding Union catalogue of fundamental rights applying to citizens and non-citizens alike. This will be all the more important as new applications for membership of the Union are considered from countries where respect for individual rights by the state is a relatively novel concept. Indeed it would not come amiss in the UK, the only Member State with neither a written Constitution nor an enforceable Bill of Rights.

THE FUTURE OF THE UNION

A highly polarised debate on the future form of the Union has taken place in Britain and a few other countries. However, there was until recently a broad consensus in most Member States that it was going in the right direction. It was assumed that the European Community would evolve with time to give the 'ever closer union among the peoples of Europe' referred to in both the original Treaty of Rome and the amending Treaty on European Union agreed at Maastricht in 1992. The Union's policy of fostering closer economic links between Member States was believed to be a guarantee against a repetition of the devastating wars of the first half of the century.

Events in the former Yugoslavia have now shown all too clearly that such links alone do not save a federation of nations from bitter conflict. Possible future enlargement of the Union to 30 or more Member States has also raised new doubts about the federal ideal. To add to this, economic recession has made the financial benefits of the Union much less obvious to the ordinary person. Popular disillusion with the 'big idea' of Europe has thus risen with increased unemployment, and called into question the direction the Union has been taking. The Union will have to deal more successfully with its outstanding problems before people are prepared to trust the promises of its leaders. Intergovernmental conferences on revising the founding treaties of the Union, such as the one preceding Maastricht, now attract a great deal more critical attention and public debate. Human rights and civil liberties need to be included in that debate.

A second major theme of this book is therefore the future reform of the Union's institutions and their legal powers. Without such reform, the commitment in the Maastricht treaty to respect the European Convention on Human Rights (see Chapter 2) cannot be taken at face value. A major defect of the treaty is that, like all its predecessors, it leaves too many matters affecting human rights to be decided in secret by representatives of national governments. There is then no possibility of democratic control beyond the notional responsibility of each government to its electorate. This is a quite inadequate safeguard where joint policies are agreed at an intergovernmental level. Community law, the European Parliament and the European Court of Justice have no role to play in some of the most sensitive areas of Union policy.

The term 'democratic deficit' is used to cover two aspects of a central problem affecting the Union in all areas of policy, whether coming under Community law or not. Firstly it describes the inability of national parliaments to exercise the control over decision-making which their governments signed away on joining the Union. The secrecy of Council decision-making means that parliaments (and hence their electorates) have little opportunity to influence negotiations between ministers. Secondly it represents the refusal of those same governments, supposedly acting in the interests of their respective parliaments and peoples, to cede an equivalent right of initiative and degree of control to the directly elected European Parliament and, in some areas, the European Court of Justice as well. This results in vital areas of policy being determined not just by the Council of Ministers, but also by powerful unelected committees and working groups. These are dominated by officials representing the Council, the Commission Secretariat-General and the individual Member States.

The need for change in many areas of policy is recognised not only by the European Parliament, which at present has little power to force an issue on to the agenda, but also by some sections of the much-maligned Commission. The latter can never push measures through a hostile Council of Ministers, and in asylum and immigration policy its proposals have been criticised for echoing the Council line too closely. However, it sometimes uses its unique power of initiating legislation to put forward proposals which enlarge the scope of social policy and respond to urgent problems. In other cases it recommends the drafting of non-binding agreements between Member States, particularly where non-citizens of the Union are concerned. Specific remedies may end up by being rejected, but the issues remain on the table for further discussion. The Commission relies on a broad range of supporting bodies to justify returning at intervals to important issues where nothing has been agreed. These include sympathetic Member States, the European Parliament, and non-governmental organisations (NGOs) of all kinds.

A further ground for hope lies in the fact that the founding treaties of the Union are periodically reviewed; the next intergovernmental conference following the Maastricht negotiations is fixed for 1996. Such a review is a window of opportunity for all those with an interest in changing the treaties, and powerful lobbies for special interest groups are active long before negotiations start. NGOs have learnt the value of such lobbying, and those that can afford it already have permanent offices in Brussels. Their aim is usually to insert into the treaties the power to make binding laws to help vulnerable groups in society and protect individual rights, where previous attempts to do so have been rejected as 'outside Union competence'. By individual or group lobbying and by supporting NGOs and joining their campaigns, everyone has a chance to influence the ultimate outcome.

SUMMARY OF CONTENTS

The book starts with a guide to the confusing decision-making structure of the Union, as amended by the Maastricht treaty. The next chapter is on the protection of human rights in Europe. It brings out the often-missed distinction between the European Union and the older Council of Europe, whose influence on the Union (particularly through its European Court of Human Rights) is far from negligible. Later chapters examine particular areas of concern: measures flowing from the abolition of internal frontiers, the treatment of refugees, immigration policy, racism and discrimination, police cooperation, and data protection. The chapters explain which individual rights are covered by Community law and capable of improvement in this way, and which are currently left to the decisions of national governments.

Particular attention is given to the 'grey area' of matters coming under Title VI of the Maastricht treaty. This covers the vital field of justice and home affairs, including highly sensitive areas of policy which remain the least accessible to democratic control by European or national parliaments. Judicial control is crucial here as well.

Discussion of these topics is then illustrated by 'snapshots' of seven Member States, selected from the 15 countries which now make up the Union (Austria, Belgium, Denmark, Finland, France, Germany, Greece, Ireland, Italy, Luxembourg, the Netherlands, Portugal, Spain, Sweden and the UK). This supplements the information in previous chapters covering all Member States. The aim here is to concentrate on the special problems facing states that fall in particular broad categories: founder members, later recruits and very new members; countries with a long history of immigration, and those for which it is a new experience. The responses of governments are discussed in the light of the differing mechanisms that exist for national monitoring of respect for human rights.

Throughout these chapters the reader will encounter words and phrases that have acquired special meanings in 'Eurospeak' as a shorthand for quite complex concepts: subsidiarity, transparency, the *acquis communautaire* and so on, not to mention the baffling acronyms that are a Brussels speciality. All these are defined where they first occur, and the location of each definition is included in the Index.

Finally, the key issues for reform emerging from earlier chapters are summarised. Throughout the book, original references drawn from various countries are given for those wishing to track information to its source and carry out further studies. As an aid to communication between interested readers and the many NGOs active in the field, an Appendix lists a selection of national and international bodies which can provide more detailed information on every topic. Nobody need feel that they are alone in wishing for change or unable to exert any influence. The only problem is getting together to work for it.

1

Europe after Maastricht

FROM COMMUNITY TO UNION

Even before the Treaty on European Union (TEU) or the Maastricht treaty came into force on 1 November 1993,[1] most people would have had difficulty in explaining to a visiting Martian exactly how the European Economic Community (as it then was) produced its new rules and regulations. The predecessor to this book[2] included a step-by-step explanation of the system in operation. After Maastricht the situation became even more complicated. As well as introducing numerous amendments to the existing Treaty of Rome,[3] the new treaty included Protocols or 'opt-outs' applying only to certain governments (particularly that of the UK). In addition, a large 'grey area' of policy-making in justice and home affairs appeared for the first time in Title VI of the treaty; in this case the normal rules of Community decision-making were not to apply. Foreign affairs, formerly covered by European Political Cooperation under Article 30 of the Single European Act, were similarly treated under Title V of the TEU. Titles V and VI formed, respectively, the second and third 'pillars' of the treaty to complement the first 'pillar' of the amended Treaty of Rome. Title VI has attracted heavy criticism from the European Parliament and from every campaigning group in the field.

To understand the problems arising in European human rights and civil liberties, we need to get to grips with the details of this treaty and its predecessors. This chapter is for those who need some help in doing so. Because certain topics were deliberately omitted from all the treaties, some of the problems now afflicting the Member States still cannot be properly tackled. This is one reason why the planned revision of the treaties in 1996 is of such importance.

The European Economic Community or EEC (the 'common market') was originally one of three associations of Member States, the others being the European Coal and Steel Community and the European Atomic Energy Community. The 1965 Brussels treaty (the 'merger treaty')[4] and the Single European Act brought all three under the umbrella of the 'European Communities'. The TEU completed the tidying-up process; the EEC was renamed the European Community (EC) to recognise that its aims were not purely economic, while the new Articles of the treaty used the words 'European Union' – a symbolic term already introduced in the preamble to the Single European Act. To avoid confusion it was agreed that the Community could commonly be referred to in future as the Union.[5]

The TEU did not change the principal institutions of the Union: the European Parliament, the Council, the Commission and the Court of Justice, with the court of Auditors now elevated to an equal status. It retained the advisory function of the Economic and Social Committee (see below and Chapter 2). However, it did change the rules regarding which topics were to be subject to Community law; which decisions required unanimous approval by Member States; and which were to be subject to 'qualified majority voting' (see below). It also introduced a new and more complex procedure of decision-making for certain topics only, and included a Protocol on Social Policy which applied to every Member State except the UK. The whole treaty was a curiously muddled product of the intense bargaining between Member States which preceded the signing ceremony.

Finally, as mentioned above, the TEU included, for the first time, specific provisions in Title VI on topics that previously had lain entirely outside the scope of the Treaty of Rome. In this field of justice and home affairs, covering sensitive topics such as policy on refugees and immigrants, cooperation had grown up in an entirely *ad hoc* manner, discussed in a plethora of intergovernmental committees that met in secret. The immediate effect of the treaty was, however, minimal: the various committees simply changed their names to accommodate the reform. The most glaring omission was the lack of any mechanism to put these areas under proper democratic scrutiny by the European Parliament and judicial control by the Court of Justice. Only for certain topics was there provision for the Court to be involved after a unanimous decision by the Council. For MEPs, the only marginal improvement was a right to ask parliamentary questions on such matters.

THE INSTITUTIONS

The *European Parliament*,[6] now enlarged to 626 seats distributed very roughly in proportion to the populations of the 15 Member States, is directly elected every five years. It meets in Strasbourg for a five-day session in every month except August, sometimes with an extra session in October to discuss the Community budget. Its administration (including research and publications) is based in Luxembourg and most other meetings (of committees, working parties and so on) take place in Brussels, where the Commission is based. Rivalry between governments has so far prevented its activities from being concentrated in one place, so the members spend a great deal of their time travelling.

Members sit not in national groups but in broad political alliances in which left and right are at present quite closely balanced; the two largest groups are the Party of European Socialists and the centre-right European People's Party. The absence of 'government' and 'opposition' parties means that the political groups spend less time abusing each other than is common in national parliaments; more often they join together to urge some course of action on the Council and Commission. The specialist committees (Chapter 2) also work more by consensus, and leave the plenary sessions of the Parliament to vote on whether to accept or reject their reports.

Unfortunately the powers of the Parliament remain limited, even after some improvements introduced at Maastricht, and the members yearn for a more meaningful role in the law-making process. On many issues the role of the Parliament is still in effect only consultative, though it can now veto certain legislative proposals; previously the Council always had the last word. The Parliament gained the right to examine each of the Member States' nominees for membership of the Commission, though (as before) it can only reject the entire Commission as a body, a drastic step which it has never taken. It also has the right to be consulted over the choice of the Commission's President.[7] In 1994 the Parliament narrowly approved Jacques Santer as the European Council's compromise candidate.

The Parliament can also reject or amend the annual budget presented to it, and has a final say on most non-agricultural spending. Drastic action involving total rejection has only rarely been taken, and critics of the system complain that the Parliament is too fond of making empty threats of this kind when it feels strongly that (for instance) it should be consulted on a topic which lies outside its usual powers. The bluff is usually called. The underlying problem is that, although directly elected, the Parliament is reluctant to be accused of being a 'loose cannon' intent only on blocking initiatives over which it has no real power. We shall return later to the major problem posed by this 'democratic deficit'.

The *Council* [8] (often called the Council of Ministers) comprises a representative of each Member State at ministerial level, which means that the composition varies with the topic: thus the different agriculture ministers make up the Agriculture Council, and so on. The presidency of the Council rotates between countries every six months. Twice a year (or exceptionally more often) there is a 'summit' meeting of the European

Council comprising the various heads of state or government, together with the President of the Commission; national foreign ministers are also present.

As explained below, the Council still retains the greatest power to make or break a proposal for new legislation. However, unlike a national government or cabinet, it is not the executive body of the Community – that is the Commission's role – and it cannot initiate new Community laws. It normally acts only in response to a detailed proposal by the Commission, though like the Parliament it can request the Commission to draft new legislation. For the intergovernmental cooperation covered by Titles V and VI of the TEU, where Community legislation is not at present envisaged, the Commission has a reduced role and the Parliament virtually none; the Council and the European Council reign supreme.

The detailed work of negotiation between Member States is done first by specialist working groups of national civil servants and then by the Committee of Permanent Representatives (COREPER),[9] composed of senior civil servants or diplomats. COREPER prepares the ground for each Council meeting, and if agreement has been reached at this level there is generally no further debate.

The *Commission*[10] (often called the European Commission[11]) has 17 members with at least one national of each Member State. Its members are, however, bound to act in the general interest of the Community and not as national representatives. This was a point never appreciated by Margaret Thatcher, who once refused (when she was UK Prime Minister) to reappoint Lord Cockfield – whose views on Europe she disliked – as a UK-nominated Commissioner. The Commission has several tasks: apart from implementing decisions approved by the Council and the Parliament, it acts as a guardian of the Community treaties. This means that it can make its own proposals for legislation to implement any aim laid down in the treaties, such as Article 119 EC which requires men and women to receive equal pay for equal work. It does not have to wait to be asked, though both the Council and (since Maastricht) the Parliament can formally request the Commission to submit proposals.[12] It can also take a Member State to the Court of Justice for a failure to implement the treaties, and investigate complaints about a Member State from any quarter, including individuals.

The Commission is thus much more than a civil service and more like an executive body, which is why its members are political appointees subject to a vote of confidence by the Parliament. Its powers are strictly limited by the treaties. Contrary to popular belief, the executive staff of the Commission (who, like most civil servants, are recruited by examination) are not very numerous; translators are, however, required in large numbers to render everything into the various official languages

– eleven at the time of writing, but likely to increase as more states join the Union. The Commission is sensitive to the accusation that it dictates policy in a non-democratic way, and considers representations from the Parliament even when not required by law to do so. It also operates a relatively open style of policy-making which commercial lobbyists from all over the world have long made use of; in recent years NGOs have also appreciated the value of maintaining an office in Brussels.

The Commission is, since Maastricht, to be appointed as a body every five years starting in 1995, in the months following the election of each new Parliament. Each Commissioner has areas of special responsibility. The staff are organised into a Secretariat-General – a powerful body, also involved in secret discussions coming under Title VI – and various Directorates-General (DGs). Each DG contains several directorates, divided further into divisions with special responsibilities.[13] The DG most relevant to this book is DGV which covers employment, industrial relations and social affairs; this includes equal opportunities for women, migration policy, and free movement of workers. DGV also works on issues such as racism and other forms of discrimination that are not yet covered by Community law. DGXV covers the operation of the internal market and also deals with data protection, a topic with ramifications beyond the limits of Community law. Human rights are only specifically mentioned in the brief of DGIA (external political relations) – a curious allocation of responsibility, implying that problems in human rights exist only outside the Union. Its small human rights division was previously part of the Secretariat-General.

The *Court of Justice*,[14] commonly called the European Court of Justice (ECJ) to avoid confusion, is based in Luxembourg. It should not be confused with the European Court of Human Rights, a Strasbourg-based body set up by the Council of Europe (Chapter 2). The ECJ consists of 13 judges, appointed for six-year terms by agreement between Member States. There is also a *Court of First Instance*,[15] set up in 1988 to reduce the backlog of cases awaiting the ECJ; it considers certain cases brought by individuals and 'legal persons' (such as companies), with a right of appeal to the ECJ on a point of law. The ECJ is assisted by six Advocates-General, whose preliminary opinions are usually followed by the Court.

The ECJ is the final arbiter on the interpretation of the treaties governing the Union, and acts as a supreme court with authority over all national courts. Where there is doubt concerning the consistency of national and Community laws, any appropriate court of a Member State may ask the ECJ for a ruling. Such a ruling can even suspend the operation of a national act of parliament, pending full adjudication on whether it conflicts with Community law; thus the ECJ has a power which in Britain (which lacks a constitutional court) the national courts do not have. If the ECJ's final decision goes against the Member State, its national legislation has to change. Under the TEU the ECJ also has a new power to levy fines on a Member State, following a complaint from the Commission over non-compliance with Community legislation.

Although the European Convention on Human Rights (Chapter 2) is not incorporated into Community law, Article F TEU does require Member States to respect the fundamental rights guaranteed by this Convention. The ECJ had already shown an increasing willingness to take the Convention into account when making its rulings, and the TEU gave further justification for this. It also left open the possibility that the ECJ would be given jurisdiction over matters at present outside its control. Under Article K.3, a Convention between Member States in the fields of judicial cooperation or police cooperation may stipulate that the ECJ has the power to interpret the Convention and rule on any disputes. All in all, its power is likely to increase with time. It is fortunate that it has so far been well respected for the correctness of its judgments.

The remaining Community bodies are the *Court of Auditors*, the *Economic and Social Committee* (abbreviated as ESC to avoid confusion with the United Nations body ECOSOC which bears the same title), the *Committee of the Regions* and the *European Investment Bank*. Only the second of these will be considered in this book.

THE DECISION-MAKING PROCESS

Community law is expressed in the ways listed below, depending on the topic:[16] the European Parliament is involved in most but not all of them.

- *Regulations*[17] are binding in their entirety and are immediately applicable to all Member States. They are not widely used in the fields covered by this book, but are more commonly issued to implement 'secondary legislation' in areas such as agricultural policy.
- *Directives* are also binding and can be addressed to all Member States, but the method of achieving the result is left to each national government; this can, for instance, be done by introducing new legislation or by amending existing laws. Many of the topics discussed here are the subject of existing or proposed Directives.
- *Decisions* are binding instructions that can be addressed to a particular government, enterprise or individual. They are also used to implement a change in the composition of the Community, as when a new Member State is admitted.

- *Recommendations, Opinions* and *Declarations*, which can be issued by the Commission alone, are not binding.
- *Resolutions,* issued jointly by the Member States after agreement within the Council, are not specified in the treaty and are also non-binding; they can, however, be significant expressions of intent by the Member States in areas not covered by Community law. The European Parliament also expresses its views by such means.

Most of the binding legal instruments are announced in the *Official Journal of the European Communities,* but long before this point is reached there will be draft proposals issued by the Commission; these may be amended and reissued during the legislative process.[18] Where binding legislation is involved, the European Parliament can be involved in one of four different ways:[19]

- *Assent,* the simplest of the four procedures, involves confirmation by the Parliament of a proposal put forward by the Council (with or without the initiative of the Commission, depending on the topic). Some topics require only a simple majority of the votes cast; others (such as the accession of a new Member State) require an absolute majority of the Parliament's membership. Without the necessary majority the proposal fails.
- *Consultation* (Figure 1 overleaf), now restricted to relatively few topics; the Parliament votes by a simple majority while the Council votes either by a qualified majority (see below) or by unanimity only (not counting abstentions). Under this procedure, the topic most relevant to this book is that of visa controls (Chapter 3).[20]
- *Cooperation* (Figure 1), a procedure introduced by the Single European Act.[21] This increases the power of the Parliament to suggest amendments to a proposal, but the last word remains with the Council if it is unanimous. In several key areas it has now been replaced by codecision (see below).
- *Codecision* (Figure 2), the new procedure devised at Maastricht.[22] Although falling short of what the Parliament hoped for, it does for the first time allow the Parliament to veto a proposal to which it remains opposed after all the necessary consultation has taken place. There is a built-in hurdle to be surmounted in this case, since the Parliament must summon up an absolute majority of its membership to exercise the veto – not an easy matter when no single political group may have an overall majority.

The last two procedures are subject to time limits for completion of the later stages of the process, but there is no limit to the time taken by the Parliament to deliver its initial Opinion. It may deliberately delay doing this and bargain with the Commission for changes.

There is also no limit to the time taken by the Council to reach its Common Position (see Figures 1 and 2). This can involve every sentence being the subject of negotiation between officials representing the Member States, and as a result it may take months or even years for a proposal to become law. The Commission may revise the proposal

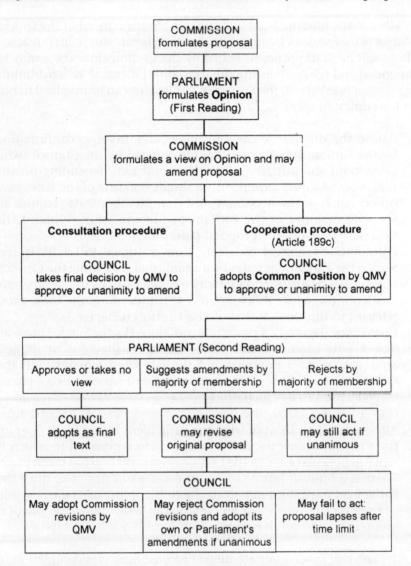

Figure 1 Consultation and cooperation; QMV = qualified majority vote (see text)

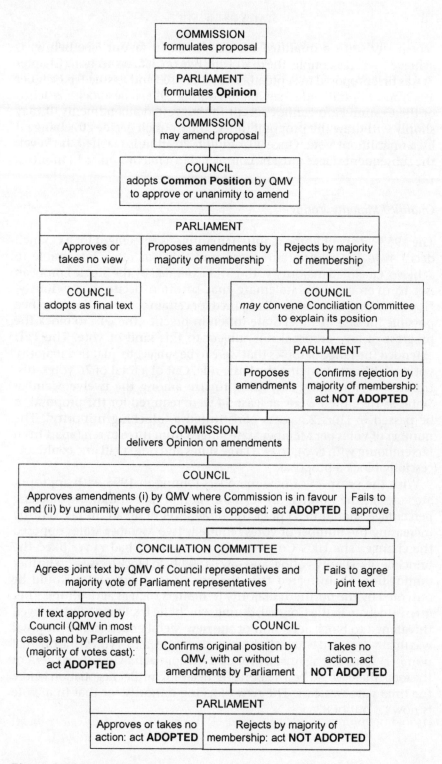

Figure 2 The new codecision procedure (Article 189b); QMV = qualified majority vote (see text)

repeatedly until a qualified majority vote in favour (see below) is achieved. As an example, the draft Directive on data protection (Chapter 7) was first proposed in September 1990, revised and reissued in October 1992, and was still under negotiation during 1995. If deadlock is reached or the Commission cannot accept the suggested amendments, it may simply withdraw the proposal unless the Council decides to change it by a unanimous vote. Once a Common Position is reached, however, the subsequent stages must be completed in a maximum of 13 months.

Qualified Majority Voting

The 1957 Treaty of Rome required unanimous agreement for a Council decision in most important areas, and this was often impossible to achieve. Qualified majority voting was extended by the Single European Act to overcome the stalemate that so often occurred previously. However, unanimity was still required for certain topics, and it remained possible for one Member State (often in practice the UK) to block the progress of any proposal not subject to this kind of vote. The TEU extended the range of topics that were to be subject to qualified majority voting, without changing the basic rule. Out of a total of 76 votes, distributed very roughly according to size among the twelve Member States as they then were, at least 54 were required for the proposal to be passed.[23] Thus 23 votes constituted a 'blocking minority'. The number of votes per Member State ranged from three to ten (apart from Luxembourg with two), so two large states and one small one could successfully block a proposal.

With the prospect of new members joining in 1995 with appropriate votes in the Council, the Commission proposed that the blocking percentage should be kept at the same level of about 30 per cent by increasing the number of votes required. Two Member States opposed the change. The UK's Conservative government had never liked the principle of majority voting, and saw its ability to block legislation further diminished. Spain feared that the poorer southern states would be outvoted by the northern majority in matters such as agriculture. After intense debate in the Council, during which the UK Prime Minister even threatened to block accession of the new Member States, the proposal was finally accepted with a declaration that if at least 23 votes (the original number) were cast against a proposal without achieving 30 per cent of the total, there would be a 'reasonable' delay for further negotiation before the final vote was cast. The new blocking minority for that final vote is now 26 out of 87.

The Legal Base

Because different voting rules apply to different Articles of the EC treaty, the question of which Article to use as the legal justification for action becomes crucial. The Commission has shown some ingenuity in trying, wherever possible, to get its proposals through under a legal base for which qualified majority voting rather than unanimity will apply. Governments opposed to particular measures have hotly disputed the choice of legal base in order to maintain a veto in the Council. This has applied in particular to social legislation, where qualified majority voting applied (before Maastricht) only to health and safety at work under Article 118a EC. This Article has been invoked for matters having only a limited relevance to health and safety; another much-used Article has been the catch-all Article 100a which applies to 'measures for the approximation of the provisions ... which have as their object the establishment and functioning of the internal market'. With the extension of qualified majority voting under the amended EC treaty and the Social Protocol (see below) the scope for disputing the legal base will diminish. However, disagreement may remain over measures where the TEU offers more than one possible legal base. The Commission has been urged by the Parliament to reintroduce a number of proposals under the optional Social Protocol (see below).[24]

The Social Protocol

One of the more bizarre features of the TEU is that a whole section that was intended to form part of the amended EC treaty now appears in the form of a Protocol to which all Member States except the UK subscribe. The Protocol on Social Policy includes an Agreement on Social Policy which, for the eleven signatories, is an alternative to the corresponding Articles of the EC treaty.[25] Its purpose is to 'continue along the path laid down in the 1989 Social Charter', the latter being a non-binding policy document that the UK had also refused to support at the time. For areas covered by the new agreement, the rule for qualified majority voting is modified to allow for exclusion of the UK. Acts adopted under the agreement are not to apply to the UK, though in practice it will not be as clear-cut as this; if multinational corporations are bound by regulations applying everywhere else in the Community, it seems likely that they will apply the same conditions to their UK operations.

The agreement specifies some new topics such as the conditions of employment for third-country nationals (people not holding citizenship of a Member State). It also expands existing Articles of the EC treaty in two areas: the relations between management and labour, and equality of pay for male and female workers for equal work. Equally importantly, the agreement provides for the cooperation procedure (see above) to apply to a number of areas where previously a unanimous vote in the Council was required. These include working conditions and the information and consultation of workers, two areas where the UK government has long maintained its opposition to Community involvement (Chapter 6). It is clear that there will be strong pressure on the UK to accept the provisions of the Social Protocol as part of the 1996 renegotiation of the TEU. The other Member States are not expected to tolerate for ever a dual standard in social policy, and this is reflected in the Commission's 1994 White Paper on the future social policy of the Union.[26]

THE THIRD PILLAR

Title VI, the 'third pillar' of the TEU, covers cooperation in the fields of justice and home affairs and formalises the cooperation that had long taken place between Member States in various intergovernmental forums. By and large there is still an almost complete absence of democratic control through the European Parliament. This is very far from what the Parliament and a few of the Member States hoped to achieve at Maastricht.

Title VI comprises a single Article K and embraces work directed by the 'K4 Committee' (see below). This is the successor to the Co-ordinators' Group, a committee of senior officials charged with overseeing the programme of work agreed at the meeting of the European Council at Rhodes in December 1988. This resulted in a definitive list of aims and target dates called the Palma Document (Chapter 3), which is still of interest because it foreshadows many of the subsequent developments that have serious implications for human rights. Article K.1 lists 'matters of common interest' that relate in particular to achieving the free movement of persons – by which it means citizens of the Union, since its main purpose is to restrict or prevent the entry and free movement of non-citizens. The topics listed include

- asylum policy,
- controls on the crossing of external borders of the Union,
- immigration policy and controls on third-country nationals,
- judicial cooperation in civil and criminal matters, and
- police and customs cooperation.

The last item covers cooperation 'for the purposes of preventing and combating terrorism, unlawful drug trafficking and other serious crime ... in connection with the organisation of a Union-wide system for exchanging information within a European Police Office (Europol)'. The Commission, which is to be 'fully associated with the work in the areas referred to in this Title', may initiate proposals in all areas except judicial cooperation in criminal matters and police or customs co-operation. On the initiative of any Member State, the Council may adopt proposals for joint action and draw up Conventions for adoption by the Member States.

The European Parliament's role in all this is extremely limited; apart from being kept informed of discussions and consulted on the principal activities carried out, the Presidency of the Council is obliged only to 'ensure that the views of the European Parliament are duly taken into consideration'. The Parliament may ask questions of the Council or make recommendations, and hold an annual debate on matters covered by Title VI – a small sop to democracy, and much less than the Parliament had long demanded. Two reports of the Parliament's Committee on Civil Liberties and Internal Affairs spelt this out. In the first,[27] it was asserted that such matters should be a joint responsibility of the national parliaments and the European Parliament, with a formal framework for cooperation between them. It also called for the Court of Justice to have jurisdiction over the whole of Title VI. The second report[28] demanded, among other things, that all international agreements and Conventions agreed under Title VI should be subject to assent (see above) by the European Parliament.

A number of options are left open in Article K that have already led to disagreement between Member States. The Council *may* decide that measures implementing joint action should be adopted by a qualified majority, and the Conventions drawn up *may* stipulate that the Court of Justice has jurisdiction to interpret their provisions and to rule on any disputes. The UK in particular has objected to giving the Court a role, since this might be seen as the thin end of a wedge designed to bring the whole area into the normal legislative procedure of the Community.

Another option is set out in Article K.9, which says that the Council *may* decide to apply Article 100c EC (which involves the European Parliament through the consultation procedure and would allow for judicial review) to some of the topics listed in Article K.1. These include asylum and immigration policy and external border controls, but not criminal justice cooperation or police matters. In a declaration attached to the TEU the Member States required the Commission to report by the end of 1993 on the possibility of implementing Article K.9 with particular reference to asylum policies. However, the Commission's report[29] concluded that, despite a number of arguments in favour (including greater 'transparency' of decision-making), 'the time is not yet right' for the change to be made.

Article K.4 sets up a Coordinating Committee, reporting to the Council, which also has the right to offer opinions to the Council on its own initiative. This 'K4 Committee' supervises the various working groups which replace those existing before Maastricht; the officials concerned have in most cases remained the same. The Commission, which now has a special directorate for justice and home affairs within the Secretariat-General, is also in a position of considerable influence. The work of the K4 Committee is organised by three Senior Steering Groups, each covering a number of working groups. The names and responsibilities of the steering groups (together with their pre-Maastricht names in square brackets) are as follows:[30]

- *Steering Group I (immigration and asylum)* [Ad Hoc Working Group on Immigration]: immigration policy, asylum, visas, control of external frontiers.
- *Steering Group II (law enforcement)* [Trevi Group and Mutual Assistance Group]: counter-terrorism, public order, serious crime, Europol, customs, drugs.
- *Steering Group III (judicial cooperation)* [European Political Cooperation]: criminal and civil judicial cooperation.

Carried over from the old structure is the *Horizontal Group on Data Processing*, also reporting to the K4 Committee, which works specifically on the European Information System (Chapter 3). Cooperation over drug trafficking continues in the *Pompidou Group*; this comes under the Council of Europe and includes non-EU nations as well.

THE DEMOCRATIC DEFICIT

The European Parliament

As we have seen, Title VI of the TEU (which involves some of the most sensitive topics where human rights are concerned) displays a particular lack of democratic accountability. There is not much improvement over the situation before Maastricht, when members of the Council concluded intergovernmental agreements in secret without any formal justification under the EC treaty. However, the 'democratic deficit' goes deeper than this, and in many respects there has been little change since the European Parliament adopted a report on the subject in 1988.[31] The Parliament's continuing dissatisfaction was expressed in a report following the signing of the TEU in 1992.[32] Apart from deploring the continuing lack of parliamentary control over Titles V and VI, the Parliament pointed out that it still lacked:

- the right to initiate legislation regardless of whether the Commission responds to a request for draft proposals,
- a genuine codecision procedure with the Council for all legislation,
- involvement in ratifying all constitutional decisions requiring ratification by Member States, and
- the right to elect the President of the Commission.

These demands had already been endorsed by the Conference of Parliaments or 'assizes' between representatives of national and European parliaments, held in Rome in 1990.

The problem will become more acute as the Union acquires new members.[33] Much will depend on the model adopted for reform of the institutions of the Union. Some changes in structure and composition will certainly be needed to avoid their becoming unwieldy and inefficient: an unreformed Parliament, for example, would ultimately have more than 1000 members. Certain Member States are suspected of wanting to enlarge the Union only as a means of weakening it,[34] so resistance to reform is to be anticipated. A move to a more federal model could avert this danger, but great care will be needed to achieve more democratic legitimacy along with operational efficiency.

National Parliaments

A basic problem is that the powers taken away from national parliaments in forming the Union have never been fully transferred to the European Parliament. The advent of qualified majority voting in the Council means that on many issues a national government has to accept a decision which neither it nor its parliament wanted. At the same time the governments of Member States have been reluctant to press for real control to pass to the European Parliament, despite the fact that it is democratically elected. The Commission has also been accused of failing to call for this logical development because it wishes to preserve its monopoly of initiating proposals for legislation.

There has been much talk of the need for 'subsidiarity' (taking decisions at a level as close as possible to the citizen). However, what some governments mean by subsidiarity is exercising executive power without necessarily involving any parliament. For intergovernmental negotiations on treaty revision (as at Maastricht) and Conventions under Titles V and VI of the TEU, governments have tended to treat such matters as demanding a high level of secret diplomacy. Parliamentary approval is then either not sought at all or limited to the entire text of the treaty, with no opportunity for amendment. While this is at least arguable for questions of foreign affairs and relations with states outside the Union, there is scant justification for applying such procedures to matters of internal affairs where the only purpose of the agreement is to harmonise national practices in a given area such as immigration or asylum.

All the national parliaments of the Union have committees charged with monitoring new and proposed legislation brought forward under the EC treaty, and they have taken an increasing interest in the further matters covered by the TEU.[35] However, in most cases they have no power to control what negotiating positions are being adopted in the Council by ministers of their respective governments. Notable exceptions to this lack of control have been the parliaments of Denmark and the Netherlands. In Denmark the European Affairs Committee of the Folketing (parliament) requires ministers to obtain a mandate from the committee before entering negotiations in the Council, though for European Council meetings only a verbal briefing is given to the members.[36] For Title VI matters the Legal Affairs Committee is also involved.[37]

In the Netherlands, the law approving the TEU specifies that any binding decision under Title VI must, before being voted upon in the Council, be submitted to the States General (the Dutch parliament). Unless the States General has failed to express an interest within fifteen days, the government may not proceed without its approval.[38] Similar rules apply to decisions taken under the Schengen Convention (Chapter 3). For a treaty or Convention such as that on Europol (Chapter 7), ratification requires the passing of a Bill of Approval by the States General. A full debate is required unless no request for one has been made within 30 days.

A more common situation is that existing in the UK, where the government is committed only to depositing draft agreements (but not working documents) under Title VI (but not Title V) for consideration by committees of the House of Commons and House of Lords. The opinions of such committees are not, however, binding on the government. There is also a resolution of the House of Commons that government ministers should not adopt a legislative proposal or a Common Position in the Council before parliamentary scrutiny has been completed.[39] The problem here is that so many proposals pass through the committees that there is not time for all of them to be examined; domestic matters still take precedence where parliamentary time is concerned. A detailed enquiry by the House of Lords, which takes a broader interest in European Union matters than the elected House of Commons, wanted both Title V and Title VI to be subject to the same degree of scrutiny, but the government rejected this.[40] The enquiry report asserted that 'we intend to be vigilant in holding ministers to account in these areas', but recommended nothing as far-reaching as the Danish or Dutch procedure.

A conference convened in 1993 by the European Parliament's Committee on Civil Liberties and Internal Affairs was attended by members of national parliamentary committees whose interests overlapped those of the civil liberties committee. The participants had much to say about their general inability to influence intergovernmental agreements entered into by their governments.[41]

Freedom of Information and Transparency

Many people would say that two prime requirements of democratic accountability are public access to all the information on which decisions are based (though this is not a view espoused by many national governments), and an open system of decision-making. This requires the debates of the legislative body and the votes cast to be a matter of public record. 'Transparency' is a word used to describe the second requirement (confusingly, it is also used to mean clarity and ease of interpretation in Community law).

Where the European Parliament and the Commission are concerned, their involvement in Community decision-making is in many respects open to public view. The Parliament has always published details of its discussions, and its plenary sessions and most committee meetings are held in public. The Commission publishes its draft proposals for Community legislation at the same time as they are transmitted to the other institutions. Even Commission working papers and internal documents are made available to those who ask for them, either officially or through a process of 'leakage' – a fact that accounts for the proliferation of lobbying organisations based in Brussels. Commission officials are often prepared to talk about present and future policy in a way that surprises those who are used to dealing with more cautious national civil servants at home. Only in matters now covered by Titles V and VI, where the Parliament is excluded from the drafting process, has secrecy ruled.

In contrast, the debates and votes cast in the Council (where the final decision to adopt an act is made) have hitherto been shrouded in secrecy. This is particularly strange when one considers that the Council is in this respect a law-making body like a national parliament. The analogy with a cabinet of government ministers is not valid, since at national level a proposal formulated by the government still has to be approved by the parliament (whatever the defects of that process in practice). The only information made public prior to decisions by the Council has come from selective leakage to journalists by its members or their staff.

The TEU included a Declaration on the Right of Access to Information which bravely stated that 'transparency of the decision-making process strengthens the democratic nature of the institutions and the public's confidence in the administration.' It went on to ask the Commission to submit to the Council no later than 1993 'a report on measures designed to improve public access to the information available to the institutions.' The Commission responded in 1992 and 1993 with a number of documents,[42] summarised in a European Parliament committee report along with other material.[43] This report identified the decision-making procedure of the Council acting as legislator as an out-standing problem, pointing out that 'no parliamentary assembly under a democratic regime takes decisions in camera or withholds the results of its votes from publication'.

In October 1993, following talks between representatives of Parliament, Council and Commission, an Interinstitutional Declaration was signed which included a promise that the voting records of Member States in the Council would in future be made public.[44] The Council was also to open some of its debates to the public and provide access to its archives. However, later publication of the Council's new Rules of Procedure[45] showed how limited an advance this would be in practice. The only debates to be open to the public (unless unanimously agreed otherwise on a case-by-case basis) are the broad policy debates on each six-monthly work programme – not the contentious debates on particular issues. The voting record is to be published automatically only when:

- the Council 'adopts rules which are legally binding in or for the Member States' (on the final vote leading to a Regulation, Directive or Decision);
- a Common Position (see above) is reached under the cooperation or codecision procedure; or
- votes are cast in the Conciliation Committee (see p. 17).

Decisions taken under Titles V and VI are only covered if there is unanimous agreement to publish the voting record – in other words, one Member State can exercise a veto.

The Rules of Procedure also make it plain that the 'archives' to be made freely available do not include the minutes of meetings. There is a blanket rule that 'the deliberations of the Council shall be covered by the obligation of professional secrecy, except in so far as the Council decides otherwise'. The publication of minutes may be authorised only for use in legal proceedings, and public access is permitted only to documents 'disclosure of which is without serious or prejudicial consequences'.

What this really meant became clear when the Council published a common code of conduct for disclosure of Commission and Council documents.[46] This included a long list of exceptions to a public right of access to documents, including a widely drawn 'protection of the public interest'. It was also laid down that the Council and Commission may refuse access 'in order to protect the institution's interest in the confidentiality of its proceedings'. It emerged that the K4 Committee (see above) had advised that 'areas of concern' in this regard included all matters coming under Titles V and VI of the TEU.[47] There was also to be a comprehensive scheme for classifying information under various grades of secrecy, together with a new system of security vetting for officials combined with sanctions (including criminal prosecution) against those who leak information.[48]

These restrictions were strongly opposed by the Dutch government, which started an action in the European Court of Justice against the scope of the rules. It had already experienced precisely this passion for secrecy in the operation of the Schengen Convention (Chapter 3). A test of the restrictions was also mounted by the UK newspaper the *Guardian*, which initially asked for (and obtained) the minutes of a Council meeting which had been discussing draft legislation on the protection of young people at work. However, when the newspaper asked for the minutes of other meetings about police and immigration matters, the President of the Council not only refused to supply them but said that the release of the earlier minutes had been an 'administrative error'. The *Guardian* then lodged its own application with the ECJ to challenge the decision, backed now by the European Parliament and both the Dutch and Danish governments.[49] Even the French government, a former defender of Council secrecy, showed signs of changing its position.[50]

It seems clear that officials working behind the scenes hold widely diverging views on the issue of secrecy; while some of them draft papers on the need for more openness, others are ready to propose draconian limitations on freedom of information. This is true even within the traditionally 'open' Commission; in 1992 there was a proposal (later withdrawn after the Parliament rejected it) for a Community-wide official secrets law, emanating from the Commission's legal service and security office. This included the same kind of vetting and criminal penalties as those later put forward for matters under Title VI (see above).[51]

The significance of the debate was not lost on the future Nordic members of the Union; Sweden, for instance, has a constitutional guarantee of freedom of information that would seem to be quite incompatible with the restrictions discussed above (Chapter 8). Sweden and Finland attached declarations to their accession agreements asserting the importance of open government and public access to documents. The existing Member States responded with a counter-declaration as follows:

> The Present Member States of the EU take note of the unilateral declaration of Sweden concerning openness and transparency. They take it for granted that, as a member of the EU, Sweden will fully comply with Community law in this respect.[52]

This was taken by observers to be a veiled reference to the Council decisions on secrecy classification of documents. It relies on the primacy of the *acquis communautaire* – a phrase defying direct translation which is used to describe the accepted body of existing Community law and practice. Even the much-vaunted principle of subsidiarity is secondary to this rule.[53] All in all, the saga outlined above suggests that there is a long way to go before the Union achieves the aims of the Maastricht promise of transparency.[54]

NOTES

1. The official text (published by the Office for Official Publications of the European Communities in Luxembourg) is confusing because it gives only the changes made to the existing Treaty of Rome, together with the additional provisions agreed at Maastricht. Consolidated texts containing the full Treaty of Rome 'as amended', together with useful commentary, are available commercially; for example Paul Beaumont and Gordon Moir, *The European Communities (Amendment) Act 1993* (London: Sweet and Maxwell, 1994) which also includes the relevant UK legislation to implement the TEU.
2. Michael Spencer, *1992 And All That: civil liberties in the balance* (London: Civil Liberties Trust, 1990).
3. For the text of the 1957 treaty as amended by the 1986 Single European Act, together with that Act and other relevant treaties and agreements or 'instruments', see *Treaties establishing the European Communities* (Luxembourg: Office for Official Publications of the

European Communities, 1987). There is a complete edition and an abridged one, the latter being adequate for most purposes.

4. *Treaty establishing a single Council and a single Commission of the European Communities.* For text see the complete edition referred to in note 3.

5. In this book the amended Treaty of Rome will be referred to as the 'EC treaty' and the word 'Community' (as in 'Community law') will be kept for all matters governed by this treaty. Articles of the EC treaty will be cited here as 'Article ... EC' and those of the TEU as 'Article ... TEU'. Articles of the TEU are distinguished by the letters A, B, C and so on, while those of the EC treaty carry numbers as they did before Maastricht. People holding full citizenship of a Member State for the purposes of Community law will be referred to as EC or EU citizens or 'nationals'. The term 'Member State' (as used in the EC treaty and TEU) will be reserved for those belonging to the Union.

6. Articles 137–44 EC. For a detailed description of its role see Francis Jacobs, Richard Corbett and Michael Shackleton, *The European Parliament*, 2nd edn (Harlow: Longman, 1992). A new edition will appear in 1995.

7. Article 158 EC.

8. Articles 145–54 EC.

9. Article 151 EC.

10. Articles 155–63 EC.

11. This term will be avoided because it invites confusion with bodies such as the European Commission of Human Rights (Chapter 2). The Commission's official title is 'Commission of the European Communities'.

12. Articles 152 and 138b EC, respectively.

13. For a detailed list of directorate responsibilities (and much other information) see *Vacher's European Companion and Consultants' Register* (Berkhamsted: Vachers Publications, published quarterly).

14. Articles 164–88 EC.

15. Article 168a EC.

16. Articles 189 and 191 EC.

17. The names of the instruments are normally capitalised to indicate their formal status.

18. For details of the different types of documentation, see for example Spencer, *1992 And All That* (note 2) Appendix V.

19. Jacobs *et al.*, *The European Parliament* (note 6) pp. 203–5. This lists under each procedure the Articles of the EC treaty to which each option applies. See also Committee on Legal Affairs and Citizens' Rights (rapporteur: M. Garcia Amigo), *Report on the transparency of*

Community legislation and the need for it to be consolidated, A3–0266/94 (European Parliament, 1994) p. 5.

20. Article 100c EC. Other topics relate to indirect taxation (Article 99), approximation of laws to achieve a common market (Article 100) and international agreements entered into by the Community (Article 228(2) and (3)).

21. Article 189c EC.

22. Article 189b EC. The Conciliation Committee referred to here is to be composed of 'the members of the Council or their representatives and an equal number of representatives of the European Parliament'. The Commission also takes part in the proceedings without having a vote.

23. Article 148 EC.

24. Committee on Legal Affairs and Citizens' Rights (rapporteur: R. Bontempi), *Report on the application of the Treaty on European Union to proposals pending before the Council on 31 October 1993 for which its entry into force will require a change in the legal base and/or a change in procedure*, A3–0013/94 (European Parliament, 1994).

25. Articles 117–22 EC.

26. Commission of the European Communities, *European social policy a way forward for the Union*, COM(94) 333 final (Luxembourg: Office for Official Publications of the European Communities, 1994).

27. Committee on Civil Liberties and Internal Affairs (rapporteur: C. Robles Piquer), *Report on cooperation in the field of justice and home affairs under the Treaty on European Union (Title VI and other provisions)*, A3–0215/93 (European Parliament, 1993).

28. Committee on Civil Liberties and Internal Affairs (rapporteur: G. Jarzembowski), *Report on participation by the European Parliament in international agreements by the Member States and the Union on co-operation in the fields of justice and home affairs*, A3–0436/93 (European Parliament, 1993).

29. Commission of the European Communities, *Report to the Council on the possibility of applying Article K.9 of the Treaty on European Union to asylum policy*, SEC(93) 1687 final (internal document, 1993).

30. House of Lords Select Committee on the European Communities, *House of Lords scrutiny of the inter-governmental pillars of the European Union*, Session 1992–93, 28th Report (London: HMSO, 1993) evidence pp. 1–5.

31. Committee on Institutional Affairs (rapporteur: M. Toussaint), *Report on the democratic deficit in the European Community*, A2–0276/87 (European Parliament, 1988).

32. Committee on Institutional Affairs (rapporteur: D. Martin), *Report on the results of the intergovernmental conferences,* A3–0123/92/Parts I & II (European Parliament, 1992); republished with additional material as *Maastricht* (Luxembourg: Office for Official Publications of the European Communities, 1992). See also David Martin, *European Union: the shattered dream?* (Broxburn: John Wheatley Centre, 1993).

33. 'Europe and the challenge of enlargement', *Bulletin of the European Communities,* Supplement 3/92 (Luxembourg: Office for Official Publications of the European Communities, 1992) p. 15.

34. Directorate-General for Research, *Enlarged Community: institutional adaptations,* 'Political Series' working paper 17 (Luxembourg: European Parliament, 1992) p. 80.

35. Directorate-General for Research, *Bodies within national parliaments specialising in European Community affairs,* 'National Parliaments' series working document W1 (Luxembourg: European Parliament, 1992). A new edition is in preparation.

36. International Department, *A description of the E.E.C. Committee* (Copenhagen: Folketinget, undated); Nicole Ameline, *Les Parlements de l'Europe: les leçons de l'expérience danoise,* Rapport d'information 1437 (Paris: Assemblée nationale, 1994).

37. European Affairs Committee, *Report submitted on May 20th 1994 regarding the Government's briefing of the Folketing on EU matters,* report no. 5 of 1993–94 (Copenhagen: Folketinget, 1994). Available in Danish, English and French.

38. Law of 17 December 1992, *Staatsblad* (1992) no. 692.

39. Resolution of 24 October 1990. See *Bodies within national parliaments* (note 35) p. 53.

40. House of Lords, *House of Lords scrutiny* (note 30). For the government response see official document Cm 2471 (London: HMSO, 1994).

41. Directorate-General for Research, *Cooperation among Member States in the fields of justice and home affairs: the 'third pillar' of the Treaty on European Union,* 'A People's Europe' series working document W4 (Luxembourg: European Parliament, 1993).

42. Commission of the European Communities, *Increased transparency in the work of the Commission,* SEC(92) 2274 final (internal document, 1992); *Public access to the institutions' documents,* COM(93) 0191 final; *Openness in the Community,* COM(93) 0258 final (Luxembourg: Office for Official Publications of the European Communities, 1993). The second of these includes a comparative survey of the practices adopted in Member States and certain other countries, together with general access laws where they exist.

43. Committee on Institutional Affairs (rapporteur: M. Duverger), *Report on openness in the Community*, A3–0153/94 (European Parliament, 1994).
44. *Official Journal of the European Communities*, C329 (6 December 1993) p. 133; see also Committee on Institutional Affairs (rapporteur: J. M. Gil-Robles Gil-Delgado), *Report on the interinstitutional declaration on democracy and transparency and the Interinstitutional Agreement on procedures for implementing the principle of subsidiarity*, A3–0356/93 (European Parliament, 1993) pp. 7–9.
45. *Ibid.*, L304 (10 December 1993) pp.1–8.
46. *Official Journal of the European Communities*, L340 (31 December 1993) pp. 41–2.
47. *Statewatch*, November–December 1993, pp. 1–2.
48. *Ibid.*, January–February 1994, p. 15.
49. *Statewatch*, September–October 1994.
50. *Guardian*, 10 December 1994.
51. *Ibid.*, 11 May 1992 and 26 January 1993.
52. *Statewatch*, May–June 1994, p.11.
53. See the Gil-Robles report (note 44) pp. 10–11.
54. For an authoritative discussion of this and other topics relating to the TEU see Deirdre Curtin, 'The constitutional structure of the Union: a Europe of bits and pieces', *Common Market Law Review*, vol. 30 (1993) pp. 17–69.

2

Guardians of Human Rights

The Member States of the European Union share a commitment to the various international agreements on human rights that were drawn up in the aftermath of the Second World War. The United Nations (UN) sponsored a Universal Declaration of Human Rights in 1948 which served as a model for a number of later texts, and also influenced the 'post-fascist' constitutions adopted by Germany, Italy and Spain. The UN was responsible for a number of other Conventions, the most relevant of which are listed below;[1] the first date given is the year of adoption and the second the year in which the Convention came into force after being ratified by the requisite number of states.[2] They are:

- the Convention Relating to the Status of Refugees (the Geneva Convention) (1951/1954),[3]
- the International Convention on the Elimination of All Forms of Racial Discrimination (1965/1969),
- the International Covenant on Economic, Social and Cultural Rights (1966/1976),
- the International Covenant on Civil and Political Rights (1966/1976),
- the International Convention on the Elimination of All Forms of Discrimination against Women (1979/1981),
- the Convention against Torture and Other Cruel, Inhuman or Degrading Treatment or Punishment (1984/1987),
- the Convention on the Rights of the Child (1989/1990), and
- the International Convention on the Protection of the Rights of All Migrant Workers and Members of their Families (1990/–).[4]

A given Convention is often supplemented by Protocols which update it or introduce additional options for contracting states, and these too are subject to ratification. A further long series of Conventions relating to the rights of workers has been adopted by the International Labour Organisation (ILO), a body which is part of the UN system.

Regional organisations of states such as the Organisation of American States and the Organisation of African Unity have adopted their own Conventions on human rights, modelled on those of the UN. In Europe this role is filled by the Council of Europe and the Organisation for Security and Cooperation in Europe (OSCE, formerly CSCE), both of which will be discussed in this and other chapters.

A problem at the heart of nearly all the Conventions drawn up by these bodies is the lack of an effective enforcement mechanism. However, in most cases there is a requirement that the contracting states submit regular reports on their adherence to the relevant Convention. These are considered by committees of international experts with the power to question government representatives, make recommendations, and in a few cases visit a country for further investigation. In some cases (subject to agreement by the state concerned) there is a right of individual petition to the supervisory committee. NGOs can bring problems to the attention of a committee, though they are not always officially recognised.[5] Member States of the European Union have not infrequently been among those criticised by international committees of this kind.

Governments are expected to respond to adverse reports by correcting any abuses. In the last resort, however, the Conventions rely on the commitment of democratic states to the moral authority of international law. Even a ruling by the UN's International Court of Justice at The Hague can simply be ignored. An inconvenient Convention on a particular topic can be de-ratified or 'denounced' by a contracting state, as happened several times when the UK under Margaret Thatcher changed its labour legislation.[6] Other Conventions never attract the full range of ratifications, even when all states have signed up in principle. International conferences on human rights have deplored these weaknesses without finding a solution.[7]

Fortunately for human rights in Europe, the Council of Europe's Convention for the Protection of Human Rights and Fundamental Freedoms (usually called the European Convention on Human Rights or ECHR) is uniquely strong in having an enforcement mechanism. As we shall see, it has its own judiciary whose authority is universally respected. Many states have also incorporated the Convention into their domestic law.

THE COUNCIL OF EUROPE

The Council of Europe is older than the European Union and remains quite distinct from it. It was founded by ten nations in 1949 and grew steadily over the years; with the admission of new members from

Eastern Europe, it stood at 33 members by the start of 1995. All the members of the European Union also belong to the Council of Europe. It was in many ways a forerunner of the Union, and in fact arose from a specially convened Congress of Europe in 1948 which strongly endorsed the idea of an ultimate union of states. Its influence on the development of the Union has been considerable and, under an agreement formalised in 1987, the two bodies have collaborated over topics of mutual interest.[8] Its mandate covers everything except military aspects of defence, but its current priorities are human rights, culture and social problems.[9]

The Council of Europe is based in Strasbourg, which adds to popular confusion about its role because this is also where the European Parliament holds its main meetings. The structure of the Council of Europe resembles that of the European Union in that it has a Parliamentary Assembly drawn from all the Member States. There is a Committee of Ministers comprising the Ministers for Foreign Affairs (or their deputies) from national governments. The Assembly makes recommendations to the Committee of Ministers, which can also (if unanimous) issue formal recommendations on specific topics which the Member States are expected to observe.

There, however, the resemblance ends. Like the European Parliament prior to 1979, the Assembly is not elected but comprises delegates from national parliaments. It has no legislative or executive power, and has only three week-long plenary sessions each year for debates. However, there are also about 50 parliamentary committees and subcommittees which meet between each full session. They report to the Assembly, which can then pass recommendations to the Committee of Ministers. Although there is a large Secretariat, its powers are in no way comparable to those of the Commission of the EC.

Much of the Council of Europe's groundwork is performed by more than 100 expert intergovernmental committees and working groups which produce reports, recommendations and draft Conventions on a wide range of topics. The Conventions, if adopted by the Committee of Ministers, are then opened for signature and ratification by the Member States. These Conventions, and the formal Recommendations that supplement them (known prior to 1979 as Resolutions), are often used implicitly or explicitly as a basis for proposals by the Commission of the EC. In some areas, particularly those of human rights and data protection, there has been almost too much reliance on standards set by the Council of Europe which were laid down in previous years and not sufficiently updated.

The ongoing work of the Council of Europe covers several areas dealt with in this book. Apart from human rights in general (see below) there is a great deal of work on migration and the problems of migrants, an area in which the European Union has shown a marked inability to come up with humane and far-sighted policies. Under the heading of legal affairs (rather than human rights) there is extensive study of the situation of refugees. Work on privacy and data protection has led to the formulation of the only international Convention of its kind (see Chapter 7) and a range of 'sectoral recommendations' on such topics as the handling of personal data by the police. Social problems of all kinds also receive detailed attention.

With all this background activity it is unfortunate that the reports and other publications of the Council of Europe are little known outside the world of experts, and not always easy to obtain even if their existence is known of. Whereas the Commission of the EC has offices in every state of the Union and others outside as well, together with a network of documentation centres in each Member State, the Council of Europe has only a headquarters in Strasbourg, an office in Paris and a small liaison bureau in Brussels. There are no national documentation centres, and only a few academic institutions stock more than a few of its publications.

To make matters worse, the system of publication is curiously fragmented: although many documents are published centrally and distributed by state publishing houses, others (including recent reports on current problems) may be available only from the Strasbourg office of the appropriate division of the organisation. Each division produces its own list of activities and publications in an apparently uncoordinated manner.

The European Convention on Human Rights

The unique achievement of the Council of Europe has been to put the UN's Universal Declaration of Human Rights into a legally enforceable form. The European Convention on Human Rights (ECHR) was signed in 1950 and has been ratified by all Member States of the Union. Eleven Protocols have been added over the years of which eight are so far in force, and new ones are still being suggested.[10] All but two Member States of the Union (Ireland and the UK) have incorporated the Convention into their national law. This means that a violation of the Convention can be argued in their domestic courts. Its main weakness is that the anti-discrimination clause (Article 14) is not a general one; although it prohibits any form of discrimination, this relates only to the enjoyment of rights and freedoms specified in the Convention (see also Chapter 6).

Any individual or group of individuals can in principle raise a complaint about the actions of government, or even the legality of an act of parliament, if these conflict with the provisions of the ECHR. Domestic remedies (appeal through the courts) must first have been exhausted. NGOs and other governments can also lodge complaints; however, NGOs can only do this when they are directly affected as victims, or when offering information in what is called an *amicus curiae* brief.

Enforcement of the Convention is in the hands of the *European Commission of Human Rights* and the *European Court of Human Rights*, though the former will ultimately disappear (see below). Both are based in Strasbourg, and neither has any connection with the Commission and Court of Justice of the Union. The members of the two bodies are drawn from persons nominated by the contracting states, but they are bound to act in an entirely independent manner. No two members can be nationals of the same state.

The Commission of Human Rights is a committee of legal experts which decides whether a case is admissible; it then tries to achieve a friendly settlement between the complainant and the government concerned. If this is not possible, it makes a report (including a legal opinion) to the Committee of Ministers and also considers whether to pass the case to the Court of Human Rights for a judicial decision. The government accused of violation can also forward the case to the Court; if neither it nor the Commission of Human Rights has done this within three months, the Committee of Ministers can decide on the merits of the case by a two-thirds majority vote.

The Court of Human Rights consists of judges elected for nine-year terms of office by the Parliamentary Assembly, from lists drawn up by the Committee of Ministers. The total number of judges is equal to the number of contracting states of the Council of Europe, but each case is considered by a panel of nine judges; the panel always includes the judge originally nominated for election by the state defending the action.

All EU Member States are among the 30 countries to have made declarations under Article 46 of the ECHR that they recognise as compulsory the jurisdiction of the Court of Human Rights. All have similarly declared under Article 25 that they accept the right of individual petition to the Commission of Human Rights, though this may be for a specific period and subject to periodic review.

Of the Protocols, five have so far been ratified by all Member States of the Union. One notable exception is No. 6 on abolition of the death penalty, which remains unratified by Belgium, Greece and the UK. Others are Nos 4 and 7, which include restrictions on the expulsion or exclusion of nationals and aliens. Several features of these Protocols appear to be in conflict with the trend of immigration policy in the Union.

Protocol No. 9 (not yet in force) would allow individuals or groups to take an admissible case before the Court, even when the Commission of Human Rights has decided not to do so.

The system suffered from its own popularity through an increasing backlog of unresolved cases; those passed to the Court were taking an average of more than five years from the initial application to final judgment. With the rapid increase in signatories to the Convention there was a clear need to reform the procedure. The first attempt to do this was the publication in 1992 of Protocol No. 10, which would have made it easier for the Committee of Ministers to decide the cases left to its jurisdiction: the previous requirement of a two-thirds majority was to be replaced by a simple majority of members entitled to sit. The Committee of Ministers had sometimes been accused of undue delay or political bias in its handling of cases left to its jurisdiction.

Protocols 9 and 10 were, however, overtaken by a much more radical reform that had long been canvassed, and which was formally recommended by the Parliamentary Assembly in 1992.[11] The Vienna Declaration adopted by a Council of Europe summit meeting in 1993 included a commitment to abolishing the two-tier system in favour of a single court.[12] It was also agreed at an earlier meeting that as part of this reform the Committee of Ministers would lose its judicial power. Its only role would then be to supervise the execution of the judgments of the Court.

A new Protocol No. 11 to put this into effect was opened for signature in May 1994,[13] though it is unlikely to come fully into effect before 1997. This will eliminate the Commission of Human Rights. Instead it introduces a new 'sifting' procedure by a committee of three members of the Court, which will then pass admissible cases to a larger Chamber of seven judges for detailed consideration. They will either negotiate a friendly settlement between the parties or issue a judgment. A Grand Chamber of 17 judges will consider cases that raise important issues of interpretation, either on referral by a Chamber or when a party to a dispute asks for a re-hearing. It thus acts as a final court of appeal.

The Protocol includes an automatic right of individual petition to the court. This initially ran into objections from the UK, which had long tried to obstruct the whole reform and then insisted that the right of petition should remain open to periodic review (every five years in the case of the UK). Human rights activists feared that this example might be followed by other countries in which an automatic right of petition would safeguard the position of vulnerable minorities.[14] As an 'amending Protocol' affecting the operation of the entire system, the reform could not go ahead without unanimous agreement. The UK government finally agreed to sign the Protocol. By the end of 1994 only four out of

30 contracting states had ratified it, but most others were expected to do so during 1995. When all of them have ratified there will be a further period of a year before the Protocol comes into effect.

The Union and the Convention on Human Rights

Article F of the TEU demands that the Union shall 'respect fundamental rights, as guaranteed by the European Convention for the Protection of Human Rights and Fundamental Freedoms ... and as they result from the constitutional traditions common to the Member States, as general principles of Community law'. This reinforces a trend already apparent in the judgments of the European Community's Court of Justice. However, it has long been argued by the Commission of the EC that the Community should accede as a body to the ECHR. Support for this idea has steadily increased over the years.

The Commission made its first proposal in 1979[15] and revived it in 1990.[16] The European Parliament, which supported both proposals, commissioned a detailed study of the matter in 1993.[17] The International Commission of Jurists (ICJ) added its support,[18] and the Brussels delegation of the International Federation of Human Rights recommended its affiliated national organisations to do the same.[19] The arguments in favour of accession may be summarised as follows:

- The institutions of the Union would, like the governments of the member states, be subject to the ECHR. Complaints against them or against member states implementing Community decisions have so far been declared inadmissible by the European Commission of Human Rights.
- Accession would underline the Union's commitment to the ideals of democracy and human rights. The Union already includes clauses on human rights in its trade agreements with the Third World (the Lomé Conventions) and Association Agreements with neighbouring countries. Accession would indicate what was expected of new Member States.
- The risk of conflicting interpretations of the ECHR by the Court of Justice and the European Court of Human Rights would be eliminated.

Resistance to the idea of accession has been confined to certain Member States, particularly the UK; having not yet incorporated the ECHR into its own law, the UK government has a persistent fear that accession by the Union will amount to 'back-door incorporation' into domestic law.

Assurances by legal advisers to the Commission in Brussels that this would not be the case have fallen on deaf ears.[20]

Another objection (also discounted by most experts) has been that there would be legal difficulties in giving the Union (which is not a sovereign state) the right to nominate its representatives on the Commission and Court of Human Rights. However, in 1993 the Council finally set up a working group to explore the possibility of mandating the Commission to open negotiations with the Council of Europe on accession to the Convention.[21] In April 1994 the Council submitted an official request to the European Court of Justice for its opinion on whether adhesion of the EC to the ECHR would be compatible with the EC treaty.[22]

Other Council of Europe Conventions

An early Council of Europe initiative was the European Social Charter of 1961, coming into force in 1965.[23] All 15 EU Member States have ratified it, together with Cyprus, Iceland, Malta, Norway and Turkey. Although much cited as a precedent in European Union declarations, it has had only a limited practical effect because it embodies no enforcement mechanism. Workers in some countries would probably be surprised to learn that their governments are committed under the Charter to ensuring fair remuneration and the right to organise and bargain collectively. However, parts of the Charter have served as a model for binding legislation under Community law.

The European Convention on the Legal Status of Migrant Workers[24] was opened for signature in 1977 but did not come into force until 1983; even now only six Member States of the Union have ratified it. Its supervisory mechanism is criticised as being far too weak, since the submission of country reports is only voluntary and there is no place in it for NGOs.[25]

A more concrete result followed adoption in 1981 of the Convention for the Protection of Individuals with Regard to Automatic Processing of Personal Data (the 'Convention on data protection').[26] It came into force in 1985, and many of the Member States of the European Union duly brought in legislation to give effect to it. Its strength lay in the requirement that each state was obliged to set up an independent supervisory body. It was only the failure of a few states to ratify the Convention that led the Commission to finally bring forward its own proposals for data protection. This subject is discussed in more detail in Chapter 7.

In 1987 the Council of Europe sponsored the European Convention for the Prevention of Torture and Inhuman or Degrading Treatment or Punishment, which came into force in 1989 and has been ratified by all Member States of the Union.[27] Under a Protocol opened for signature in 1993, non-Member States of the Council of Europe may also be invited to accede to the Convention.

The Convention builds on Article 3 of the ECHR to set up a European Committee for the Prevention of Torture and Inhuman or Degrading Treatment or Punishment (the CPT). The committee is authorised to make regular visits to all contracting states and report on any abuses relating to 'persons deprived of their liberty by a public authority'. This is a much more effective power than that given to the UN's Committee Against Torture, which under the relevant Convention (see above) can only take this course if there are 'well-founded indications that torture is being systematically practised'; even then it can only visit the country concerned with the agreement of its government.

The visits by the European committee are mostly to police stations and civil prisons, but psychiatric establishments are also included. The reports and government responses are confidential to the governments concerned unless they request publication. If a government refuses to respond to criticism the CPT can issue a public statement. This was done in the case of Turkey, when the CPT said that 'the practice of torture and other forms of severe ill-treatment of persons in police custody remains widespread in Turkey'.[28] The reports of the CPT can thus be used in assessing whether an applicant for membership of the European Union is adequately committed to the protection of human rights.

THE OSCE

The Organisation for Security and Cooperation in Europe, formerly the Conference on Security and Cooperation in Europe (CSCE),[29] was set up in 1975 with US involvement in an effort to defuse the Cold War, and the Helsinki Final Act included broad commitments on respect for human rights, cooperation between states and the resolution of conflicts.[30] In 1987 the Human Dimension Mechanism was established in the form of a four-stage intergovernmental procedure, under which states could raise and discuss general or individual issues of human rights abuse in other signatory states. The 1990 Charter of Paris outlined areas of future work and established a permanent secretariat in Prague. Regular follow-up meetings were arranged,[31] and non-governmental monitoring groups were formed in the shape of the Prague-based Helsinki Citizens' Assembly and various national committees. In 1992 agreement was reached on the use of investigating missions to report on particular problems, if necessary without the consent of the investigated state. More than 50 countries now belong to the OSCE, and it has taken a particular interest in the protection of national minority groups.[32] This will be discussed further in Chapter 6.

The complex nature of the OSCE system, in which successive conferences have led to further revision of the rules for examining complaints, renders it a poorly understood mechanism for protecting human rights; it also lacks a channel for individuals to state their case independently of governments. Nevertheless it has some unique features not offered by the more rigid UN and Council of Europe structures. Though its decisions and documents carry no legal force, this means that states that might otherwise refuse to cooperate are more willing to engage in a dialogue not only on individual cases, but also on broader issues with a political content.[33]

EUROPEAN UNION WATCHDOGS

As mentioned in Chapter 1, the Commission of the EC has no specific brief to monitor the adherence of Member States to international standards of human rights. Its human rights division can only help to formulate a Commission response to issues of human rights both inside and outside the Union, and to ensure policy consistency throughout the Commission. The amended EC treaty instructs the European Parliament to appoint an Ombudsman,[34] but the powers of this official are limited to investigating 'maladministration in the activities of the Community institutions or bodies, with the exception of the Court of Justice and the Court of First Instance acting in their judicial roles'. The Court of Justice can invoke the principles of the ECHR in its judgments, but only where points of Community law are concerned. It is not involved in testing each new proposal for new legislation against such standards, and in the vital area of Title VI it so far has no power at all. Within the Union, this leaves the European Parliament and the Economic and Social Committee with the unwritten task of looking after the interests of the individual.

The ESC has a purely consultative role in examining proposals for new Community legislation.[35] The membership is supposed to reflect a broad range of backgrounds: 'producers, farmers, carriers, workers, dealers, craftsmen, professional occupations and representatives of the general public', a revealing indication of the order of importance assigned to special interest groups in the Community. The members are nominated by Member States and appointed by the Council, but they are expected to act 'in the general interest of the Community'.

In giving an opinion on each new proposal the ESC can raise objections to any neglect of the rights of a particular group. Like the Committee of the Regions and the European Parliament, the ESC can now (under the TEU) enquire into any issue on its own initiative. However, some observers feel that its function has gradually been superseded by that of the elected Parliament. In practice the Parliament, with its range of specialist committees, has played by far the most important role in monitoring individual rights.

Since the Parliament is not restricted to examining proposals for legislation, it can also enquire into agreements between governments that fall outside the EC treaty. Sensitive matters like asylum and immigration policy, police powers, racism and so on are not excluded. The Parliament has an honourable record of raising issues that many national governments would rather not see discussed for political reasons.

At a more fundamental level, the Parliament has long been arguing for the adoption by the Union of its own Bill of Rights. In 1989 it adopted a Declaration of Fundamental Rights and Freedoms[36] and urged the other Community institutions and the Member States to follow suit.

In 1994 it went further and recommended the adoption of a draft Constitution of the European Union which included, among much else, a catalogue of human rights to be guaranteed by the Union.[37] These rights would apply to any person, including a non-citizen of the Union, with the sole exception of the right to form political parties. The Court of Justice would be competent to rule on any action brought by an individual for violation of human rights by the Union.

The list of rights is an interesting amalgam of the previous Declaration with elements of the European Social Charter and other international instruments. It includes some radical proposals which certain governments would object to: a right of conscientious objectors to refuse military service, an unqualified right of workers to strike, and a ban on the surveillance of individuals and organisations unless duly authorised by a judicial authority.

Committees of the European Parliament

The Parliament has set up a number of specialist committees which consider each piece of draft legislation submitted to it. Often more than one committee examines the same proposal. Each committee may call expert witnesses, and a rapporteur is appointed to draft a report and a resolution for submission to a plenary session of the Parliament.[38]

The committee then votes on the draft resolution, and the full Parliament may amend this before passing it to the Commission and the Council; exceptionally, it may reject the resolution or refer it back to the committee for redrafting. The Parliament's official opinion is expressed by the resolution as amended, while the explanatory statement in the report (which may be quite long) is regarded as the responsibility of the rapporteur alone. Such reports often contain a wealth of information and analysis, and form a basis for future discussion of the issue concerned.

The committees most relevant to human rights and civil liberties are those for Legal Affairs and Citizens' Rights; Social Affairs, Employment and the Working Environment; Development and Co-operation; Civil Liberties and Internal Affairs; Institutional Affairs; Women's Rights; and Petitions.

The last committee, set up in 1987, was only given legal status through the last revision of the EC treaty.[39] It considers complaints from individuals or groups about injustice or maladministration and passes them on to the appropriate quarter, but has no other power. Its function is now largely duplicated by that of the new parliamentary Ombudsman (see above), who similarly lacks any power of enforcement. There is also a Subcommittee on Human Rights reporting to the Committee on Foreign Affairs and Security, but it deals only with human rights outside the Union.

Although most reports deal with proposals for legislation passed on by the Commission and Council, many are 'own initiative' reports that can (and do) deal with matters outside Community law. This is particularly true of the civil liberties committee. Such reports highlight areas of concern and keep up the pressure for their future incorporation into the treaties. An own-initiative report automatically lapses if not approved by the Parliament by the end of its five-year term of office; the subject has to be considered anew by the newly elected body.

The civil liberties committee dates only from February 1992, but in its short existence has produced a large number of reports, most of which will be cited in this book. There has been some rivalry with the legal affairs committee, which suspects the new committee of poaching on its preserve. This is hardly justified, since the former committee has mostly restricted itself to matters of Community law.

The reports of the civil liberties committee, chaired until 1994 by a British Conservative MEP who earned the hostility of some of his party at home, have often been radical in their proposals. In January 1993 the first of its annual reports on respect for human rights in the Community was published.[40] Like its successor in 1994,[41] it aroused objections from some MEPs whose countries featured unfavourably in the report.

NGOs

Non-governmental organisations are usually organised on a national basis and find it difficult (for financial and other reasons) to form effective international networks. This makes it hard for them to match the lobbying power of multinationals and other commercial interest groups, let alone the armies of officials deployed by governments to further their interests. Nevertheless, NGOs are increasingly recognising the need to join forces. At all levels, from the UN downwards, they are pressing for improved levels of protection under the various international Conventions. While recognising the weakness of many of the existing Conventions, it is argued that

> ... international Conventions and their supervisory instruments are useful and powerful instruments in the hands of individuals and NGOs. They offer protection in addition to national laws and practices, provide for friendly settlements and remedies for victims, oblige states to adapt their legislation to international norms, have a preventive effect on states' behaviour and offer possibilities of having public and parliamentary debates on the efforts of states to comply with international human rights standards.[42]

NGOs whose concerns are recognised by the EC treaty (such as environmental protection) are able to obtain Community funding through grants reserved for such topics. Others find this more difficult. In the field of human rights there are a few organisations which support modest offices in Brussels and which try to influence Union policy by issuing reports and recommendations. The most well-known of these is Amnesty International, whose International Secretariat (based in London) issues regular reports on violations of human rights in European countries.[43] Its reports on Member States of the European Union have voiced concern about many different abuses:

• extrajudicial execution by security forces,
• ill-treatment, torture and deaths in police custody and prisons,
• imprisonment of conscientious objectors,
• violations of freedom of expression,
• religious discrimination,
• prolonged solitary confinement of prisoners, and
• unfair trials.

A particular concern of Amnesty International and many national NGOs has been the trend of asylum policy in the European Union (Chapter 4). This is also monitored closely by ECRE, the European Council [formerly Consultation] on Refugees and Exiles.

Amnesty's reports are a sobering reminder that although the abuses are not as serious as in other parts of the world, not all is well in the field of human rights in Europe. They reinforce the arguments for a more firmly based system of protection and an effective means of redress for the individual.

NOTES

1. For collected texts of all but the first and last Conventions listed, see *Human rights in international law: basic texts* (Strasbourg: Council of Europe, 1992) (also published in French). See also Leah Levin, *Human rights: questions and answers* (Paris: UNESCO, 1995).
2. An international treaty is first signed by representatives of the states concerned but does not come into force until a minimum number of them (as specified in the treaty) have also ratified it. This is a detailed commitment which can be subject to reservations or derogations by the contracting state, where this is permitted by the treaty. These 'opt-out clauses' demand careful study, since they sometimes allow the ratifying state to avoid all but the least onerous requirements of the agreement. An annually updated list of the state of ratification of all international instruments relating to human rights is prepared by the International Institute of Human Rights in Strasbourg; for the situation at 1 January 1994 see *Human Rights Law Journal*, vol. 15 (1994) pp. 51–67.
3. For full text including the 1967 Protocol (Chapter 4), see for example Richard Plender (ed.), *Basic documents on international migration law* (Dordrecht: Nijhoff, 1988) pp. 87–105.
4. Not yet in force. For full text see United Nations General Assembly Resolution 45/158 (1990); for summary and discussion see *Proclaiming migrants' rights*, Briefing Paper no. 3 (Brussels: Churches' Committee for Migrants in Europe, Geneva: World Council of Churches, 1991).
5. For a full description of procedures applying to UN Conventions see David Johnson, 'The reporting procedure under the United Nations human rights Instruments', in Julie Cator and Jan Niessen (eds), *The use of international Conventions to protect the rights of migrants and ethnic minorities*, proceedings of seminar: Strasbourg, November 1993 (Brussels: Churches' Committee for Migrants in Europe, 1994) pp. 124–8.
6. Keith Ewing, *Britain and the ILO* (London: Institute of Employment Rights, 1994).
7. See for example 'The reform of international institutions for the protection of human rights: La Laguna Declaration', in *Declaración*

de La Laguna (La Cuesta, Tenerife: Universidad de La Laguna, 1993) pp. 75–103; also Ineke Boerefijn and Koen Davidse, 'Every cloud … ? The World Conference on Human Rights and supervision of implementation of human rights', *Netherlands Quarterly of Human Rights*, vol. 11 (1993) pp. 457–68.

8. *Arrangement between the Council of Europe and the European Community, concluded on 16 June 1987* (Strasbourg: Council of Europe, 1987).

9. Commission of the European Communities, *Commission Communication to the Council on relations between the Community and the Council of Europe*, COM(89) 124 final (Luxembourg: Office for Official Publications of the European Communities, 1989).

10. For the text of the Convention and Protocols 1, 2, 4, 6, 7 and 9 see *Human rights in international law* (note 1) pp. 159–210. See also Luke Clements, *European Human Rights: Taking a Case under the Convention* (London: Sweet and Maxwell, 1994).

11. Recommendation 1194 (1992) of the Parliamentary Assembly of the Council of Europe.

12. *Netherlands Quarterly of Human Rights*, vol. 11 (1993) pp. 513–20.

13. Protocol No. 11 to the European Convention on Human Rights and explanatory report, document H (94) 5 (Strasbourg: Human Rights Information Centre, Council of Europe, 1994). This includes an interesting history of the proposal. For more explanatory material see *Human Rights Law Journal*, vol. 15 (1994) pp. 81–131 (also published as *Revue universelle des droits de l'homme* and *Europäische Grundrechte-Zeitschrift*).

14. *Guardian*, 18 March 1994.

15. *Bulletin of the European Communities*, Supplement 2/79 (1979).

16. Commission of the European Communities, *Commission Communication on Community accession to the European Convention for the Protection of Human Rights and Fundamental Freedoms and some of its Protocols*, SEC(90) 2087 final (internal document, 1990).

17. Committee on Legal Affairs and Citizens' Rights (rapporteur: R. Bontempi), *Report on Community accession to the European Convention on Human Rights*, A3–0431/93 (European Parliament, 1993).

18. *The accession of the European Communities to the European Convention on Human Rights* (Geneva: International Commission of Jurists, 1993).

19. *Etat de la question de l'adhésion des Communautés Européennes à la C.E.D.H.* (Paris: Fédération Internationale des Droits de l'Homme, 1993).

20. House of Lords Select Committee on the European Communities, *Human rights re-examined*, Session 1992–93, 3rd Report (London: HMSO, 1992).

21. *Netherlands Quarterly of Human Rights*, vol. 11 (1993) pp. 489–90.
22. ECJ register no. 461807 (26 April 1994).
23. *Human Rights in International Law* (note 1) pp. 211–52.
24. *European Treaty Series*, no. 93 (Strasbourg: Council of Europe, 1985).
25. Jan Niessen and Henri de Lary de Latour, 'Equality of treatment: the European Social Charter and the European Convention on the Legal Status of Migrant Workers', in *The use of international Conventions* (note 5) pp. 93–101.
26. *European Treaty Series*, no. 108 (Strasbourg: Council of Europe, 1982).
27. *Human rights in international law* (note 1) pp. 253–63.
28. *3rd general report on the CPT's activities covering the period 1 January to 31 December 1992*, CPT/Inf(93) 12 (Strasbourg: Directorate of Human Rights, Council of Europe) p. 7.
29. The Budapest summit meeting at the end of 1994 decided on the change of title to reflect the organisation's developing role.
30. For extracts from this and subsequent declarations see *Human rights in international law* (note 1) pp. 363–465; for a comprehensive account of organisation's history see Rachel Brett, *Is more better? An exploration of the CSCE Human Dimension Mechanism and its relationship to other systems for the promotion and protection of human rights* (Colchester: University of Essex, Human Rights Centre, 1994).
31. Rachel Brett, *The challenges of change: report of the Helsinki follow-up meeting of the CSCE* (Colchester: University of Essex, Human Rights Centre, 1992).
32. Urban Gibson and Jan Niessen, *The CSCE and the protection of the rights of migrants, refugees and minorities*, Briefing Paper no. 11 (Brussels: Churches' Committee for Migrants in Europe, 1993).
33. For more discussion see A. H. Robertson and J. G. Merrills, *Human rights in Europe*, 3rd edn (Manchester: Manchester University Press, 1993).
34. Article 138e EC.
35. Articles 193–8 EC.
36. Committee on Institutional Affairs (rapporteur: K. De Gucht), *Report on the Declaration of Fundamental Rights and Freedoms*, A2–3/89/Parts A and B (European Parliament, 1989); *Official Journal of the European Communities*, C120 (16 May 1989) pp. 51–7.
37. Committee on Institutional Affairs (rapporteur: F. Herman), *Second report on the Constitution of the European Union*, A3–0064/94 (European Parliament, 1994); *Official Journal of the European Communities*, C61 (28 February 1994) pp. 155–70.

38. For a full description of how they operate see Francis Jacobs, Richard Corbett and Michael Shackleton, *The European Parliament*, 2nd edn (Harlow: Longman, 1992) pp. 97–135.
39. Articles 8d and 138d EC; Epamimondas Marias, 'Growing appeal of appealing', *European Brief*, December 1994, pp. 31–3.
40. Committee on Civil Liberties and Internal Affairs (rapporteur: K. De Gucht), *Annual report on respect for human rights in the European Community*, A3–0025/93 (European Parliament, 1993).
41. Committee on Civil Liberties and Internal Affairs (rapporteur: E. Newman), *Annual report on respect for human rights in the European Union*, A3–0200/94 (European Parliament, 1994).
42. Jan Niessen, in *The use of international Conventions* (note 5) p. 5.
43. *Concerns in Europe* (London: Amnesty International). Issued twice a year.

3

Abolishing Border Controls

FREEDOM OF MOVEMENT

The Single European Act (SEA) of 1987 was intended to give new impetus to a process which is still not completed: that of achieving a free circulation of people throughout the European Union. To do this the SEA inserted into the EC treaty a new Article 8a (re-numbered as 7a by the TEU) which has probably caused more controversy than any other. This laid down that the EC should adopt 'measures with the aim of progressively establishing the internal market over a period expiring on 31 December 1992'. It went on to define the internal market as 'an area without internal frontiers in which the free movement of goods, persons, services and capital is ensured in accordance with the provisions of the Treaty'.

In this context 'persons' appeared to imply people of all nationalities, not just citizens of Member States. This was certainly the view taken by the Commission in its role as guardian of the EC treaty. The Article did not, however, say what non-citizens could do with their freedom of movement; where movement to take up residence or employment were concerned, only nationals of Member States had guaranteed rights. A new Article 8a in the amended EC treaty promises a qualified right of both free movement and residence to all citizens of the Union, but not to anyone else.[1]

There was no difficulty in meeting the 1992 deadline for services and capital, and for goods the problems were not insurmountable; it was the people that gave rise to fundamental objections. Visions of an uncontrollable invasion by criminals and unwanted immigrants began to haunt the politicians of certain countries. In some cases these fears were fed by a mistrust of Member States with which they shared a land border. If state A was too lax in policing its external borders with the non-EU world, what was there to stop undesirables flooding in and across the border with state B? For nations with extensive coastlines like Denmark, Greece, Ireland and the UK there was also a conviction that nothing could be as effective as the existing entry controls at ports and airports. The British government signed the SEA but insisted on the insertion of a General Declaration which has been much quoted since:

> Nothing in these provisions shall affect the right of the Member States to take such measures as they consider necessary for the purpose of controlling immigration from third [non-EC] countries, and to combat terrorism, the traffic in drugs and illicit trading in works of art and antiques.[2]

This was intended to justify the continuance of border controls for as long as any government thought necessary, and in particular the right to subject non-EC nationals to detailed checks at the border. The scene was set for a lively battle of wills in subsequent years involving the Commission, the European Parliament and recalcitrant Member States.

Threats of Enforcement

Matters appeared to be coming to a head in early 1992 when Martin Bangemann, the Commissioner responsible for the internal market, issued a stern warning aimed largely at the UK. He said that if systematic checks at ports and airports did not cease by the end of 1992, the Commission would consider action in the Court of Justice against offending Member States. Even their own citizens would be encouraged to bring actions. 'We will fight like lions', he declared, 'against anyone violating these rules.'[3] This was followed by a legalistic broadside from the Commission[4] which argued that 'a declaration can never deprive an Article of the Treaty of its practical effectiveness'. It stated bluntly that 'the Commission ... hereby declares that it is resolutely determined to use all the legal and political means at its disposal to ensure that the work programme stemming from Article 8a [now 7a] is carried out in full'.

Following this robust statement of intent, it was something of a let-down when Mr Bangemann stated in September 1992 that he had no interest in a legal wrangle with the UK government over the abolition of border controls. He said that while he differed with the UK on the issue, it was time to 'get to grips pragmatically' with the general aim of abolishing regular checks on EC citizens.[5] He went on to imply that a compromise solution might be acceptable for a transitional period, pending negotiation of the planned Convention on external border controls (see below).[6]

This softening of tone came after some stormy Council meetings earlier in the year at which the matter was discussed. The Internal Market Council then issued a statement that pointedly failed to endorse the

Commission's position on border controls.[7] A compromise with the UK emerged under which EC citizens could simply raise their passports unopened as they passed through port and airport controls (the 'Bangemann wave').

During this period the European Parliament became increasingly restive at the lack of action. One of its committees had drawn up a lengthy report in 1991 which deplored the slow progress in achieving full freedom of movement, and insisted that the Commission had the power to enforce compliance by Member States.[8] It also warned the Commission to expect a legal challenge from the Parliament if it failed to act. This would be based on Article 175 EC which empowers any Member State, any institution of the Community or any 'natural or legal person' (an individual or a corporate body) to bring an action before the Court of Justice.

In October 1992 the Parliament adopted a second report on the same theme.[9] The report accepted the need for some internal controls as the price of opening up the borders, but urged Member States to avoid sacrificing individual rights in the process. The committee clearly felt that granting unrestricted freedom of movement to every non-EC national was going too far, but it pointed to the injustice of denying such freedom to those who had long been resident in the Community. The resolution accompanying the report ended with a renewed threat of legal action against the Commission for failing to act.

In July 1993 the Parliament finally made good its threat. Its President wrote to the Commission demanding that it 'define its position' within the two months allowed by Article 175 EC. The Commission denied in its response that it had failed to act in accordance with the treaty. The Parliament then instituted an action before the Court of Justice.[10] This asked for a declaration that the Commission had in fact failed to implement Articles 7a and 155 EC (the latter being a requirement that the Commission must 'ensure the proper functioning and development of the common market'). Judgment in the case was not expected before Easter 1995.

Meanwhile, to the ordinary citizen the debate appeared increasingly academic. Far from decreasing after 1992, some controls at internal frontiers seemed actually to be increasing. At international airports not only were people subjected to intense security checks of themselves and their luggage, but their passports were repeatedly demanded by airline officials. This was a response to the laws introduced by some states which exacted heavy penalties from carriers that allowed anyone to travel on false or invalid documents (Chapter 4). The dream of free movement seemed rather divorced from reality.

The Hidden Agenda

Whatever their disagreements about the interpretation of Article 7a, the governments of Member States have always been at one over the need for measures to offset the loss of control implied by the abolition of internal frontier checks. The principal concern has always been to construct an impregnable external boundary to the Union, so as to exclude all those who might constitute a threat to its internal stability.

The measures to be adopted were discussed at length in secret meetings of the Council and the European Council and elaborated by working groups of officials. In many of these the Commission also had a role. The topics under discussion were summarised in a public report by the Commission in 1988.[11] This promised a number of Commission initiatives, including a Directive on the harmonisation of asylum policy. However, this and other proposals never saw the light of day; the Council insisted (as it still does) that such matters lay outside the scope of Community law, and could only be settled by intergovernmental agreement.

The European Parliament was thus excluded from the process of policy-making in these areas, a decision which it has bitterly disputed ever since.[12] The Commission's 'steadily diminishing ambitions' were seen by the Parliament as a betrayal of the democratic principles of the Community, since the supposed guardian of the EC treaty was reduced to the role of merely working under the direction of the Member States.[13]

The Commission's 1988 report was a somewhat anodyne collection of proposals to which few people could object. A more detailed agenda emerged (with minimal publicity) after the European Council meeting at Madrid in 1989, in the form of the Palma Document.[14] This was drawn up by a group of senior officials from Member States, together with a Vice-President of the Commission. It was named the Co-ordinators' Group and continued to work under this title until it was reborn as the 'K4 Committee' (Chapter 1).

The Palma Document can now be seen to have set in motion a progressive erosion of fundamental rights, all in the name of achieving freedom of movement within the Community. This lay not so much in the formal Conventions that subsequently emerged, such as the Dublin Convention on asylum requests (Chapter 4), but in a series of secretly negotiated ministerial agreements. These resulted in coordinated changes in national law and policy towards asylum seekers and immigrants. Some of them, such as 'recourse to a simplified or priority procedure, according to national legislation, in the case of unfounded applications', are clearly spelt out in the Palma Document.

Another area in which the document gives a foretaste of things to come is that of information exchange – a necessary process but one that, if not properly regulated, can do untold harm to individuals. It lists as 'essential' a number of systems for exchanging information on

- persons who are wanted or 'inadmissible',
- the removal of citizens of third countries that 'represent a possible terrorist danger to security', and
- known members of, and activities of, terrorist groups in one of the Member States 'when the security interests of another Member State may be affected'.

Among 'desirable' measures are:

- a European drug-addiction information system,
- a central instrument for the collection and evaluation of intelligence concerning terrorism,
- computerisation of the exchange of information needed in visa processing, and
- a data bank for storing information on the places and dates of submission of applications for asylum; this would also cover 'other matters such as refusal to grant visas and forged papers'.

A curious omission is the creation of a central police organisation, an idea that was certainly being discussed at the time[15] and which later came to pass (Chapter 7). Soon after the drafting of the Palma Document, the data protection commissioners of the EC nations issued a warning about the dangers inherent in transborder exchanges of the kind envisaged.[16] They strongly recommended

- the adoption of 'appropriate legal instruments' to ensure that the principles of the Council of Europe Convention on data protection were binding on all Member States and on the EC institutions themselves, and
- the creation of an independent authority to advise the EC institutions on all data protection issues.

What the commissioners did not foresee was that the data protection Directive later drafted by the Commission (Chapter 7) would not apply to any of the systems listed above.

SCHENGEN

Soon after publication of the Palma Document, a new Convention on the abolition of internal frontiers was signed quite independently in

1990 by five Member States of the EC: France, Germany and the Benelux countries (Belgium, Luxembourg and the Netherlands).[17] As its title indicates, this was a detailed treaty to implement an agreement first signed in 1985.[18] The latter followed earlier precedents for the abolition of border controls on persons: the 1960 agreement between the Benelux countries and the 1984 Saarbrücken Accord between France and Germany.[19] Its importance cannot be overemphasised; it has variously been described as a 'blueprint for the ending of border controls', a 'laboratory experiment' and a 'pilot project'.[20] The Commission of the EC has taken a back seat with only observer status at meetings between representatives of the Member States concerned, but clearly regards Schengen as a useful precedent. Others have been much less sanguine about the outcome of the processes set in motion.

The earlier Schengen Agreement was at first sight a harmless declaration of intent. Its aims (in apparent order of importance) were to give freedom of movement to nationals of all Member States of the EC (not just the Schengen signatories), and to facilitate the movement of goods and services. Few observers took much notice of a section of the Agreement headed 'measures applicable in the long term'. However, included in a list of harmonisation measures were such items as 'arrangements for police cooperation on the prevention of delinquency' and the harmonisation of visa policies. Controls at the common frontiers were to be transferred to the external frontiers of the Schengen group, and states were to take 'complementary measures to safeguard security and combat illegal immigration by nationals of states that are not members of the European Communities'. No details were given of how this was to be achieved.

Such was the lack of interest that only the Netherlands government put the Agreement to its parliament for ratification, and this was achieved without a debate. NGOs were also slow to wake up to the significance of the Agreement, and the UN High Commissioner for Refugees did not formally ask to be consulted until 1989.[21] In retrospect this is not too hard to understand, since the 1985 Agreement made no mention at all of refugees; the idea that they were a potential problem did not arise.

Alarm bells started to ring as the outcome of negotiations on the 'complementary measures' began to leak out. By 1989 the data protection commissioners of European countries, who had also been left out of the negotiations until 1988, were disturbed by the implications of the proposed information exchange system (see below). They warned that it could 'substantially affect the rights of citizens',[22] and commissioned one of their number to report on the matter.[23]

The final text of the Schengen Convention[24] is very different to that of the 1985 Agreement. The focus has shifted dramatically from freedom of movement to its control; only two Articles in the Convention give guarantees to travellers, while most of the remaining 140 are devoted either to tightening external border controls or to a comprehensive system of internal surveillance. Worst of all, there is a marked absence of accountability to any independent judicial or parliamentary body. The Convention was drafted by technocrats and wastes no space on declarations about the importance of safeguarding human rights or democracy.[25] The Convention contains no provision for a state to opt out of the arrangement; there is only an acknowledgement of the fact that in due course it may be superseded by Conventions involving all Member States of the Union.

Elements of the Convention

The Convention covers the same ground as three separate EU Conventions that are discussed elsewhere in this book: the Dublin Convention on asylum requests (Chapter 4) and two others relating to external border controls, considered later in this chapter. The Schengen Convention may be regarded as a model for all of them, though they must have been worked on simultaneously. In its explicit linkage of two areas of concern – one supposedly humanitarian and the other to do with exclusion – it brings out all too clearly the underlying philosophy of those who drafted all three Conventions. Unfortunately, defects in the Schengen Convention have been faithfully reproduced in the other two, in spite of urgent pleading from jurists and NGOs. The main features of the Schengen rules are as follows:

- Internal border checks on persons will be abolished except when 'public policy or national security so require' (Article 2), but there will be increased policing of external borders (Article 6). There will be detailed checks on those entering from outside the Schengen area, covering not only personal identity and 'other conditions governing entry, residence, work and exit' but also 'checks to detect and prevent threats to the national security and public policy of the Contracting Parties'.
- All aliens (defined as non-EC nationals) must be subject to thorough checks not only on entering but also on leaving (Article 6). On arrival they may be required to submit documents 'substantiating the purpose and the conditions of the planned visit', and may have to demonstrate adequate means of support and funds for an onward

or return journey. An alien will be refused entry if he or she has been 'reported as a person not to be permitted entry' or is 'considered to be a threat to public policy, national security or the international relations of any of the Contracting Parties' (Article 5).

- Carriers by air, sea or land are obliged to take back any alien who is refused entry. They must check the validity of travel documents (including visas) and must be penalised for carrying aliens travelling without them (Article 26).
- Visits by aliens are limited to three months for the entire Schengen area. Aliens from countries on an agreed list will require a visa; for short visits this will have a uniform format and will be valid in the entire area. Visas for longer periods will be valid only in the territory of the issuing state (Articles 9–18).
- Aliens allowed entry are free to move between Schengen states but must register with the authorities of each state entered (Article 22). Both aliens and non-aliens must be registered when staying in hotels, lodging houses and even on camping sites or hired boats (Article 45).
- An alien who no longer fulfils the conditions of entry for a short stay must leave 'without delay' or be expelled (Article 23). Even a person with a residence permit to stay in one state may have this withdrawn if another Schengen state puts that person on its national list of banned individuals; this is subject to consultation between the states concerned. A residence permit may be issued to a banned person only 'on serious grounds, in particular of a humanitarian nature or pursuant to international obligations' (Article 25).
- Detailed provision is made for the allocation of requests for asylum. Only one Schengen state will handle a given application, with complex rules as to which country should be responsible (Articles 28–36). A person refused asylum cannot then apply for it to a second Schengen state. Subject to its obligations under the Geneva Convention, a state may expel or refuse entry to an applicant 'on the basis of its national provisions'. Subject to certain rules on data protection, states will exchange information on all applicants (Article 38). This will include personal data, places stayed at and routes followed before arrival, and details of any previous applications for asylum.
- Police authorities will assist each other and respond to requests that do not involve 'the application of coercive measures' (Article 39). Subject to authorisation, officers who are keeping under observation 'a person who is presumed to have taken part in a criminal offence to which extradition may apply' may continue their surveillance in another state (Article 40). Cross-border 'hot pursuit' is also allowed, subject to bilateral agreements between the states sharing borders (Article 41). Pursuing officers may apprehend a person until local officers arrive to take over. Firearms may be used only in self-defence.

- Mutual assistance in criminal matters such as legal proceedings and customs offences (Articles 48–53) and in extradition (Articles 59–66) is based on existing international Conventions. Safeguards against double prosecution for the same offence (the *non bis in idem* principle) are laid down (Articles 54–8).
- Cooperation is demanded of all states in combating offences relating to 'narcotic drugs and psychotropic substances of whatever type, including cannabis', a wording evidently aimed at the more liberal policy of the Netherlands (Articles 70–6). 'Monitored deliveries' of drugs are to be allowed. Laws relating to firearms are to be brought into line with detailed requirements (Articles 77–91).
- A computerised Schengen Information System (SIS) is to be set up for exchanging data on a wide range of matters (Articles 92–119). Each state will have a national computer system connected to a central 'technical support function' located in Strasbourg. This will hold data transmitted by each state for automatic access by other states. The subjects covered include wanted or missing persons, vehicles and other items stolen or missing, persons to be extradited or expelled, and persons or vehicles under covert surveillance. The grounds for including details of a person are widely drawn. Apart from those 'reported for the purpose of being refused entry' (Article 96) and those suspected of being about to commit 'extremely serious offences' which are not defined, anyone deemed to pose 'serious threats to internal or external State security' may be listed as requiring surveillance (Article 99). Only asylum seekers are excluded from the SIS, although nothing is said about their status when an application has been refused. Access to the system is available to officials dealing with border checks, police and customs checks within each country, visa applications, residence permits and the internal movements of aliens (Article 101). Data protection rules are specified for these and other uses of personal data (Articles 114–18 and 126–30).
- An Executive Committee will implement the Convention (Articles 131–3). It will comprise a minister from each of the Schengen governments and will draw up its own rules of procedure.
- The Convention comes into force after all states have ratified or otherwise accepted its terms, and certain other conditions are fulfilled. Any other Member State of the EC can join, subject to ratification by all the existing members (Articles 139–40).

Technical Hitches

Soon after the signing of the Convention in 1990 the founding members were joined by Italy, followed by Spain and Portugal (1991) and then

Greece (1992). However, the essential process of ratification proceeded much more slowly. The five original members harboured doubts about the ability of the new members to control their borders, and were in no hurry to ratify their adhesion.

Quite apart from this, four out of the five governments (France,[26] Germany,[27] Belgium[28] and the Netherlands[29]) were facing objections from their own parliaments or constitutional courts – a direct consequence of having failed to consult them in the first place. In France[30] and in Germany[31] the government responded by pushing through an amendment to the Constitution. In Portugal, President Soares initially refused on constitutional grounds to sign the ratification bill passed by his parliament, but finally did so after a delay of nine months.[32] For many observers, the process of ratification by the Schengen states was a shameful saga in which constitutional principles were repeatedly sacrificed to political expediency.

By September 1993, the five founding members of the Schengen group had deposited their instruments of ratification with the Luxembourg government as required by the Convention, and 1 December 1993 was agreed as the date on which it would come into force in those states.[33] France had still to amend its Constitution (see above) and its ministers remained highly critical of the drug policies of the Netherlands,[34] but it was hoped that the problems could be resolved in time. It then began to emerge that there were serious technical difficulties that would probably make the deadline impossible to meet.

The first of these related to international airports, where it was necessary to arrange for passengers travelling only between Schengen states to do so without passport checks. This involved expensive building work to segregate such passengers from those arriving from outside. Only Frankfurt airport had completed the work by November 1993.[35]

A far more serious problem emerged in connection with the SIS, without which the Convention could not be implemented. To enable data stored in each national (N.SIS) system to be made available to other national systems through the central (C.SIS) one, personal names in particular need to be transcribed into a uniform format with standardised spelling. An obvious difficulty arises with the Greek, Chinese and other alphabets. Even within one alphabet, other more subtle differences (like the double surnames in Spain and Portugal) make it difficult to arrange names in a common alphabetical order. In August 1993 it was reported that about 50 per cent of the reporting of persons to be refused entry at external borders was not functioning properly.[36]

Successive postponements in the starting date were announced until in January 1994 the attempt to fix a deadline was abandoned for the time being.[37] Meanwhile, politicians of the different countries were starting to blame each other for the fiasco.[38] Some experts doubted whether the system would ever work, and suggested that a further two to three years might be needed to set up a new one.[39]

As 1994 progressed it began to look as if Schengen, despite the interest shown by Austria and Denmark in joining,[40] was running out of steam. However, at the end of the year the SIS was pronounced functional and the Executive Committee announced that seven of the contracting states (excluding Greece and Italy) would 'irreversibly' put the Convention into effect from 26 March 1995. Doubts remained about the willingness of the French government to actually abolish its border checks on that date.[41]

Schengen and Human Rights

The Schengen Convention remains important as a precedent for Union-wide agreements, and will be considered here in more detail because it has attracted the most detailed critiques of its defects. Once the terms of the Convention became known, legal experts and NGOs were not slow to express alarm. Among these, the Dutch-based Standing Committee of Experts on International Immigration, Refugee and Criminal Law (the 'Meijers committee') offered the most detailed and authoritative analysis.[42] The committee also maintains a network of foreign correspondents in other EU countries. Its arguments on Schengen were primarily aimed at the Dutch government and parliament (which was quicker to show disquiet about the issues than its Schengen counterparts), but were reproduced in English for a wider public.

The committee's criticism centres above all on the lack of real control by any parliamentary or judicial body. Enormous power is vested in the Executive Committee, whose accountability (like that of the Council of the EU) is restricted to that of its constituent ministers to their respective parliaments. Power to rule on the interpretation of the Convention is not assigned to any supreme court such as the European Court of Justice, so national courts or appeal tribunals are the only channel of complaint for the individual. Although there is a joint supervisory body for the SIS, it is not empowered to investigate individual complaints about data protection; this, like much else, is left to national laws that vary between states.

The experts regard as ominous the omission from the Convention of any reference to the European Convention on Human Rights (ECHR). This is particularly surprising in view of the many aspects of Schengen that could give rise to infringement of the ECHR. As it was pointed out before the Convention was finalised, even data protection is essentially a matter of privacy as an aspect of human rights and should take account of its norms.[43]

The committee concludes that the cumulative effect of all the Schengen provisions is to increase the collective power of the governments and their law-enforcement agencies, while denying the individual any corresponding benefit except the notional freedom to cross an internal border without showing a passport. An example cited is the legal assistance which states will increasingly provide to one another in the prosecution of crimes, backed up by police cooperation in the collection of evidence.[44] There is no obligation to inform defence lawyers of the nature of such cooperation, making it difficult to determine whether evidence from another country was legally obtained or not. Comparable facilities for assistance and information collection are not available to the defence, so the scales are weighted against the accused.

The apparently detailed attention to data protection is also found wanting, a view shared by other experts.[45] The Convention does reproduce several provisions of the Council of Europe Convention on data protection (Chapter 7), and extends this to cover manual as well as computerised files. It also refers to the Council of Europe's important Recommendation R (87) 15 on police data. However, it embodies no obligation to inform a person that personal data have been exchanged. This, like the right of access to data and the mechanism for correcting errors, is left to national laws which are notoriously weak where police and security service files are concerned.[46] Evidence has already begun to accumulate of the extreme difficulties faced by persons wrongly identified as dangerous criminals because of faulty exchanges of data between police forces (Chapter 7). A further problem is that police cooperation has so far been allowed to develop without any regulating framework of international law. It has been claimed that the police indulge in 'an increasing amount of activities of which the legitimacy … is open to serious doubt, or which even form a direct contravention of law'.[47] It remains to be seen whether the detailed rules laid down by the Convention will change this, or whether there will be pressure to modify them as being too restrictive in practice.

So far as asylum is concerned, the committee believes that the Schengen rules fall seriously short of the standards demanded by the Geneva Convention and the ECHR. Far from eliminating the problem of the 'refugee in orbit', the Convention offers no guarantee that any of its signatories will offer even temporary refuge; Article 29 specifically states that every state retains the right to refuse entry or to expel an applicant for asylum. The 'one chance only' rule, combined with visa requirements and carrier sanctions (Chapter 4), leads to the conclusion that 'their opportunities to find a country of asylum in these European parts are not being increased. On the contrary, they will dramatically be reduced'.[48]

The committee is heavily critical of the 1991 'readmission agreement' between the Schengen states and Poland.[49] This was the forerunner of many other agreements between EU states and those lying between them and the refugee-producing countries (Chapter 4). It obliges Poland to take back any person who has entered that country from a non-Schengen state and who, on crossing its border with the Schengen area, is found to be 'irregular' in any of the Schengen states. The agreement also applies to Polish nationals. The committee points out that through agreements such as this 'the Eastern European States lighten the burdensome task of controlling the land borders of the Schengen territory. These States, however, are under no obligation to guarantee any legal protection. Nor are they to give account of their way of exercising the controls.'

The committee's concerns about the powers of the Schengen Executive Committee were amplified in a later document. This criticised the draft rules of procedure of the Executive Committee in strong terms:

> The Executive Committee has unique powers. These powers are unique in the field of international organisations because they are so sweeping. They are sweeping in three ways, namely: the nature and extent of the subject matter on which the Executive Committee can make binding decisions; the absence of international parliamentary and judicial control; and the kind of people to which those decisions can be addressed: individuals, mainly aliens and persons subject to criminal law ... The agreement in the first place addresses the rights and duties of individuals ... and not the rights and duties of states, which perhaps have less need of protection by an international parliament and an international court.[50]

The rules of procedure that were subsequently adopted[51] confirmed the fears of the experts. The meetings of the Executive Committee are not to be in public unless otherwise decided, and its deliberations are similarly covered by an obligation of secrecy. Even the manner of announcing its decisions, which is to be governed by national laws, may be restricted by the 'confidential character' of the decisions. The work of the committee is to be prepared by a Central Group of high officials with wide powers to set up working parties and carry out 'other work which it judges necessary'; the analogy with the K4 Committee of the EU (Chapter 1) is obvious. The Commission of the EC is invited to attend meetings, though the Executive Committee may nevertheless meet in its absence.

The Dutch parliament responded to these concerns by passing an Act of Approval with the crucial safeguard that the Dutch representative cannot agree to a binding decision by the Executive Committee without the approval of both chambers of the Dutch parliament; the Belgian and Italian parliaments also obtained a more limited measure of control.[52] The Meijers committee wanted much earlier publication of a draft decision and background documents, so that the Dutch minister concerned could adequately consult the parliament.

Under pressure from Belgium, Italy and the Netherlands, the Executive Committee agreed in 1992 at least to study the idea of giving judicial competence to the European Court of Justice. Other states later supported the idea, and only France remained totally opposed.[53] In this connection, one option suggested by a British expert in Community law is that a new court attached to the ECJ could specialise in all matters involving asylum, immigration, police cooperation, data protection and any other matters relating to the movement of persons in the internal market.[54] It would thus cover all the sensitive issues arising out of both Schengen and Title VI of the TEU. A similar view was adopted by a committee of the UK House of Lords,[55] but other experts have deemed this unnecessary.[56]

Other prominent critics of Schengen have included the United Nations High Commissioner for Refugees (UNHCR) and the European Parliament. UNHCR tempered its criticism with a welcome for the safeguards that were in place, but warned that carrier sanctions and strict visa requirements were both liable to harm the interests of refugees:

> Visa requisites, such as having an address in the country of refuge, monetary sums, a return air ticket or family ties, are prerequisites a refugee will very often have difficulty meeting. For some refugees, the very real danger which lies in even approaching governmental authorities for visas considerably hinders their search for protection.[57]

The European Parliament was much less restrained in its criticism. It accepted the function of Schengen as a testing ground for the whole Union, but realised that this precedent could lead to exclusion of the Parliament from any control over what was decided in future. A resolution deploring the way things were going was passed in 1989.[58] This was followed in 1992 by a detailed report from one of its committees.[59] The criticisms listed above are forcefully repeated in the report and some others added.

The legality of an important adjunct of the SIS, the SIRENE system,[60] is seriously questioned on the grounds that it is not provided for in the Schengen Convention. SIRENE, like the SIS, is an information exchange system in which each country has its own system operated by the police. Its purpose is to supplement the automated exchanges of limited data through the SIS by direct 'free text' communication between national systems, mainly by using electronic mail for the exchange of documents. This is regarded by some observers as extremely dangerous from the point of view of civil liberties.[61] A manual regulating its use was approved by the Executive Committee in December 1992 but its contents remain secret.

The report also criticises the secrecy surrounding the joint list of countries whose nationals would require a visa to enter the Schengen area. This forms part of a confidential appendix to the common consular instruction manual. In 1989 it was believed to contain 98 countries.[62] After publication of the report it emerged that the list had grown to 120, nearly all of them in the Third World.[63]

The report ends by emphasising the Parliament's long-held belief that the matters covered by Schengen should all along have been handled by the Commission and subjected to the normal rules of decision-making laid down in the EC treaty. As mentioned above, the Commission also held this view at one time but retreated in the face of opposition from the Council. As the report says:

> For the moment, the Member States are in the ascendant in their long-standing rivalry with the Commission. The introduction of the third pillar is evidence of this. It ought to be realised that much power is being transferred to national officials. This is a threat to a democratic Europe; it definitely represents a step backwards and cannot be accepted without protest.[64]

THE EXTERNAL FRONTIERS CONVENTION

Four years after the signing of the Schengen Convention, the process of producing corresponding Conventions for the whole EU was still in progress. Refugee issues were covered by the Dublin Convention on the allocation of requests for asylum (Chapter 4). This was signed in 1990, but by the end of 1994 it had still not been ratified by all Member States. Those parts of Schengen that relate to external borders were to be covered by two Conventions: one on external frontier controls and the other on an information exchange system based on the SIS, the European Information System (EIS). The draft EIS Convention was still the subject of negotiations during 1994 (see below). The external frontiers Convention was first drafted in 1991, but a bizarre dispute between Spain and the UK prevented it proceeding any further for another three years. The point at issue was the status of Gibraltar, and in particular its port and airport. Spain wanted these to be subject to joint police and customs control, in recognition of the historic dispute with Britain concerning sovereignty over Gibraltar.[65]

Before adoption of the TEU the draft Convention remained in the hands of an intergovernmental working party,[66] and was regarded by the Council (though not the European Parliament) as outside the scope of Community law. After Maastricht the situation changed somewhat, though not as much as the Parliament wished. Under Article K.1 TEU, rules on external border controls are specified as a legitimate matter of common interest (Chapter 1). Article K.3(2) lays out options which include the adoption of Conventions between the Member States. It also gives the Commission a right of initiative in this and certain other areas. The Parliament is to be consulted and kept informed of discussions, but has no other power.

In an attempt to break the deadlock, the Commission availed itself of its new powers and proposed that most of the draft Convention should be incorporated into a Council Decision (see Chapter 1 for definition of its legal status).[67] In this way the Council would recommend Member States to adopt the Convention 'in accordance with their respective constitutional requirements'. However, one section of the previous draft was treated differently. The new Article 100c EC places two matters firmly under Community law: determining a list of countries whose nationals require a visa to enter the Union, and deciding on a uniform format for visas. The Commission therefore proposed that the visa list should be issued in the form of a binding Regulation.[68] Under Article 100c this would still require only 'consultation' of the Parliament, rather than coming under cooperation or codecision procedures. By the end of 1994 there was still no progress on the Convention: the Gibraltar issue was even further from resolution, and new areas of disagreement had emerged.[69]

The New Convention

As finally unveiled, the draft Convention bears a remarkable resemblance to the corresponding parts of the Schengen Convention, though the Commission makes no reference to the fact. The Articles have been rearranged in a different order, but the effect is unchanged. All the essential features are there: detailed entry restrictions for aliens, exclusion or expulsion of those on a joint list of undesirables, and penalties on carriers accepting passengers without valid documents. 'Short stay' visas are to be issued for visits totalling no more than three months in a six-month period starting on the first day of entry.

In contrast with Schengen, a residence permit for one Member State will not entitle a third-country national or certain family members to more than a 'short stay' (defined as above) in another Member State.[70]

The vague but sweeping criteria for exclusion – that a person represents 'a threat to the public policy, national security or international relations of Member States' – are identical to those of Schengen. About the only things missing are the obligation for aliens to register with the authorities on moving between Member States, and for owners of hotels etc. to register the names of visitors.

There are, however, two welcome provisions that were absent from both Schengen and the earlier draft Convention. The ECHR is now mentioned (in the preamble and in Article 27) as a treaty that should take precedence over the Convention, in addition to the previously cited Geneva Convention. Secondly, Article 29 proposes that the ECJ should have jurisdiction in two areas: to give preliminary rulings on interpretation of the Convention (as in Article 177 EC), and to rule on disputes over implementation. The last innovation was based on Article K.3 TEU which allows such a provision, but it aroused immediate opposition from at least one Member State (see below). Finally, the contentious Article 30 on 'territorial extent' is left blank, so that Spain and the UK can try again to settle the issue of Gibraltar.

The Visa List

The draft Regulation lists 126 countries on what the Commission chooses to call the 'negative list'. In an explanatory memorandum the Commission claims that Article 100c EC implies a corresponding 'positive list' of countries whose nationals are guaranteed to be free of visa requirements; however, this is made impossible by the large number of states for which some but not all Member States demand visas. The Schengen states have 31 states in this third category and had intended to make them either 'positive' or 'negative' by the middle of 1993,[71] but this was never achieved. Under questioning, Commission officials admitted in 1994 that their negative list of 126 was simply the latest version of the Schengen list; the other 96 countries in the world were in the third category which allowed Member States to take unilateral decisions.[72]

The draft Regulation optimistically gives 30 June 1996 as a deadline for eliminating discrepancies between national visa lists. It seems likely that the negative list can only increase during these further negotiations. The only positive feature of this catalogue of exclusion is that the draft Regulation demands an end to the secrecy surrounding visa lists: all national lists, and any change in either the joint list or a national list, will have to be published in the Community's Official Journal.

Parliamentary Critics

The European Parliament was not slow to criticise both the draft Convention and the proposed visa list. Among many proposed amendments to the Convention, the civil liberties committee[73] wanted to delete altogether the requirement for carrier sanctions (Article 14) on the grounds that it is contrary to the aims and the spirit of the Geneva Convention. It also proposed that from 1996 onwards the three-month limit for short-stay visas should be replaced by a period of one year.

The committee wanted many other rules concerning visas to be changed, and the provision for visas valid in only one country (Article 24) to be deleted as inconsistent with freedom of movement within the Union. At the instigation of the legal affairs committee, the report also suggested inserting a reference to the primacy of the Council of Europe Convention on data protection (Chapter 7). The report also demanded a right of consultation over any decisions needed to implement the Convention.

In a companion report,[74] criticisms of the visa rules were amplified and a shorter transitional period proposed for abolishing discrepancies between national visa lists. However, the Commission rejected the suggested date of 31 December 1995 as unattainable, since qualified majority voting in the Council on this issue will only start on 1 January 1996. Until that happens, the requirement for unanimity over the joint visa list will make agreement unlikely.[75]

The committee also suggested the important safeguard of a right of appeal against a refusal to issue one of the proposed uniform visas; these will be valid in all Member States, so there is likely to be a 'one chance only' rule for visa applications, just as in the case of asylum requests. Finally, the committee deplored the vague criteria for adding countries to the visa list 'according to their political and economic situation and according to their relations with the Community and the Member States, taking into account the degree of harmonisation achieved at Member State level'. The foreign affairs committee had commented that this gave 'an unfavourable image of the Union's external policy'. Instead, a new preamble was suggested which demanded 'clearly understood, objective and publicly stated criteria'.

In the UK, the House of Lords launched one of its thoroughgoing inquiries into the draft proposals.[76] Evidence was taken from Commission officials, MEPs, UK civil servants, international lawyers, NGOs and those concerned with airports. All except the first category were highly critical of different aspects. British civil servants reiterated their government's rooted objection to giving the ECJ jurisdiction over this or any other Convention drawn up under the TEU.

NGOs representing refugees, immigrants and their lawyers took the opposite view on this, and voiced numerous concerns about the dangers to human rights. All were critical of the requirement for carrier sanctions and the wider imposition of visas, and all deplored the absence of democratic control by any parliament, whether national or European. They insisted that all third-country nationals with permanent residence in a Member State should have freedom of movement on the same basis as citizens of the Union and the other states in the European Economic Area (Iceland and Norway, probably joined by Liechtenstein in 1995).

Particular doubts were expressed about the wide and ill-defined grounds that can be invoked for putting somebody on the exclusion list, leading to the risk of a person being excluded or expelled on the basis of unreliable or false information. Commission officials cross-questioned by the committee chairman seemed unconcerned about this, saying that all this was a matter for Member States; they also dismissed the idea that a person should have a right to be told as soon as his or her name was put on the list.[77] Just before this, however, a report in the Dutch press had illustrated the problems likely to arise from this purely national control of the joint list. Greece had expelled a foreign correspondent from a non-EU newspaper for criticising the government's refusal to recognise the former Yugoslav republic of Macedonia; had the joint list been in operation, the correspondent could have been excluded from all other EU countries.[78]

Quite apart from these concerns, expert witnesses expressed widely varying views on a constitutional question inherent in the Convention: as a new and hybrid species of international treaty, initiated by the Commission under Article K.3 TEU, did it preclude Member States from concluding their own such treaties independently? This seemed likely to occupy international lawyers for some time to come.

The House of Lords committee concludes by supporting the general aim of strengthening entry controls, but comes out strongly in support of ECJ jurisdiction and other safeguards for the individual. It recommends an explicit requirement for judicial remedies against a national decision to withdraw a residence permit. While not opposing carrier sanctions, it says they should be restricted to cases of actual negligence by airlines (Chapter 4).

The report provides an invaluable archive for future historians, and an insight into the problems and official attitudes that need to be addressed at future conferences on revision of the TEU. However, as a means of immediately influencing either the Council or the UK government its value is limited. The committee has no illusions on that score: it cites a 1993 statement by the immigration ministers of Member States to the effect that

... any changes made to the draft Convention to bring it into line with the Treaty on European Union should be technical in character and confined to what is strictly necessary; there is no question of reopening negotiations on any other Articles than those which need to be revised for that purpose.[79]

THE EUROPEAN INFORMATION SYSTEM

Article 13 of the external frontiers Convention specified that in order to set up a joint list of undesirable persons it would be necessary to have a computerised system of information exchange, the European Information System (EIS). This was to be regulated by a separate Convention incorporating rules on data protection. In 1994 the Schengen Executive Committee announced its willingness to allow the SIS to be integrated into the proposed EIS, to avoid unnecessary duplication[80] – though in view of the problems experienced in setting up the SIS, this seemed a somewhat dubious advantage.

A draft Convention was prepared by the Horizontal Group on Data Processing, reporting directly to the K4 Committee.[81] Like the external frontiers Convention, it was presented as an annex to a draft Council Decision recommending adoption by the Member States. Unlike the other Convention, it included no clause assigning jurisdiction to the European Court of Justice; the fact that this draft was prepared by a body working under the Council rather than the Commission may have had something to do with it. The draft makes no bones about its primary purpose, which is to exchange information about persons so as to 'enable public order and security to be maintained and illegal immigration to be effectively countered'.

The draft is a virtually word-for-word copy of the Articles in the Schengen Convention that deal with the SIS (Articles 92–119) with some rearrangement, together with all the Articles on data protection and the setting up of an Executive Committee. The central computer system will be based in Strasbourg like that of the SIS. The only insertion is a couple of paragraphs that are added to Article 108 of Schengen. These legitimate the national SIRENE systems (see above) and allow for their being controlled separately from the national EIS ones.

Under these rules the SIRENE systems will exchange 'such further information as is necessary to identify the persons or objects reported as well as other information and documentation relevant to the follow-up action taken'. This is supposed to be subject to data protection rules similar to those governing automated EIS data. However, the real problem is likely to be that of instilling into some police and security forces a stronger respect for individual rights and privacy. As with the SIS, no rule book will be of much use if officers feel justified in bypassing it in their legitimate aim of combating crime.

Negotiations on the draft Convention continued throughout 1994 but became blocked on several points. The Spanish delegation wanted the Convention to spell out more clearly (as in the Schengen Convention) the obligation of states to cooperate closely in all aspects of police and judicial matters. Three states (Denmark, Ireland and the UK) objected to the inclusion of 'manual data' in the rules for data protection.

Greece had continuing problems with the rules for entering names in the automated lists, and ended up by insisting that all EIS entries should 'respect the alphabet of the Member States'. Technical problems inherent in transmitting the Greek alphabet as well as the other European ones were dismissed as 'not serious' in view of the rapid advance of information technology. Nothing was said about the likely bafflement of foreign recipients of such entries.

Perhaps more serious in the long run was the division between Member States over the omission of a role for the ECJ. Italy and the Netherlands, in particular, attach great importance to giving it jurisdiction while the UK is virtually alone in being opposed to this. The scene seems to be set for another bruising confrontation with Britain over a matter of principle.

PROSPECTS

Few people doubt that the abolition of internal frontiers must entail some increase in controls at the external borders. What is at issue is the way in which these have been planned, and the apparent readiness of governments to jettison long-standing principles of respect for individual liberty and human rights. The 1989 Palma Document said in that 'in keeping with the traditional values of the Member States of the Community, the Co-ordinators insist that the stepping-up of controls at external frontiers should not go beyond what is strictly necessary for safeguarding security and law and order in the Member States'. As later chapters will make clear, the commitment of governments to this principle is seriously open to question where three groups of people are concerned: refugees, immigrants and the many third-country nationals who already live and work in the Union. Even citizens of Member States – particularly if their skin colour is other than white – may be subjected to more unwelcome attention from police and other officials than was the case before.

Is freedom of movement for citizens really so essential that a price must be paid in terms of human rights? Since the process of change is now irreversible, this is a redundant question. What is needed is a reassertion of the principle stated above, which the authors of the Palma Document appear to have understood more clearly than their political masters. Some underlying attitudes need changing. Resistance to parliamentary and judicial supervision of measures of control is expected of a dictatorship, but not of a democratically chosen government. In the same way, secret diplomacy is not appropriate to agreements which, though concluded between states, bear directly on the rights and freedoms of ordinary people. The ways in which the trend might be reversed are considered further in the chapters that follow.

NOTES

1. The re-numbering of the old Article 8a has led to confusion in the literature, since both relate to freedom of movement. Some studies published soon after Maastricht continued to use the old numbering for the new Article 7a.
2. *Treaties Establishing the European Communities*, abridged edition (Luxembourg: Office for Official Publications of the European Communities, 1987) p. 588.
3. *Guardian*, 26 February 1992; John Lewis, 'Border controls', *New Law Journal*, vol. 142 (1992) pp. 1584–6.
4. Commission of the European Communities, *Abolition of border controls: Commission Communication to the Council and to Parliament*, SEC(92) 877 final (internal document).
5. *The Week in Europe* (London: Commission of the European Communities) 10 September 1992.
6. *Guardian*, 3 September 1992; *Migration News Sheet*, October 1992.
7. *Migration News Sheet*, June 1992.
8. Committee on Legal Affairs and Citizens' Rights (rapporteur: K. Malangré), *Report on freedom of movement for persons and problems relating to national security in the Community*, A3–0199/91 (European Parliament, 1991).
9. Committee on Civil Liberties and Internal Affairs (rapporteur: K. Tsimas), *Report on the abolition of controls at internal borders and free movement of persons within the European Community*, A3–0284/92 (European Parliament, 1992).
10. Case C–445/93; *Official Journal of the European Communities*, C1 (4 January 1994) pp. 12–13.
11. Commission of the European Communities, *Commission report on the abolition of controls at intra-Community borders*, COM(88) 640

(Luxembourg: Office for Official Publications of the European Communities, 1988).

12. See for example the Tsimas report (note 9).
13. See the Malangré report (note 8) p. 14.
14. *Free movement of persons: report to the European Council by the Co-ordinators' Group*. For the full text see House of Lords Select Committee on the European Communities, *1992: border controls of people*, Session 1988–89, 22nd Report (London: HMSO, 1989) Appendix 5; for a summary see Michael Spencer, *1992 And All That: civil liberties in the balance* (London: Civil Liberties Trust, 1990) pp. 158–9.
15. Spencer, *1992 And All That* (note 14) pp. 88–9.
16. Statement added to the resolution adopted at the international conference of data protection commissioners, Berlin, August 1989.
17. *Convention applying the Schengen Agreement of 14 June 1985 between the governments of the states of the Benelux Economic Union, the Federal Republic of Germany and the French Republic, on the gradual abolition of checks at their common borders*. The Benelux secretariat in Brussels supplies texts in Dutch, French and German and also an unofficial translation into English. The French text is reproduced in Alexis Pauly (ed.) *Les accords de Schengen: abolition des frontières ou menace pour les libertés publiques?* (Maastricht: Institut européen d'admin-istration publique, 1993) pp. 187–269. The English translation was also published in *Commercial Laws of Europe, Part I* (1992) pp. 33–100.
18. For an English text of the 1985 Schengen Agreement see House of Lords, *1992: border controls of people* (note 14) Appendix 3.
19. Antonio Cruz, *Schengen, ad hoc Immigration Group and other European intergovernmental bodies*, Briefing Paper no. 12 (Brussels: Churches' Committee for Migrants in Europe, 1993) p. 5.
20. House of Commons Home Affairs Committee, *Practical police co-operation in the European Community*, Session 1989–90, 7th Report, vol. I (London: HMSO, 1990) p. xiv.
21. Cruz, *Schengen* ... (note 19) p. 3.
22. *Transnational Data and Communications Report*, June/July 1989, p. 27.
23. Jaques Thyraud, 'Communication on the report on the Schengen Agreement'. Reprinted in Douwe Korff, 'The Schengen Information System: also a question of data protection', in G.P.M.F. Mols (ed.) *Dissonanten bij het akkoord van Schengen* (Deventer: Kluwer, 1990) pp. 67–96. See also Charles D. Raab, 'Police cooperation: the prospects for privacy', in Malcolm Anderson and Monica den Boer (eds), *Policing across national boundaries* (London: Pinter, 1994) pp. 121–36.

24. Some writers refer to the 1990 Convention as the Schengen 'Supplementary Agreement' or 'Additional Agreement'. This is not, however, justified by its title.
25. See for example Lode van Outrive, 'Une vue de l'extérieur ... mais combien valable!', in *Europe: montrez patte blanche!* (Geneva: Centre Europe – Tiers Monde, 1994) pp. 5–20.
26. *Migration News Sheet*, July 1991 and January 1992.
27. *Ibid.*, February 1992.
28. *Ibid.*, October 1992.
29. *Statewatch*, March–April 1991; *Migration News Sheet*, March 1993.
30. *Platform Fortress Europe?*, December 1993–January 1994.
31. *Migration News Sheet*, June 1993.
32. *Ibid.*, November 1993.
33. *Ibid.*, September 1993.
34. *Platform Fortress Europe?*, June 1993.
35. *Migration News Sheet*, November 1993.
36. *Ibid.*, August 1993.
37. *Ibid.*, February 1994.
38. *Observer*, 13 March 1994.
39. For a fuller history of the controversy see *Platform Fortress Europe?*, March 1994 and *Statewatch*, May–June 1994.
40. *Statewatch*, March–April 1994; *Fortress Europe?*, July–August 1994.
41. *Migration News Sheet*, December 1994 and January 1995.
42. H. Meijers (ed.), *Schengen: internationalisation of central chapters of the law on aliens, refugees, privacy, security and the police*, 2nd edn (Leiden: Stichting NJCM, 1992).
43. Korff, 'The Schengen Information System' (note 23).
44. A.H.J. Swart, 'Police and security in the Schengen Agreement and Schengen Convention, in *Schengen* (note 42) pp. 96–109.
45. Martin Baldwin-Edwards and Bill Hebenton, 'Will SIS be Europe's Big Brother?', in *Policing across national boundaries* (note 23) pp. 137–57.
46. L.F.M. Verhey, 'Privacy aspects of the Convention', in *Schengen* (note 42) pp. 110–34.
47. Swart, 'Police and security' (note 44) p. 101.
48. José J. Bolten, 'From Schengen to Dublin: the new frontiers of refugee law', in *Schengen* (note 42) pp. 8–36.
49. 'Commentary to the readmission agreement between the Schengen countries and Poland', *ibid.* pp. 165–8 and 215–7 (the French text of the agreement).
50. *Schengen: rules of procedure of the 'Executive Committee'*, document CM93–207 (1993). Issued by the Secretariat, Standing Committee

of Experts on International Immigration, Refugee and Criminal Law, Utrecht.

51. *Réglement intérieur du Comité Executif institué en vertu du titre VII de la Convention d'application de Schengen*, document SCH/Com-ex (93) 1 rév 2 (issued 14 December 1993); *Tractatenblad* (1994) no. 39.

52. *Statewatch*, July–August 1994.

53. P. Boeles, R. Fernhout, C.A. Groenendijk, E. Guild, A. Kuijer, H. Meijers, Th. de Roos, J.D.M. Steenbergen and A.H.J. Swart, *A new immigration law for Europe?* (Utrecht: Dutch Centre for Immigrants, 1993) pp. 51–2.

54. David O'Keeffe, 'European immigration law and policy: the Schengen Conventions and European Community law', in *Les accords de Schengen* (note 17) pp. 171–83; see also *Yearbook of European Law*, vol. 11 (1991) pp. 212–3.

55. House of Lords Select Committee on the European Communities, *Community policy on migration*, Session 1992–93, 10th Report (London: HMSO, 1993) report para. 73, p. 25.

56. Boeles *et al.*, *A new immigration law for Europe?* (note 53) p. 51.

57. Luise Drüke, 'Refugee protection in the post cold war Europe: asylum in the Schengen and EC harmonization process', in *Les accords de Schengen* (note 17) pp. 105–69. A shorter version was published as *Asylum policies in a European Community without internal borders*, Briefing Paper no. 9 (Brussels: Churches' Committee for Migrants in Europe, 1992).

58. *Official Journal of the European Communities*, C323 (27 December 1989) pp. 98–9.

59. Committee on Civil Liberties and Internal Affairs (rapporteur: L. van Outrive), *Second report on the entry into force of the Schengen Agreements*, A3–0336/92 (European Parliament, 1992). The first report (A3–0288/92) contains the same explanatory statement but was referred back to the committee after disagreements over the resolution.

60. *Supplément d'Information Requis à l'Entrée Nationale*. The official but rather clumsy English translation (as used in the EIS Convention discussed later) is 'Supplementary Information Required for the National Entry'.

61. Beat Leuthardt, 'Le SIS et les libertés fondamentales: les nouveaux ennemis', in *Europe: montrez patte blanche!* (note 25) pp. 98–112.

62. See *Official Journal* (note 58).

63. *Migration News Sheet*, January 1993; Cruz, *Schengen*, … (note 19) p. 30.

64. van Outrive report (note 59) p. 28.

65. *Migration News Sheet*, June 1992; see also the Tsimas report (note 9) and Committee on Civil Liberties and Internal Affairs (rapporteur:

J.P. Beazley), *Report on the crossing of the EC external borders*, A3–0253/93 (European Parliament, 1993).

66. Ad Hoc Working Group on Immigration, *Convention between the Member States of the European Communities on the crossing of their external frontiers*, WGI 829 (1991). Deposited with national parliaments but never officially published.

67. *Commission Communication to the Council and the European Parliament*, COM(93) 684 final (Luxembourg: Office for Official Publications of the European Communities, 1993) part (a).

68. *Ibid.*, part (b).

69. *Migration News Sheet*, January 1995.

70. Ann Dummett and Jan Niessen, *Immigration and citizenship in the European Union*, Briefing Paper no. 14 (Brussels: Churches' Committee for Migrants in Europe, 1993) pp. 16 and 22. The restriction will not apply to citizens of Iceland and Norway (probably joined by Liechtenstein during 1995), countries which belong to the European Economic Area but not the EU. They have had freedom of movement in the Union (but not full rights) since 1 January 1994.

71. Cruz, *Schengen*, ... (note 19) p. 30.

72. House of Lords Select Committee on the European Communities, *Visas and control of external borders of the Member States*, Session 1993–94, 14th Report (London: HMSO, 1994) evidence pp. 22–33, QQ 112, 121 and 137 .

73. Committee on Civil Liberties and Internal Affairs (rapporteur: C. Beazley), *Report on the communication of the Commission containing a proposal for ... a Convention on the crossing of the external frontiers of the Member States*, A3–0190/94 (European Parliament, 1994).

74. Committee on Civil Liberties and Internal Affairs (rapporteur: F. Froment-Meurice), *Report on the Commission proposal for a Council Regulation determining the third countries whose nationals must be in possession of a visa when crossing the external borders of the Member States*, A3–0193/94 (European Parliament, 1994).

75. *Migration News Sheet*, May 1994.

76. House of Lords, *Visas and control of external borders* (note 72).

77. *Ibid.*, evidence pp. 61–70.

78. *Kleintje Muurkrant*, 17 February 1994. Quoted in *Statewatch*, March–April 1994.

79. House of Lords, *Visas and control of external borders* (note 72) report p. 8.

80. *Migration News Sheet*, July 1994.

81. Council document 9925/93 dated 10 November 1993 (unpublished). For a summary and other comments see *Fortress Europe?*, May 1994.

4

Refugees

The Union's internal debate on asylum policy must be viewed in the wider world context of refugee movements. The number of refugees in the world was 2.5 million in 1970. This rose to 11 million in 1982 and in 1994 it reached 23 million, not counting 26 million displaced persons in a refugee-like situation in their own countries. Until recently most of these were in non-European countries, but in the collapse of Yugoslavia six million people fled from or were driven from their homes. Of these some 600,000 obtained protection (however temporary) in countries of the European Union.[1] Official figures for 13 European states[2] show that the total number of asylum-seekers rose from 65,400 in 1983 to a peak of some 680,000 in 1992 at the height of the Bosnian exodus; in 1994 there were likely to be only half that number,[3] representing 1.5 per cent of the world's refugees.

The topic of refugees has deliberately been separated from that of immigration in this book. NGOs in these two areas were mostly set up on the presumption that refugees and immigrants have quite different origins and needs, requiring separate representation of their interests. The layman tends to support this view, and to have an instinctive sympathy for anyone to whom the term 'refugee' can be applied; the media also use the term loosely to describe anyone fleeing from conditions that they find intolerable, whatever the cause. In contrast, European governments tend to treat refugees and immigrants as components of one big problem that can only be solved by restricting the entry of both categories. This ignores the fact that national and international laws demand special protection for refugees, and it allows politicians and sections of the media to label both categories as equally undeserving. The truth is far more complex.

Governments have always been reluctant to surrender national jurisdiction to any supranational authority where the entry of aliens is concerned. This is why the Schengen and external frontiers Conventions are strictly intergovernmental in character. When international agreements on asylum for refugees are drawn up, great care is taken to restrict the definition of a refugee to narrow categories. This leaves all those outside these categories without the protection of international law; instead they are subject to national immigration policies, determined by economic and political motives rather than humanitarian ones.

In more liberal times this did not prevent states from extending protection to those who did not satisfy all the criteria, and until recently some 80 per cent of those refused full protection have probably been allowed in one way or another to remain in the country of application.[4] However, the rules are rapidly being tightened up, and European politicians tend nowadays to categorise people who seek asylum but who fall outside the strict definition as 'bogus refugees'. This exposes them to denigration and racial hatred, as recent events in several countries have shown. A bitter argument, in which there are few relevant facts beyond the bare statistics, continues to rage over this issue. On one side are those who claim that 'the asylum instrument ... has become a major channel for permanent immigration by non-refugees'.[5] On the other side, NGOs concerned with human rights in general and refugees in particular believe that individuals in real need of protection are being turned away.

REFUGEES AND HUMAN RIGHTS

The Universal Declaration of Human Rights (Chapter 2) says, in Article 14(1), that 'everyone has the right to seek and enjoy in other countries asylum from persecution'. However, neither this nor any other treaty obliges any state to grant that asylum. This has given rise to the shameful spectacle of the 'refugee in orbit', shuttling between states in search of asylum. What the treaties do forbid is the returning of a refugee to a country where the person's life or freedom may be at risk – an action called *refoulement*.[6] This became the cornerstone of the Geneva Convention (see below) that deals specifically with refugees.

The UN's Convention Against Torture and Other Cruel, Inhuman or Degrading Treatment or Punishment specifically prohibits returning a person to a country 'where there are substantial grounds for believing that he would be in danger of being subjected to torture'. The International Covenant on Civil and Political Rights and the European Convention on Human Rights both assert that 'no one shall be subjected to torture or to cruel, inhuman or degrading treatment or punishment'. In view of all this, it is remarkable that governments of Member States of the Union now seem prepared to send asylum seekers to so-called 'safe third countries' (see below) where there is no real guarantee that they will not be forced to return to the countries from which they fled.

The Convention on the Rights of the Child came into force in 1990, and has now been ratified by all EU Member States except the Netherlands (where protection for children is in practice good). It contains several references to the special needs of refugee children, and emphasises their right to make a claim for asylum regardless of whether they are accompanied by an adult.

THE GENEVA CONVENTION

Who Qualifies?

The Convention Relating to the Status of Refugees[7] was originally intended to protect both stateless persons and those at risk in their own countries. However, the text that finally emerged from the drafting conference was far from fulfilling that aim. In the words of one commentator, 'the deliberations had at one time given the impression that it was a conference for the protection of helpless sovereign states from the wicked refugee'.[8] The atmosphere was not helped by the walk-out of the Soviet bloc after a dispute over the scope of protection.

The result was a highly politicised text in which the definition of a refugee (Article 1A) precisely fitted a person who might wish to escape from a communist state because of 'well-founded fear of being persecuted for reasons of race, religion, nationality, membership of a particular social group or political opinion'. The definition thus excludes all those who flee from their homes because of war, famine or natural disaster – in other words, most of the world's refugees. Fortunately for the victims, developing countries have been less restrictive in practice, and they have accepted movements of refugees from neighbouring states on a scale that would be inconceivable in Europe. Only recently has the cataclysm in the former Yugoslavia forced a temporary relaxation of the rules insisted on within the Union.

The 1951 text of the Convention contained a further restriction to causative events occurring before 1 January 1951. This was deleted by a Protocol in 1967. What remained was a crucial requirement that, in order to qualify, a person has to be outside the country of his or her nationality or country of habitual residence (for those having no nationality). For those who are already in another country when the risk of persecution at home becomes apparent (called refugees *sur place*) this is not a problem. For those who are still in their home country the situation is very different: they must first get across the border with another state. Since the whole trend of current Union policy is to make this increasingly difficult, even the most 'genuine' refugee now faces a daunting barrier to surmount.

The Convention excludes a number of categories of people from refugee status, including war criminals and those who have previously committed 'a serious non-political crime' (Article 1F). There are also 'cessation clauses' (Article 1C) under which refugee status may be withdrawn; the most important ground for this is that 'the circumstances in connection with which he has been recognised as a refugee have ceased to exist'. A refugee lawfully in the territory may be expelled on the familiar grounds of 'national security or public order', but only after a due process of law. Apart from this, the Convention lays down various rules regarding the civil, political and social rights of recognised refugees.

Article 33(1) lays down an explicit prohibition of *refoulement*, defined as expelling or returning a refugee 'in any manner whatsoever to the frontiers of territories where his life or freedom would be threatened on account of his race, religion, nationality, membership of a particular social group or political opinion'. This principle is increasingly endangered by the current trend of asylum policy in the Union.

For those unable to qualify as 'Convention refugees' there are many second-class categories in which, depending on the state concerned, an asylum seeker may be placed and given permission to stay (see below). The degree of protection afforded to these *de facto* refugees varies widely, as do the criteria for acceptance.[9] As a further complication, the four European 'post-fascist' states (Germany, Italy, Portugal and Spain) celebrated their return to democracy by enshrining protection for refugees in their Constitutions. The criteria used were, however, different to those of the Geneva Convention, and such constitutional provisions have recently been under attack – generally to the detriment of refugee rights.

The arrival of large groups of refugees seeking to escape civil war and generalised violence has forced the issue on to the political agenda of all European countries, and the defects of the Geneva definition have become painfully apparent. Because of the wide variations between Member States of the Union in their degree of generosity and their criteria for *de facto* status, this matter will have to be addressed if the Union is ever to evolve a fair and uniform policy on asylum. The ever-present danger is that, as in some other areas, 'harmonisation' may become a euphemism for 'restriction'.

Interpretation of the Convention

The organisation headed by the United Nations High Commissioner for Refugees (UNHCR) has an international mandate which is quite independent of the Convention, and it has other roles like directing emergency aid to the victims of war. UNHCR also advises states on how they should interpret the Convention, but has no power to enforce compliance – a serious weakness at a time like the present, when the pressure to bypass it is so strong. When intergovernmental Conventions are being drawn up, UNHCR has in some cases been consulted too late to be of much use: the Schengen and Dublin Conventions (Chapter 3 and below) are examples of this. Its advice, even when sought, is not always taken.

In 1979 UNHCR published a comprehensive *Handbook on Procedures and Criteria for Determining Refugee Status*, aimed at providing guidance on borderline cases and ensuring uniform interpretation. The handbook was produced at the request of the national delegates on UNHCR's Executive Committee (EXCOM), so one might expect its rules to be respected. However, there is once again a wide variation between states in how much regard is paid to the handbook. In no country has it been fully integrated into national law.[10]

The only other source of guidance on the Convention is the series of formal Conclusions produced at intervals by EXCOM. These have addressed particular problems such as 'manifestly unfounded' applications for asylum, a subject of increasing sensitivity. Apart from this, the Committee of Ministers of the Council of Europe issues its own recommendations on refugee issues, such as R (81) 16 on the harmonisation of national procedures relating to asylum. As explained below, this particular recommendation conflicts with the new procedures based on the Schengen Convention and now spreading to the whole of the Union.

The Need for Reform

The obvious gaps in the Geneva Convention are compounded by the lack of any judicial body to interpret its provisions in a binding manner. Despite periodic moves by UNHCR and the Executive Committee to clarify particular issues, ambiguities remain. However, there seems to be a feeling that, whatever the deficiencies of the Convention, any attempt to reform it might end up with something worse; certainly the states responsible for the Union measures discussed below might well produce a majority in favour of weakening its provisions. The other problem is that of reaching any agreement among the many nations that have ratified it (121 by 1994).

There is no reason, however, why a regional agreement between states should not build on the Geneva Convention to construct a more comprehensive and equitable set of rules for that area. For Europe this has been suggested in full detail by more than one organisation. Their proposals will be summarised at the end of this chapter, by which point it should be all too clear that the need for reform is very urgent.

REFUGEES IN THE EUROPEAN UNION

Facts and Figures

National policies on asylum vary so widely, and are in such a rapid state of change, that a current survey would give only a 'snapshot' of little future validity.[11] Statistics can also be a trap for the unwary, since national systems of compiling them vary so widely. Even the criteria for counting asylum seekers vary; a recent report lists six sources of variation, and concludes that when this is combined with variations in the extent to which statistics are available at all, it becomes 'practically impossible to compile asylum statistics for the European Union as a whole'.[12]

When it comes to comparing acceptance or rejection rates the situation is even worse, and no attempt will be made here to do that. One problem is that apart from 'Convention refugees' satisfying the strict Geneva criteria (and even here states vary in how they apply them), there are many kinds of *de facto* or humanitarian status (see below) that may not all be included in the statistics; in some cases they constitute a majority of those allowed to stay. Refugees from the former Yugoslavia are in some countries processed by the normal asylum procedure and in others they are treated quite separately. Another difficulty is that decisions on acceptance often relate to an earlier year of application, so one cannot compare applications and acceptances for the same year.

Subject to the reservations mentioned above, Table 1 gives a rough comparison of asylum requests in 1991–93 for 17 European countries including all members of the Union.[13] It does show clearly that Germany received by far the greatest number of applications in all three years; hence the insistence of the German government on the need for more 'burden sharing' in the future.[14] The table also shows that some of the smaller or less populous countries have received relatively large numbers of applications. The Netherlands, Sweden and Switzerland are among these, and the available data show that, as well as taking those who satisfy the Geneva criteria, they offer non-Convention status to many others as well.[15] Declarations by other governments that 'the boat is full' need to be seen in this perspective, and treated more as political statements than irrefutable fact.

Table 1 Number of persons requesting asylum[a]

Country	1991	Year 1992	1993
Austria	27,300	16,200	4,356
Belgium	15,200	17,754	26,883
Denmark	4,600	13,884	14,351
Finland	2,100	3,634	2,023
France[b]	46,500	28,872	27,564
Germany	256,000	438,191	322,599
Greece[b]	2,572	1,972	789
Ireland	31	39	91
Italy	31,700	2,589	1,323
Luxembourg	238	120	225
Netherlands	21,600	20,346	35,399
Norway	4,600	5,238	12,876
Portugal[b]	233	688	1,659
Spain	8,100	11,700	12,615
Sweden	27,300	84,018	37,581
Switzerland	41,600	17,960	24,739
UK[c]	73,400	32,300	28,500
Total	563,074	695,505	553,573

[a] For sources see note 13.
[b] Not including dependants.
[c] Annual data adjusted later to include dependants.

Few statistics are available on how many rejected asylum seekers are actually deported, and those that are show the proportions to be fairly low.[16] National officials are reluctant to admit to exercising undue tolerance, and NGOs have no wish to publicise it for fear of harming those involved. In a few countries (Germany[17] and Sweden in particular) there are well-organised sanctuary movements, often church-based, which shelter some rejected asylum-seekers while further appeals are made on their behalf.[18] In many states, however, there are signs of a toughening of official attitudes and a determination to enforce more deportations.

Barring another disaster on the scale of that afflicting the former Yugoslavia, the figures for 1992 seem likely to represent a peak in asylum applications to countries of the Union. As explained below, numerous measures are being put in place that will progressively limit the ability of refugees to reach the country of their choice, let alone achieve refugee status when they arrive. The present position is that national asylum policies vary so widely that 'upward harmonisation' is unlikely to be achieved. Every government insists that it cannot possibly take more refugees than it already does, so in practice only the lowest common denominator is chosen as a future standard. Even where discretion is left to national governments, none is likely to step out of line for fear of attracting a higher proportion of applicants. The very concept of harmonisation, in theory a desirable aim, thus carries within it a threat to the future prospects of refugees.

Unaccompanied Children

Although most refugee children arrive as part of a family, a small but significant number come unaccompanied. Statistics are few and far between because such children are not often separately recorded, but estimates for 1991 indicate that more than 2000 arrived in Germany; Italy followed with 1277 and Austria with 807. Other Member States received fewer than 500 each.[19] National arrangements for dealing with them vary, but they have not so far been a target for harmonisation. There is certainly an argument for setting a higher minimum standard of treatment; at present most countries officially permit the detention and return of children, and unaccompanied children rarely achieve full refugee status. It is clear that unaccompanied children need sensitive and sympathetic treatment because of the traumas they have often experienced.[20]

Who Decides Policy?

The Commission has made periodic attempts to influence the asylum policies of the Union. In 1985 it announced that by 1988 at the latest there would be a Directive on the subject, but this never saw the light of day; instead the Ad Hoc Working Group on Immigration (a purely intergovernmental body) agreed in principle to prevent people from claiming asylum in more than one country.[21] This was followed in 1989 by the Palma Document[22] in which the shape of future policy became clear: the aims of the 1990 Dublin Convention (see below) and the external frontiers Convention (Chapter 3) were put on the agenda. The European Parliament commissioned a report and protested strongly both at the way things were going and about its exclusion from the discussions, but to no avail.[23]

The Commission's next foray into the field was in 1991, when it issued a purely advisory report on the need for a harmonisation of asylum policies.[24] This seemed to accept the intergovernmental agenda without question, and stated bluntly that recourse to the asylum procedure by those who are not political refugees under the Geneva Convention is 'an abuse of the asylum procedure aimed at circumventing the restrictions on immigration for employment purposes which Member States have brought in'. This blanket condemnation was only softened by a reference to the existence of *de facto* refugees, defined as those who are allowed to stay 'temporarily' on humanitarian grounds. The document pointed out that 'certain elements of the concept of refugee as defined by the Convention give rise to different, not to say divergent interpretations by the national authorities responsible for examining asylum requests' – a crucial dilemma that has still not been adequately addressed. There was a reference to a questionnaire on national policies which was sent to Member States, but the results were never made public.[25]

The Ad Hoc Working Group then drew up a report to the European Council[26] which outlined many of the measures that were faithfully adopted later (see below): action against 'clearly unjustified' applications, the definition of 'safe' countries to which asylum-seekers could be returned, the forcing of 'first host countries' to take back asylum-seekers, the fingerprinting of asylum seekers and so on. Once again, reference was made (without any supporting figures) to a 'massive increase in the number of unjustified applications'. Once again, the need for a harmonisation of national asylum rules was stressed.

The ball returned to the Commission's court in 1993 when, in accordance with the Declaration on Asylum attached to the Treaty on European Union (TEU), it prepared a report to the Council on the advisability of bringing the harmonisation of national asylum policies into the ambit of Community law.[27] This would, for the first time, demand formal consultation with the European Parliament. The change was allowed for in Article K.9 TEU and the new Article 100c EC (Chapter 1). After listing a number of concrete advantages of following this course, the Commission came to the rather lame conclusion that 'the time is not yet right', although the issue should be examined again 'in the light of experience'. Meanwhile the intergovernmental juggernaut rolled on with its own brand of harmonisation. The European Parliament followed with another angry complaint about its continuing impotence in this area.[28]

Early in 1994, following the entry into force of the TEU, the Commission attempted to launch a further debate on both immigration and asylum. This new report[29] gives a dispassionate account of the restrictive measures introduced by Member States, but points out that the intergovernmental procedure of adopting non-binding resolutions has led to 'approximation rather than harmonisation of asylum policies'. In particular, 'no significant progress has been made in the attempt to reach a harmonised interpretation of the definition of refugee according to Article 1A of the Geneva Convention'.[30] There is a plaintive reminder that ministers have had a survey of national practices available to them since 1991 (see above), and have done nothing more than identify the problem as a 'matter of priority'. The previously ignored recommendations of the European Parliament are now listed, and the Commission's 1991 suggestion of a common judicial machinery to eliminate disparities of interpretation is repeated. No concrete suggestion on this is made: 'it should be noted that no such examination or studies have been started yet'.

It looks as if the Commission, emboldened by the thought of ultimately acquiring new powers (see above), has at last seen the folly of going along so meekly with the intergovernmental process, which it presumably did for the sake of maintaining its non-voting seat at the conference table. It seems brutally clear that a majority of Member State governments do not really care about true harmonisation, so long as the flow of refugees can be stemmed. This sobering conclusion serves to strengthen the argument for a mandatory transfer of the whole procedure to the democratic machinery of the Union.

THE NEW EUROPEAN ORDER

In 1990 and 1992 a series of intergovernmental agreements emerged which set the tone of Union asylum and immigration policies. One was a formal Convention between Member States; the others were drawn up by immigration ministers of the Member States (without any involvement of the Parliament), and were variously described as 'resolutions', 'conclusions' or 'recommendations'. They were none the less effective in practice, since they embodied or implied a commitment by Member States to change their national laws.

The Dublin Convention

The centrepiece of the new system of refugee control is the Convention signed in Dublin in June 1990.[31] By the end of 1994 it was still not legally in force, having been ratified by only nine of the twelve signatories. Belgium, Ireland and the Netherlands were still holding back.[32] This did not prevent some governments from embracing the principle with enthusiasm and modifying their national laws accordingly. A very similar 'parallel Convention' intended for non-EU states was subsequently drafted but shelved for the time being.[33]

The Dublin Convention closely resembles the asylum provisions of the Schengen Convention (Chapter 3) in its rules for determining which Member State should examine an application for asylum (Articles 3–8). These rules are exhaustive, and include such factors as whether a family member is already resident there as a recognised refugee; whether the state has issued the person a residence permit or a visa; whether the Member State allowed the person to cross its border 'irregularly'; and whether the application was made while in transit through an airport in its territory.[34]

The overriding principle is that only one application is allowed; if rejected by one state, the asylum seeker cannot apply to any other Member State of the Union. Article 3(5) gives a state the right to send an applicant to a 'third state' outside the Union, subject only to compliance with unspecified provisions of the Geneva Convention (presumably meaning the ban on *refoulement*). This later became the subject of detailed rules (see below).

As in the Schengen Convention, states are to exchange information about applicants under certain headings (Article 15): personal details such as name, nationality and date and place of birth; details of identity and travel papers; 'other information necessary for establishing the identity of the applicant'; places of residence and routes travelled; residence permits or visas issued by a Member State; the place where the application was lodged; and details of any previous applications. The 'other information' clause was evidently inserted to cover the later development of the EURODAC system for exchanging the fingerprints of asylum seekers.[35]

Article 15 also includes some rules on data protection and gives the applicant a right to know what information has been exchanged, and to have errors corrected or inadmissible data erased. Information exchanged 'shall enjoy at least the same protection as is given to similar information in the Member State which receives it', a vague and not very reassuring criterion. Computerised data must be protected by national laws according to the 1981 Council of Europe Convention on data protection (Chapter 7); if data are not processed automatically, 'every Member State shall take the appropriate measures to ensure compliance with this Article by means of effective controls'.

These rules are distinctly sketchy in view of the extreme sensitivity of data concerning asylum-seekers. The person concerned may not want it known that he or she has left the country of origin, let alone what route was taken. If information such as this leaks back to the authorities at home, the possible consequences for friends and relatives left behind may well be imagined. Although the Dublin Convention makes no mention of it, it has always been assumed that there would be a separate Convention to cover the special protection required in this and other sensitive areas of cooperation in justice and home affairs. The idea of such a Convention was mentioned at intervals in the work programmes of the Council, but the Corfu meeting of the European Council in June 1994 failed to do so; it merely emphasised that 'the problem of data protection must be given particular attention' and expressed the hope that a progress report would be received in six months' time.

Other features of the Convention include the setting up of a committee similar to the Schengen Executive Committee, with similar powers to write its own rules and interpret the Convention. No reference is made to the European Court of Justice, and only the Geneva Convention is mentioned as an international standard to be followed. The European Convention on Human Rights is conspicuous by its absence, though its inclusion was floated as a possibility in the draft of the parallel Convention mentioned above.

'Manifestly Unfounded' Applications

A meeting of immigration ministers held in London at the end of 1992 agreed on a set of rules which would enable them to quickly reject any asylum application that could be called 'manifestly unfounded'.[36] The supposed basis for these rules was a conclusion adopted by UNHCR's Executive Committee, which defined such an application as 'clearly fraudulent or not related to the criteria laid down in the 1951 United Nations Convention relating to the Status of Refugees nor to any other criteria justifying the granting of asylum'.[37] However, the ministers' resolution goes well beyond this definition, and its interpretation by some Member States goes clearly against the EXCOM statement.

The grounds for rejection fall under three headings: 'no substance to claim to fear persecution', 'deliberate deception or abuse of asylum procedure', and the existence of a 'host third country' to which the person may safely be sent (see below). Under the first two headings the application may be put through an 'accelerated procedure', and if asylum is refused 'the Member State will ensure that the applicant leaves Community territory'. There is no mention of an appeal procedure, which is quite contrary to the EXCOM statement that 'an unsuccessful applicant should be enabled to have a negative decision reviewed before rejection at the frontier or forcible removal from the territory'.[38]

The first heading encompasses claims where the applicant fails to invoke a fear of persecution as defined in the Geneva Convention, and instead gives reasons such as the search for a job or better living conditions. No mention is made of the 'other criteria justifying the granting of asylum' mentioned by EXCOM. Where this leaves the refugee from war or famine is not elucidated, though a list of 'conclusions' agreed by the ministers appears to allow the possibility of accepting refugees generated by an event like a violent coup.[39]

The heading also covers any claim of fear of persecution that is 'totally lacking in substance' or 'manifestly lacking in any credibility'. There is at least a requirement that a negative decision be made by 'a competent authority at the appropriate level fully qualified in asylum or refugee matters', though this does not have to be the 'central authority' demanded by the Council of Europe's recommendation on asylum procedures.[40] It leaves open the possibility that frontier guards with a minimum of training in such matters could be given the task, and there is evidence that this does occur.[41]

Two other reasons are given for deciding that there are no grounds for a fear of persecution. One is that the person could avoid persecution by moving to another part of the same country – the 'internal flight' alternative. The other is that the whole country is one in which there is 'in general terms no serious risk of persecution'. According to the ministers' list of conclusions, the decision that this is the case will be based on 'as wide a range of sources of information as possible'; UNHCR, though mentioned in this connection, is not given the authority to make such a decision. It is thus left to the government concerned.

The second category of 'manifestly unfounded' applications ('deliberate deception or abuse or asylum procedures') covers those based on a false identity or forged documents, where the applicant maintains that they are genuine when challenged; 'deliberately made or false representations' made after applying for asylum; and destruction or damage of any relevant document such as a passport or ticket 'in bad faith'.

Finally, this category includes anyone who submits an application in one of the Member States after having a similar application rejected by a non-EU country 'following an examination comprising adequate procedural guarantees and in accordance with the Geneva Convention'. This in effect extends the 'one chance only' rule of the Dublin Convention to countries outside the Union in a unilateral manner and without their agreement. It implies a uniform application of the Geneva principles that does not exist inside the Union, let alone outside it.

Host Third Countries

The second resolution agreed by immigration ministers at their 1992 London meeting[42] concerned an item that occupied only one sentence of the Dublin Convention: the right of a Member State to send an applicant to a 'host third country' or 'safe third country' (see above). As expanded by the ministers, this turns out to be a rule that if any country exists to which an asylum-seeker can be sent without contravening the Geneva Convention, it should be done without even considering the substance of a claim to asylum in the Union. The ministers agreed to change their national laws accordingly, 'at the latest by the time of the entry into force of the Dublin Convention'. National governments needed no second bidding to put this into effect, and set off a series of bitter controversies over the changes involved.

The resolution thus ignores the spirit of the Geneva Convention, made more explicit by an EXCOM conclusion that 'regard should be had to the concept that asylum should not be refused solely on the ground that it could be sought from another State ...'.[43] It states the more obvious exceptions to the rule of transfer to a third country, such as a risk of exposure there to persecution or other gross infringements of human rights. The most significant clause, however, embodies two alternative excuses for turning a person away.

The first of these is that the person must either have already been granted protection in the third country or had an opportunity to seek it there, at or inside the border. The other all-embracing alternative, which does not require the applicant to have been anywhere near the third country, is that 'there is clear evidence of his admissibility to a third country'. The only safeguard is that there must be effective protection in the host third country against *refoulement*. Again it is left to the Member State, with advice from UNHCR and elsewhere, to decide whether that condition is satisfied; it is not necessary to ask the state concerned for a specific guarantee. Once disposed of in this way, the asylum seeker is out of sight and out of mind so far as the Member State is concerned.

Readmission Agreements

Following precedents dating back as far as 1955, the 1990s saw an explosive proliferation of agreements between Member States of the Union and supposedly 'safe' third countries around their borders and further afield.[44] Such agreements are designed to guarantee the return to a third country of anyone rejected or expelled after travelling from there to a Member State. Such 'buffer states' have in turn negotiated agreements with each other and with more distant countries, ensuring the displacement of the victims to ever more remote parts of the globe.

The 1993 Budapest conference of immigration ministers (Chapter 5) urged the adoption of multilateral agreements like that between the Schengen states and Poland (Chapter 3). In the event, however, only bilateral agreements have been reached. By the beginning of 1995 there were more than 60 of them either agreed or under negotiation between the various Member States of the Union and other countries, and a similar number between pairs of non-EU states.[45]

In November 1994 the EU's Justice and Home Affairs Council adopted a recommendation for a model readmission agreement which led to an immediate protest from UNHCR.[46] It warned that agreements following this model could lead to asylum-seekers being returned to countries where they faced persecution and other violations of basic human rights, in contravention of Article 33 of the Geneva Convention (see above). UNHCR called for additional safeguards to be incorporated so as to guarantee examination of any asylum claim and avoid its summary rejection by the state 'readmitting' the person concerned.

Expulsion

The 1992 resolutions of the immigration ministers were complemented by a joint recommendation[47] which endeavoured to ensure that no rejected asylum-seeker would slip through the net and remain in a Member State by default. Subject to the Geneva Convention and (in this case only) the European Convention on Human Rights, Member States are urged to expel anyone who is found to have 'entered or remained unlawfully' unless their stay has been regularised; also anyone 'liable to expulsion on grounds of public policy or national security' and anyone found to have 'failed definitively in an application for asylum and to have no other claim to remain'.

Ignoring any scruples that might arise on civil liberty grounds, the ministers state that 'there should be power in appropriate circumstances to restrict the personal liberty of people liable to expulsion'. Expulsion is to be 'to the country of origin or to any other country to which the individual may be admitted' – no specific safeguards are mentioned here, since the person is taken by definition to be undeserving of protection. This echoes a similar provision in Article 15(2) of the external frontiers Convention (Chapter 3).

For good measure there is provision for punishing (and if possible expelling) people who knowingly facilitate illegal entry or 'harbour those who have entered or remain unlawfully'. This is so widely drawn that it could be used to justify the prosecution not only of those working for profit, but also of organisations or individuals acting on humanitarian principles.

Finally, the recommendation refers to the need to exchange information on the traffic in illegal immigrants. It suggests making use of the Centre for Information, Discussion and Exchange on the Crossing of Frontiers and Immigration (CIREFI). This is one of two 'clearing houses' set up by the Ad Hoc Working Group on Immigration and taken over by the corresponding Steering Group under the K4 Committee (Chapter 1). The other is the Centre for Information, Discussion and Exchange on Asylum (CIREA). The latter has the influential role of collecting information and submitting reports on countries from which asylum-seekers come, and also on those to which they may be sent as 'host third countries'.[48]

Carrier Sanctions

Carrier sanctions are fines laid down by national laws that make it an offence for any international carrier (usually an airline) to allow a person without valid documents to have boarded a flight from another country. They are perhaps the earliest example of the way Member State governments have introduced a creeping harmonisation of national legislation without any open discussion or involvement of Community law. In this case they did so in the face of early and insistent warnings from UNHCR that the process would damage the fundamental rights of refugees.

The origin of the process is to be found tucked away in a 1988 Commission report on the abolition of internal border controls.[49] This records the fact that immigration ministers of the Member States set up a working party in 1986 to 'look into ways of developing a common policy to end abuses of the asylum process'. In April 1987 they 'agreed on a series of measures to assign greater responsibility to air carriers bringing in asylum-seekers, to curb the activities of operators organising traffic in refugees, and to coordinate the processing of asylum requests'. There was never any doubt, therefore, about the purpose of the measures.

It was therefore no coincidence that in 1987 four Member States (Belgium, Denmark, Germany and the UK) introduced new laws on the subject; by the end of 1994 they had been joined by France, Greece, Italy, the Netherlands and Portugal.[50] Both the Schengen Convention and the draft external frontiers Convention (Chapter 3) require signatory states to bring in some such legislation, but no details are specified.

These laws go further than the common practice of requiring carriers to take back, at their own expense, people refused entry to the country. They impose a duty on the carrier to check all the person's documentation: passport, visa and any stamp denoting immigration status. If any of these is found to be out of order by immigration officers, the carrier becomes liable in principle to a fine. Member States vary in the level of fines and the rigour with which the principle is applied. In 1994 the UK led the field with a penalty of £2000 per passenger, having levied more than £55 million in fines by June 1993.[51] Belgium then raised the stakes by trebling its fine to BF 150,000 (about £3000).[52] Airlines bitterly resisted paying up.

The Member States knew perfectly well in 1987 that such laws would conflict with their obligations under the 1944 Chicago Convention on International Civil Aviation, administered by the International Civil Aviation Organisation (ICAO). Annex 9 to this Convention included the rule that carriers 'shall not be fined in the event that any control documents in possession of a passenger are found by a Contracting State to be inadequate ...'. There was simply a requirement that operators should take precautions to avoid this happening. The Member States therefore set in motion an attempt to change the rules of Annex 9.

The chance to do this arose at a 1988 meeting called to consider a general updating of Annex 9. However, by then a group of experts under the auspices of the NGO network ECRE had published an analysis of the effects that carrier sanctions were already having on refugees.[53] UNHCR was also alerted to what was happening, and it presented to the meeting a forceful argument against carrier sanctions which it has reiterated at intervals ever since:

> Carrier sanctions legislation threatens to undermine basic principles of refugee protection, the operation of the asylum process, procedural guarantees of due process and international cooperation to resolve refugee problems in full respect for the human rights of the individuals involved. While States have a legitimate interest in controlling irregular migration and a right to do so through border measures, they are in breach of international obligations towards refugees where such measures hinder the access of refugees both to status determination procedures and to asylum from persecution.[54]

UNHCR clearly foresaw what did in fact occur on a wide scale when the laws came into effect: that carriers, rather than risk incurring fines, would take all possible steps to prevent passengers with suspect papers from ever starting the journey. The fact that they might have had no alternative to using forged papers to get out of their country was irrelevant. There were also cases where asylum-seekers who managed to reach their destination were forcibly restrained by airline staff and taken back without having an opportunity to claim asylum. In some instances they subsequently suffered arrest and torture by police in their home country.[55]

Despite the efforts of UNHCR the Annex 9 rules were in fact changed, though not as much as Member States wanted. Fines were for the first time authorised, but only when there was 'evidence to suggest that the carrier was negligent in taking precautions to the end that passengers complied with the documentary requirements for entry into the receiving State'.[56] A specific note was inserted to emphasise the overriding obligation to avoid *refoulement.*

This left a gap, which still remains, between the limitations laid down by Annex 9 and the law and practice of Member States. Some of them ignore the 'negligence' criterion and fine indiscriminately, and the burden of proof is placed on carriers rather than on the state as the rules imply. Although airlines have protested at being turned into an arm of their country's immigration department, they have had to accept 'training' by immigration officials who are posted abroad to help them in their task of weeding out potential offenders at source. Worst of all, Member States continue to ignore the accumulating evidence that a large but unquantifiable number of asylum seekers are prevented from escaping persecution or worse in their home countries.

International Zones

It only remains to mention briefly a further avenue that has been explored by some Member States as a possible means of rejecting unwanted immigrants and asylum-seekers without having any regard for international standards such as the Geneva Convention. It was part of the plan for abolishing internal frontiers that passengers on flights within the Union should be physically separated at airports from those arriving from outside, whose credentials would have to be carefully checked. This gave rise to expensive conversion work about which airport authorities are still complaining (Chapter 3). Some governments went further and took this opportunity to declare their international arrival areas and transit zones to be somehow outside the scope of their obligations under national or international law, since passengers were not deemed to have arrived until they passed through immigration control.

Following complaints by individuals about false imprisonment in such a zone, or a failure to observe the law on asylum, this legal fiction was firmly knocked on the head in two Member States by the courts in France and the UK.[57] The judges pointed to the absurdity of pretending that a part of the state's territory was outside judicial control; there had never been any claim that the state did not police the areas concerned, and individuals were certainly not outside the law when they were there. The episode illustrates the lengths to which some governments are prepared to go in justifying their actions. In 1994 the Council of Europe issued a recommendation aimed at ensuring proper treatment of asylum-seekers arriving at airports, but this carries no legal force.[58]

FUTURE REFUGEE POLICY

Dublin and its Aftermath

The successive measures devised and implemented by governments since 1990 have attracted sustained criticism and protest from legal experts and NGOs alike. The Dublin Convention was denounced on several grounds. The most obvious objection, as explained by UNHCR,[59] is the gross unfairness of restricting the application to one Member State with no choice open to the applicant, when the different states are nowhere near to a harmonisation of their asylum procedures or a uniform interpretation of the Geneva Convention. Some experts pointed out that this rule also contradicts the position taken by EXCOM, which recognised that 'a decision by a Contracting State not to recognise refugee status does not preclude another Contracting State from examining a new request for refugee status by the person concerned.'[60]

Other objections centred on the deficiencies in data protection and the fact that the Convention does not obviate the risk of *refoulement*; a state may send an asylum-seeker to a 'third state' (outside the Union) without being obliged to ensure its adherence to the necessary standards of protection. In 1991, Amnesty International reported that it knew of many cases where asylum-seekers had been sent to third states which then returned them to countries where they faced serious violations of human rights.[61] Far from solving the problem of the 'refugee in orbit', the Convention merely ensures that the orbit will lie outside the borders of the Union.

The ministerial resolutions of 1992 and their consequences for indi-viduals were unanimously condemned in even stronger terms by many NGOs and other experts, and it would be superfluous to list separately the points made by each of them. Instead a summary is given below, followed by the main proposals for reform. The groups included Amnesty International,[62] the European Parliament[63] and the Meijers committee of Dutch legal experts who dissected the Schengen Convention (Chapter 3).[64] There was some unusually blunt criticism from UNHCR,[65] which generally prefers persuasion to admonition for the sake of maintaining cooperation with governments. The Commission also warned that under the new regime 'Member States, unless they take great care, may involuntarily find themselves violating the principle of non-refoulement'; it added the severely pragmatic point that '... would-be asylum seekers may turn to illegal immigration if asylum procedures are no longer accessible to all. It is unlikely that the costs involved in effectively countering such illegal movements would be any less than actual costs of dealing with the asylum requests.'[66]

National NGOs concerned with refugees expressed alarm to their respective governments about the laws that put the resolutions into effect (see Chapter 8 for some examples). ECRE, the international network to which most of them belong, lobbied the immigration ministers of the Union (without success) before the resolutions were adopted.[67] It later drew up a detailed set of recommendations for reform.[68] Carrier sanctions were singled out for special criticism by all concerned.[69] Legal experts stressed the importance of overall judicial control by a court such as the ECJ,[70] echoing a general point made by the UK House of Lords: 'There is now developing a body of common rules which require machinery to ensure uniform interpretation ... Rules on these subjects, adopted on a common basis by the Member States, are unlikely to be applied in a uniform and equitable manner in the absence of some common machinery for the resolution of differences between one Member State and another or between individuals and national authorities'.[71]

Defining a Refugee

The underlying assumption of all the recent intergovernmental agreements on asylum is that the Geneva Convention provides the only binding definition of a true refugee. This ignores the trend of international developments over the last 40 years, and makes it all the more urgent to draft a new definition that is universally accepted. If this is not done, countless asylum-seekers whose claims are irrefutable on humanitarian grounds will be exposed to the direct or indirect risk of *refoulement*. Decisions by Member States will continue to rest on varying interpretations of the discretion allowed to them.

There is no shortage of models for a more rational definition of refugee status.[72] As early as 1969, the Organisation of African Unity (OAU) broadened the definition to include those who are compelled to leave their country 'owing to external aggression, occupation, foreign domination or events seriously disturbing public order'.[73] A number of Latin American states did the same in the 1984 Cartagena Declaration, which covers those threatened by 'generalised violence, foreign aggression, internal conflicts, massive violations of human rights or other circumstances which have seriously disturbed public order'.[74] Nearer home, the Parliamentary Assembly of the Council of Europe recommended in 1988 that the Committee of Ministers should examine the possibility of preparing a European Convention to deal with *de facto* refugees 'on whose fate the Council of Europe ... has been proposing concrete measures for many years'.[75]

The idea of a new European Convention, to be agreed as a first step by Member States of the Union, has been developed by ECRE. A comprehensive definition of a refugee is proposed which includes both political refugees and those fleeing for other reasons, and which covers refugees *sur place*. The recommended categories are:

- persons who have fled their country, or who are unable or unwilling to return there, because their lives, safety or freedom are threatened by generalised violence, foreign aggression, internal conflicts, massive violations of human rights or other circumstances which have seriously disturbed public order; and
- persons who have fled their country, or who are unwilling to return there, owing to well-founded fear of being tortured or of being subjected to inhuman or degrading treatment or punishment or violations of other fundamental human rights.[76]

ECRE insists that under this definition all categories of refugee should be equally treated in every way: their requests for asylum should be handled by the same central authority and they should have equal rights after recognition. In particular, the arbitrary decision that some groups merit only temporary protection should be abandoned; the Geneva Convention already contains provision for the withdrawal of refugee status when the circumstances that justify it no longer apply, and it is never possible to predict how long a 'temporary' status will be needed. ECRE suggests that in the absence of a new definition, temporary status should be subject to strict safeguards for the individual and a possibility of transfer to permanent status after not more than two years.[77]

Abuses and Remedies

Member States have rushed to bring in laws to deal quickly with 'manifestly unfounded' applications, and the safeguards against *refoulement* are often minimal.[78] Border police or immigration officials are in many cases allowed to return asylum-seekers to any 'safe third country' through which they have passed, without even considering their claim to asylum. The right of appeal is either non-existent or subject to a time limit for submission that may be as short as 24 hours; in addition it may not have suspensive effect, so that the person has to appeal from outside the country of asylum. There is no requirement to check that a 'safe third country' will consider the person's asylum claim, nor to ask for a guarantee that he or she will not be sent back to the country of origin. Reforms that have been demanded include the following points:

- all decisions to be made by a central competent authority and not by border officials;
- all applicants to be given a fair and complete oral hearing;
- access to be guaranteed to legal advice and an interpreter at every stage, coupled with the right to ask UNHCR for help;
- instructions to be given to all officials on the need to follow the UNHCR handbook on asylum procedures, together with proper training in the special problems of asylum seekers;
- account to be taken of the asylum seeker's preference for a given country of asylum;
- special consideration to be given to the needs of unaccompanied children, with strict attention to UNHCR guidelines on the subject;
- all decisions to be subject to an appeal with suspensive effect to an independent body;
- consultation to take place with UNHCR and NGOs on 'manifestly unfounded' decisions;
- no automatic rejection to be stipulated for a person who passed through a 'safe third country';
- no asylum seeker to be sent on to a third country unless the person has relevant links with that country;
- assessments of 'safe country of origin' and 'safe third country' status to be made by an independent body, based on impartial information and open to inspection;
- strict limitations to be imposed on the use of detention, with guaranteed access to advice and legal aid;
- restrictions to be laid down on the taking and storage of fingerprints;
- no asylum-seeker to be returned or expelled to a third country without guarantees of full protection of human rights and personal safety;
- carrier sanctions to be abolished; alternatively, liability restricted to cases of actual negligence or not applied to undocumented passengers who seek asylum; carriers also to be instructed not to prevent travel by unaccompanied children seeking asylum;
- no absolute requirement for a visa to be imposed where difficulties in obtaining one may affect an asylum-seeker's ability to leave the country of origin;
- no 'international zones' to be allowed in which the rights of asylum-seekers are limited;

- family reunification to be facilitated for all categories accepted for asylum or residence on humanitarian grounds;[79]
- all intergovernmental agreements on asylum policy to be subject to scrutiny by the European Parliament;
- judicial control to be instituted over the interpretation and implementation of treaties such as the Dublin Convention and other measures of harmonisation, exercised either by the European Court of Justice or by a specially constituted court;
- UNHCR and NGOs to be actively involved in the development of asylum policy;
- legislation and other action to be adopted at national level to counter the racism and xenophobia that severely affect asylum-seekers in the present climate of opinion.

The length of this list of necessary reforms indicates how far down the road the Union has gone in denying a fair and thorough examination of asylum claims to one of the most vulnerable groups of human beings that exists. None of the proposals can be dismissed as being too radical or too impractical. Most of them simply restate principles that were thought to be universally accepted in international refugee law. The fact that these principles have so easily been undermined in such a short space of time illustrates the crucial importance of ending once and for all the present intergovernmental system of 'harmonising' national laws in the absence of overall judicial and parliamentary control. Each government has forced legislation through its own parliament with alarmist predictions about the consequences of failing to 'stem the tide', and heavy hints that any country failing to follow the trend will attract the unwanted hordes of refugees rejected by other states. The word 'conspiracy' is not too harsh a term for this kind of concerted action. It says little for the commitment of politicians in power to the protection of fundamental human rights.

The last word should go to the UN High Commissioner for Refugees, speaking in 1992:

> As we move into the nineties there is no doubt that Europe is at a crossroads. Will Europe turn its back on those who are forced to move, or will it strengthen its long tradition of safeguarding the rights of the oppressed and the uprooted? Will Europe build new walls, knowing that walls did not stop those who were fleeing totalitarian persecution in the past? Or will Europe help to bridge the abyss which now separates East from West and North from South? Will Europe and the rest of the industrialised world have the courage to commit themselves politically and economically to attack severe poverty, underdevelopment and social injustice which leads to oppression, violence and

displacement? The path which we follow will create the kind of world we bestow on future generations.[80]

NOTES

1. Statement by Sadako Ogata, UN High Commissioner for Refugees, 24 November 1992; other data from UNHCR, London.
2. *Summary descriptions of asylum procedures in states in Europe, North America and Australia* (Geneva: Inter-governmental Consultations on Asylum, Refugee and Migration Policies ['Informal Consultations'], 1994) Annex 3.A. This covers all EU Member States except Luxembourg, Greece, Ireland and Portugal but includes Norway and Switzerland.
3. Provisional estimates from Informal Consultations (note 2) 10 November 1994.
4. Jonas Widgren, *The key to Europe: a comparative analysis of entry and asylum policies in Western countries*, Swedish Government Official Reports 1994:135 (Stockholm: Fritzes, 1994) p. 18.
5. *Ibid.*, pp. 55–6.
6. For a full list of relevant international instruments see *Asylum in Europe, vol. I: an introduction* (London: European Consultation on Refugees and Exiles, 1993) pp. 29–31. See also John Murray and Jan Niessen, *The Council of Europe and the protection of migrants, refugees and minorities*, Briefing Paper no. 13 (Brussels: Churches' Committee for Migrants in Europe, 1993).
7. For the full text with that of the 1967 Protocol see Richard Plender, *Basic documents on international migration law* (Dordrecht: Nijhoff, 1988) pp. 87–105.
8. James C. Hathaway, 'Re-interpreting the Convention refugee definition in the post-cold war period', in Peter R. Baehr and Geza Tessenyi (eds), *The new refugee hosting countries: call for experience – space for innovation*, SIM Special no. 11 (Utrecht: Netherlands Institute of Human Rights, 1991) pp. 38–44.
9. *Working paper on the need for a supplementary refugee definition* (London: European Council on Refugees and Exiles, 1993).
10. Thomas Spijkerboer, *A bird's eye view of asylum law in eight European countries* (Amsterdam: Dutch Refugee Council, 1993). Countries covered are Belgium, Denmark, France, Germany, Ireland, Italy, the Netherlands and the UK.
11. For a historical overview see Daniéle Joly with Clive Nettleton and Hugh Poulton, *Refugees: Asylum in Europe?* (London: Minority Rights Group, 1992). For concise country comparisons, see for instance

Spijkerboer, *A bird's eye view* (note 8); Jim Gillespie, *Report on immigration and asylum procedure and appeal rights in the 12 Member States of the European Community* (London: Immigration Law Practitioners' Association, 1993); and *Refugees and the 'new' Europe* (London: World University Service, 1994). Comprehensive information on this and related topics for all Member States except Greece, Ireland, Luxembourg and Portugal (but including Norway and Switzerland) is available in *Summary descriptions of asylum procedures* (note 2). Details for Denmark, Finland, Germany, Hungary and Switzerland are given in *Asylum in Europe, vol. II: review of refugee laws and procedures in selected European Countries* (London: European Council on Refugees and Exiles, 1994). For Belgium, Germany, Italy, the Netherlands, Sweden, Switzerland and the UK see Ruth Mason and David Forbes, *Nearest place of safety: the erosion of the right of asylum and the response of the voluntary sector* (Brussels: Quaker Council for European Affairs, 1994).

12. 'Asylum-seekers in the EU: better data needed', *Rapid Reports: Population and Social Conditions*, 1994 no. 1 (Luxembourg: Eurostat).
13. Data for Greece, Ireland, Luxembourg and Portugal are from *Minutes and conference papers from the ECRE biannual general meeting, Amsterdam, April 1994* (London: European Council on Refugees and Exiles, 1994) part 1: plenary meeting, p.1. All other figures are those updated by Informal Consulations (note 2) to 9 November 1994.
14. *Guardian*, 5 July 1994; *ESMV List of Events* (Utrecht) August 1994.
15. *Minutes and conference papers* (note 13), part 2: country reports.
16. *Return of rejected asylum-seekers*, IGC/RET/03/93 (Geneva: Inter-governmental Consultations on Asylum, Refugee and Migration Policies, 1993).
17. *Migration News Sheet*, July 1994.
18. Mason and Forbes, *Nearest place of safety* (note 11) pp. 54–61.
19. *Children or refugees? A survey of West European policies on unaccompanied refugee children* (London: Children's Legal Centre, 1992) p. 20.
20. *Child refugees in Europe*, report from the European Seminar on Protection of Refugee Children, Stockholm – Åland Islands, September 1989 (Stockholm: Swedish Refugee Council/European Consultation on Refugees and Exiles, 1992).
21. Michael Spencer, *1992 And All That: civil liberties in the balance* (London: Civil Liberties Trust, 1990) p. 40.
22. *Ibid.*, pp. 158–9; see also Chapter 3.
23. Committee on Legal Affairs and Citizens' Rights (rapporteur: H. O. Vetter), *Report on the right of asylum*, A2–227/86 parts A and B

(European Parliament, 1987); *Official Journal of the European Communities*, C99 (12 March 1987) pp. 167–71; *ibid.* C190 (18 June 1987) pp. 105–6.

24. Commission of the European Communities, *Communication from the Commission to the Council and the European Parliament on the right to asylum*, SEC(91) 1857 final (internal document, 1991).

25. See Thomas Spijkerboer, *A bird's eye view* (note 10) pp. 10 and 83–94 for some light on the probable contents.

26. *Report from the Ministers responsible for immigration to the European Council meeting in Maastricht on immigration and asylum policy*, WGI 930 (3 December 1991), unpublished.

27. Commission of the European Communities, *Report to the Council on the possibility of applying Article K.9 of the Treaty on European Union to asylum policy*, SEC(93) 1687 final (internal document, 1993).

28. Committee on Civil Liberties and Internal Affairs (rapporteur: P. Lambrias), *Report on the general principles of a European refugee policy*, A3–0402/93 (European Parliament, 1993).

29. Commission of the European Communities, *Communication from the Commission to the Council and the European Parliament on immigration and asylum policies*, COM(94) 23 final (Luxembourg: Office for Official Publications of the European Communities, 1994).

30. See also *Migration News Sheet*, May 1994.

31. *Convention determining the state responsible for examining applications for asylum lodged in one of the Member States of the European Communities*. For the English text see H. Meijers (ed.), *Schengen: internationalisation of central chapters of the law on aliens, refugees, privacy, security and the police*, 2nd edn (Leiden: Stichting NJCM, 1992) pp. 171–6; also *International Journal of Refugee Law*, vol. 2 (1990) pp. 469–83.

32. *Migration News Sheet*, July and October 1994.

33. Ad Hoc Working Group on Immigration, document WGI 1008 dated 8 May 1992 (unpublished).

34. See *Asylum in Europe, vol. I* (note 6) pp. 76–81 for more details.

35. *Guardian*, 21 June 1994; *Migration News Sheet*, July 1994.

36. Ad Hoc Working Group on Immigration, *Resolution on manifestly unfounded applications for asylum*, WGI 1282 (1992). For text see P. Boeles, R. Fernhout, C.A. Groenendijk, E. Guild, A. Kuijer, H. Meijers, Th. de Roos, J.D.M. Steenbergen and A.H.J. Swart, *A new immigration law for Europe?* (Utrecht: Dutch Centre for Immigrants, 1993) pp. 69–72.

37. EXCOM Conclusion no. 30 (XXXIV): *The problem of manifestly unfounded or abusive applications for refugee status or asylum* (1983).

38. *Ibid.*
39. Boeles *et al.*, *A new immigration law for Europe?* (note 36) pp. 76–7.
40. Committee of Ministers of the Council of Europe, *The harmonisation of national procedures relating to asylum*, Recommendation R (81) 16 (Strasbourg: Council of Europe, 1982).
41. *Europe: the need for minimum standards in asylum procedures* (Brussels: Amnesty International EU Association, 1994) pp.15–17.
42. Ad Hoc Working Group on Immigration, *Resolution on a harmonised approach to questions concerning host third countries*, WGI 1283 (1992). For text see Boeles *et al.*, *A new immigration law for Europe?* (note 36) pp. 73–5.
43. *Europe: the need for minimum standards* (note 41) p. 8; Eva Kjærgaard, *The concept of 'safe third country' in contemporary European refugee law* (London: European Council on Refugees and Exiles, 1993).
44. United Nations High Commissioner for Refugees, *Overview of re-admission agreements in Central Europe* (September 1993); *Readmission agreements, 'protection elsewhere' and asylum policy* (August 1994); *Fair and expeditious asylum procedures* (November 1994). See also Liz Fekete and Frances Webber, *Inside racist Europe* (London: Institute of Race Relations, 1994) pp. 32–4.
45. Data from a table supplied in November 1994 by the International Centre for Migration Policy Development, Vienna.
46. Press release from the Brussels office of UNHCR, 1 December 1994.
47. Ad Hoc Working Group on Immigration, *Draft recommendation regarding practices followed by Member States on expulsion*, WGI 1266 (1992). For text see Boeles *et al.*, *A new immigration law for Europe?* (note 36) pp. 83–7.
48. Boeles *et al.*, *A new immigration law for Europe?* (note 36) pp. 22–3.
49. Commission of the European Communities, *Commission report on the abolition of controls at intra-Community borders*, COM(88) 640 (Luxembourg: Office for Official Publications of the European Communities, 1988).
50. Antonio Cruz, *Carrier liability in the Member States of the European Union*, Briefing Paper no. 17 (Brussels: Churches' Committee for Migrants in Europe, 1994).
51. *Migration News Sheet*, July 1993.
52. *Ibid.*, January 1995.
53. *The role of airline companies in the asylum procedure* (Copenhagen: Danish Refugee Council/European Consultation on Refugees and Exiles, 1988).
54. Jens Vedsted-Hansen, 'Amendments to the ICAO standards on carriers' liability in relation to immigration control', in *The effects of carrier sanctions on the asylum system* (Copenhagen: Danish Refugee

Council/Danish Center of Human Rights/European Consultation on Refugees and Exiles, 1991) pp. 23–6.

55. Anne la Cour Bødtcher and Jane Hughes, 'The effects of legislation imposing fines on airlines for transporting undocumented passengers', *ibid.* pp. 6–13.

56. See Cruz, *Carrier liability* (note 50) and Vedsted-Hansen, 'Amendments to the ICAO standards' (note 54).

57. Nancy C. Etzwiler, 'The treatment of asylum seekers at ports of entry and the concept of "international zones"', in *The effects of carrier sanctions* (note 54) pp. 14–22; also *Working paper on airport procedures in Europe* (London: European Council on Refugees and Exiles, 1993).

58. Committee of Ministers of the Council of Europe, *On guidelines to inspire practices of the member states of the Council of Europe concerning the arrival of asylum-seekers at European airports*, Recommendation R (94) 5 (Strasbourg: Council of Europe, 1994).

59. *UNHCR's position on Conventions recently concluded in Europe (Dublin and Schengen Conventions)* (Geneva: UNHCR, 1991).

60. EXCOM Conclusion no. 12 (XXIX): *Extraterritorial effect of the determination of refugee status* (October 1978).

61. *Europe: human rights and the need for a fair asylum policy*, AI Index EUR 01/03/91 (London: Amnesty International, 1991).

62. *Europe: harmonization of asylum policy. Accelerated procedures for 'manifestly unfounded' asylum claims and the 'safe country' concept* (Brussels: Amnesty International EU Project, 1992); also *Europe: the need for minimum standards* (note 37). Both reports include details of national laws and practices, and the second also gives case studies of human rights abuses that have arisen as a result of their application.

63. See the 1993 Lambrias report (note 28); also Committee on Civil Liberties and Internal Affairs (rapporteur: P. Cooney), *Report on the harmonization within the European Communities of asylum law and practice*, A3–0337/92 parts A and B (European Parliament, 1992).

64. Boeles *et al.*, *A new immigration law for Europe?* (note 36).

65. *An overview of protection issues in Western Europe: legislative trends and positions taken by UNHCR* (Geneva: UNHCR, 1994). See also Luise Drüke, 'Refugee protection in the post cold war Europe: asylum in the Schengen and EC harmonization process', in Alexis Pauly (ed.), *Les accords de Schengen: abolition des frontiéres ou menace pour les libertés publiques?* (Maastricht: Institut européen d'administration publique, 1993) pp. 105–69, and Antonio Fortin, *The 'safe third country' policy in the light of the international obligations of countries* vis-à-vis *refugees and asylum-seekers* (London: UNHCR, 1993) .

66. Commission of the European Communities, *Communication from the Commission ... on the right to asylum* (note 24) pp. 23–4.
67. *Memorandum to EC ministers responsible for immigration, European parliamentarians, UNHCR and the press* (London: European Consultation on Refugees and Exiles, 20 November 1992).
68. *A European refugee policy in the light of established principles* (London: European Council on Refugees and Exiles, 1994). An Introductory Statement is printed separately from the policy paper.
69. See Cruz, *Carrier liability* (note 50) and *The role of airline companies* (note 53); also Committee on Civil Liberties and Internal Affairs (rapporteur: D. Martin), *Report on the incompatibility of passport checks carried out by certain airlines with Article 7a of the EC Treaty*, A3–0081/94 (European Parliament, 1994).
70. Luise Drüke, 'Harmonisation and judicial control of asylum under the Third Pillar', in proceedings of a conference at the College of Europe, Brugge, September 1994 (to be published). This also contains details of ECJ case-law in other areas of public policy such as freedom of movement. See also C.A. Groenendijk, 'The competence of the EC Court of Justice', in Boeles *et al.*, *A new immigration law for Europe?* (note 36) pp. 45–53.
71. House of Lords Select Committee on the European Communities, *Community policy on migration*, Session 1992–93, 10th Report (London: HMSO, 1992) report p. 25.
72. See *Working paper* (note 9).
73. *Convention of the Organisation of African Unity governing the specific aspects of refugee problems in Africa*, Article I(2).
74. *Cartagena Declaration on Refugees*, Conclusion 3.
75. Recommendation 1088 (Strasbourg: Parliamentary Assembly of the Council of Europe, 1988).
76. *Working paper* (note 9) p. 5.
77. *A European refugee policy* (note 68) p. 3.
78. For details see *Europe: the need for minimum standards* (note 41).
79. *Family reunification for refugees in Europe* (Copenhagen: Danish Refugee Council/European Council on Refugees and Exiles, 1994) pp. 5–7.
80. Statement by Sadako Ogata at the international conference *Fortress Europe? Refugees and migrants: their human rights and dignity*, Graz, Austria, 23 May 1992.

5

Immigration

DEFINING TERMS

In the last few years the terms 'immigrant' and 'migrant' have come to be widely used in policy documents to describe a person who originates from a 'third country' outside the Union, though some governments avoid the terms altogether on the fictitious grounds that their states are not countries of immigration; they use instead the words 'alien' or 'foreigner'. While citizens of one Member State who move to another are normally listed along with other groups in national statistics for immigration and emigration, they are officially regarded only as EU citizens exercising their right to freedom of movement. Not only is this confusing, but it also serves all too often to single out the non-EU immigrant as someone allowed in on sufferance, permanently suspected of being a drain on the country's resources or a source of unfair competition for low-wage employment.

This stigmatisation is made worse by the fact that the term is often extended to include not only people who have recently arrived in a country, but also those who are born there as children of the first immigrants – the so-called 'second-generation immigrants' – and even their descendants in turn. In the media and in the speeches of politicians, the word has become synonymous with 'non-white'. The fact that in some countries the majority of such people have long since acquired full citizenship does not protect them from hostility.

It is now impossible to separate public attitudes to 'immigrants' from the racism and xenophobia (hatred of foreigners) that have become a topic of much discussion in the Union but little action (Chapter 6). This dangerous trend has its roots in the failure of European states to adjust to the fact that their historical role as countries of emigration – either to more prosperous European states or to other continents – has long since been superseded. In recent decades, Europe has attracted increasing numbers of would-be immigrants from the poorer nations of the world. Although they were at one time welcomed as a solution to temporary shortages of labour, the idea that such immigrants might wish to remain and construct a new family life in their adopted country was put aside.

It later became apparent that the process of settlement and integration (however partial) had gone too far to be reversed without wholesale deportation that would violate human rights on a massive scale. Only the extreme right has been prepared to advocate this, though schemes for 'voluntary' repatriation have been set up in some countries and the International Organisation for Migration operates resettlement programmes. Instead of addressing the causes of increased migration, governments have initiated the progressive erection of barriers to entry. As explained in the previous chapter, both refugees and immigrants are increasingly treated as a threat to the stability of European society. Basic standards of respect for human rights – particularly the right to family life – have been openly treated as secondary to the need to limit immigration. Non-EU nationals who are legal residents of long standing are affected as well. It is hardly surprising that popular prejudice against immigrants (both past and present) has increased in proportion.

This chapter attempts to separate the factors that make immigration such a politically sensitive topic. It is a surprising fact that, despite the years of debate, the true extent of net immigration into Europe is still a matter of dispute. The reasons for this need to be understood, if only because official statistics can easily be misquoted to generate undue alarm. The measures agreed by governments also need examining; they are clear enough in their motivation and in the consequences for individuals, but their compliance with standards of human rights is open to question. The causes of migration pressure, and the role of Western governments in unwittingly creating that pressure, comprise another factor that is central to any attempt to reduce it. For many immigrants and their descendants already living in the Union, a crucial factor is the lack of equal rights that derives from their inability to acquire full citizenship. For all of them, the factor most affecting their daily life and their prospects in society is the deep-rooted racism that they often experience, extending from attitudes in the street to their treatment by the authorities. All these problems could be openly tackled on a Union-wide basis if the founding treaties were reformed.

MIGRATION FLOWS AND POPULATION

Annual statistics for net immigration into a given country or the Union as a whole are even less complete and reliable than those for asylum seekers.[1] A major complication is the paucity of reliable information on emigration, without which it is impossible to work out the net increase in population due to migration flows. While most countries attempt to monitor immigration as closely as they can, many have little or no idea of how many people leave the country and fail to return. The information is sometimes obtained indirectly from sources such as surveys of the labour force and data on airline passengers, in which small random samples of people are asked their purpose for travelling.[2] Some countries derive their net immigration data from changes in the total population, after allowing for the difference between births and deaths. Other estimates are even less firmly based.

Several further factors render it impossible to make a reliable comparison between the statistics compiled by different governments. First of all, it is necessary to exclude from immigration statistics the visitors and temporary residents who greatly outnumber long-term immigrants. However, countries differ widely in their cut-off point in terms of the length of stay: some count as an immigrant everyone holding a residence permit whatever the duration of stay, while others specify an expected minimum stay that varies between three months and a year. Similar differences exist in the definitions of emigration. This problem is graphically illustrated when a comparison is made between the data for emigration from a given country (tabulated by destination) and the immigration data of others (tabulated by country of previous residence). For movements between a given pair of countries the two sources should give the same answer. However, even between Member States of the Union there are very large discrepancies.

Another problem, particularly relevant at present, is that asylum-seekers are included in some national totals for immigration but not in others. Other factors are peculiar to certain countries. When Spain and Italy passed laws to regularise illegal immigrants in 1989 and 1990 respectively, large numbers of people appeared in the immigration statistics although they had been in the country concerned for some time. German statistics have shown surprisingly large inflows of German nationals because many were *Aussiedler,* people of German descent from the former Soviet bloc who are regarded as citizens; in 1990 nearly 400,000 entered Germany, declining later to about 200,000 per year.[3]

Attempts are slowly being made to put the statistics on a more reliable footing. Eurostat (the Union's own statistical service) is trying to get Member States to improve and harmonise their methods, using as a starting point some long-standing but widely ignored UN recommendations. The intergovernmental Centre for Information, Discussion and Exchange on the Crossing of Frontiers and Immigration (CIREFI) is currently more concerned with statistics for illegal immigration,[4] a matter on which few experts are prepared to hazard a guess.[5]

In view of all these difficulties, only a few statements can be made with any confidence. Eurostat data indicate a net immigration of roughly 1 million per year into the twelve EU states during 1990–92,[6] representing annually about 0.3 per cent of the total population. The net figures represent about half those for gross inflows. As in the case of asylum applications, Germany has had by far the largest share of immigrants even when *Aussiedler* are discounted. By 1991 there were some 10 million non-EU nationals legally resident in the twelve Member States then making up the Union.[7] This represented some 3 per cent of the total population, with national figures (excluding Ireland) varying between 0.5 per cent (Spain) and nearly 7 per cent (Germany).

Immigration statistics are sometimes seized upon as proof that without further drastic restriction of those seeking work or asylum in the Union, the proportion of non-EU nationals will soon rise to unacceptable levels. However, this kind of immigration is not the only reason for coming to Europe; for instance, almost comparable numbers arrived in 1991 under rules allowing family reunification (see below) with established immigrants and refugees.[8] Total numbers in recent years have been inflated by a number of exceptional factors such as the Yugoslav exodus and the inflow of those guaranteed entry because of ethnic links (Germany), colonial obligations (France, the Netherlands and the UK) and other reasons (Finns returning from the former Soviet Union). Numbers in these categories seem likely to fall in the future.

This is not the place for a complex demographic argument about future trends and the consequences of further immigration, and experts differ widely in their predictions. The figures do not in any case support a 'doomsday scenario' of such magnitude that considerations of basic human rights can be dismissed as a luxury.

UNION POLICY ON IMMIGRANTS

The Changing Climate

In 1985 the Commission, in an optimistic mood concerning its competence to intervene in such matters, suggested some principles that should guide the harmonisation of Community law and practice regarding all migrants (both EC and non-EC nationals) already living and working in Member States.[9] It declared that 'it is a constant factor of the Community approach that the aim should be equality of treatment in living and working conditions for all migrants, whatever their origin, and workers who are nationals.' This principle derived not so much from a concern for human rights as from a conviction shared by the European Court of Justice: that the logic of the internal market demands the same minimum standards of treatment for all its workers.

Although mainly concerned with workers from one Member State moving to another, the document drew attention to two problems affecting immigrants from outside the Community which remain unsolved ten years later: the access to employment of a spouse joining a worker, and the risk of losing both residence and work permits when a worker becomes unemployed. In 1990 an experts' report to the Commission pursued the same theme of taking positive action to foster integration and prevent discrimination against immigrants in areas such as employment and housing. It issued a prescient warning of the consequences of failing to act:

> If today's immigrants were left to fend for themselves they would continue to occupy the bottom rungs of society ... The larger surrounding society turns hostile, develops rejection and stigmatisation mechanisms and resorts to uncivilised policing, thus reinforcing the vicious circle of exclusion breeding marginality.[10]

Developments in later years, however, showed that most of the governments of Member States had quite different preoccupations. Their approach to immigration was to treat it as an adjunct of police and security policy. The main emphasis was put on restricting entry to the Union, with ever-growing visa requirements that affected immigrants and asylum-seekers alike (Chapters 3 and 4). The draft external frontiers Convention, following the Schengen precedent, imposed strict limits on the movement of such people within the Union and left long-term residents who were non-EU nationals to the vagaries of national laws. Other measures, agreed between Member States outside the rule of Community law, were aimed at limiting the rights of non-EU nationals to employment and family reunification.

The Commission, too, was apparently drawn into accepting these priorities; in a 1991 document,[11] issued only one year after the experts' report described above, integration is no longer treated as something to be tackled as a prime requirement of policy. Instead it is asserted that discussions between Member States on a common approach have established the principle that 'integration of immigrants [can] only be achieved by controlling migration flows', and most of the discussion centres on the obstacles to achieving such control. There is a call for prompt action to compensate for the abolition of checks at internal borders, the lack of which will otherwise 'render any control of immigration impossible'. The overriding principle is stated as being that 'the goal of free movement of persons justifies such joint measures'.

This document, like its companion dealing with asylum policy (Chapter 4), uses a new and frankly alarmist language to describe the perceived problems. It uses the imagery of the popular press to liken immigration to a flood that threatens to drown the citizens of Europe. There are references to asylum procedures being 'increasingly used by potential emigrants for purposes other than those for which they were originally designed', and 'swamped by persons seeking the social rights ... granted to asylum applicants but no longer being granted in other cases as a consequence of the halting of economic immigration'. As always there are no data to support this analysis, other than a reference to the increasing rates of refusal of refugee status; the possibility that the increase in asylum applications might reflect a real humanitarian need is not even discussed.

There is a dire warning that citizens of Eastern and Central Europe, once freed of Soviet domination and no longer eligible for asylum, could develop 'such a desire to emigrate as to overwhelm the economic and legal structures of the host countries'. That scenario, at least, was not to develop as expected; whatever the attractions of the prosperous West, most citizens of other European countries preferred to face privation at home than abandon their country, its language and its culture. The belief persisted, however, that if large numbers of people from other parts of the world continued to knock at Europe's doors, their motives were most likely to be economic.

The concrete proposals made in the Commission's 1991 Communication are an accurate forecast of what the Member States would soon adopt as priorities: harmonisation of policies on asylum, family reunification and temporary work contracts; action against illegal residents and 'undeclared work' by immigrants, whether legally resident or not; readmission agreements for the deportation of 'immigrants in an irregular situation' to a non-EU country (Chapter 4); and last in the list, action to ensure equal treatment and better security of residence for those legally resident. There is repeated reference to the dangers inherent in allowing public opinion to turn against legal immigrants because of fears about uncontrolled immigration, but the language used is hardly conducive to allaying such fears.

There is also the introduction of a hypothesis that has since been developed further by the Commission:[12] that economic development of the poorer countries, fostered by Community aid and cooperation projects, could counter the migration pressures that drive people to come to Europe. Unfortunately this assumption, self-evident though it seems, is not borne out by experience; development experts seem to agree that in the 'short' (10–20 year) term, economic development programmes can actually increase migration.[13]

Employment Restrictions

The secret agreements revealed in 1992 were mostly aimed at keeping out asylum-seekers, and have already been discussed (Chapter 4). Two, however, were directed at the few non-EU nationals still recruited for employment and at the families of those who were already legally resident. Both were drafted as resolutions for adoption by the immigration ministers of the Member States, acting outside the framework of Community law in spite of the specific provisions of the EC treaty regarding employment and social policy. The excuse for doing this was that the resolutions related to the admission of non-EU nationals, rather than to their treatment inside the Union.

The first resolution[14] underwent substantial changes before its final adoption in 1994, and was an obvious compromise designed to allow Member States to continue with most current practices. The general principle is that admission should only be permitted when a vacancy cannot be filled 'by national and Community manpower or by non-Community manpower lawfully resident on a permanent basis in that Member State ...'. However, exceptions are allowed on a temporary basis for certain categories: named workers with specialist skills or those urgently needed because of a temporary manpower shortage, seasonal workers, trainees, frontier workers, and 'intra-corporate transferees being transferred temporarily by their company as key personnel'.

Third-country nationals are only to be admitted after issue of a work permit, and this will normally be limited to employment in a specific job with a specified employer. Seasonal workers are to be admitted for no more than six months in a twelve-month period and must then leave for six months before being readmitted. For all categories there are time limits and restrictions on changing jobs, though extensions of stay may be authorised. The Member States 'will examine the desirability of issuing a permanent residence permit to third-country nationals who have had restrictions on their employment lifted'.

The danger is that these conditions could place all those concerned in the position of indentured labourers with no freedom of action beyond that of leaving the country again. The restrictions deny the workers concerned any parity of rights with those of national workers; worse still, they are left open to exploitation because they are prevented from seeking alternative employment. The resolution sets no minimum standards of treatment, and since it is not legally binding there is nothing to stop a Member State varying the rules to satisfy fluctuating demands for cheap labour. In the hands of unscrupulous employers the workers could end up as a permanent underclass, liable to instant deportation if they step out of line and criticise their treatment.

Family Reunification

The last agreement reached in the 1992–93 bout of intergovernmental activity related to family reunification policy.[15] This is certainly an area where national policies vary widely[16], and a more consistently humane approach would have been welcome. Once again, however, the resolution sets only the most minimal standard, though this is claimed to be consistent with international Conventions on the subject. It is quite frank about the reason, which is 'the need to control migration flows into the territories of the Member States'. An exception is made for recognised refugees, for whom more favourable rules remain possible.

The resolution recommends that a non-EU national who is lawfully resident 'on a basis which affords ... an expectation of permanent or long-term residence' may be joined by a spouse who is 'legally bound to him or her in a marriage recognised by the host Member State'. Children of the couple are eligible if they are under an age limit of 16 to 18, depending on national rules. Adopted children or those related to only one partner are admitted solely at the discretion of the Member State. The spouse and children may be admitted 'only for the purpose of living together with the resident'. Other family members may only be admitted 'for compelling reasons which justify the presence of the person concerned'.

Perhaps most ominously, Member States 'reserve the right to determine whether a marriage was contracted solely or principally for the purpose of enabling the spouse to enter and take up residence in a Member State, and to refuse permission to enter and stay accordingly'. This means an extension to the whole Union of the notorious 'primary purpose rule' which immigration officials in the UK have applied with such zeal over the years.[17] It led at one time to potential brides of immigrants from the Indian subcontinent being subjected to virginity tests, a practice finally banned as degrading and unjustified. The same immigration service also tried to determine the true ages of children applying to join their parents by the scientifically flawed (and potentially dangerous) method of bone radiography by X-rays. Applications were commonly refused on the grounds that the children were not in fact related to the parents, and the rate of refusal only fell when DNA analysis (for which parents had to pay) became available to prove otherwise.[18]

These examples serve to illustrate how readily a government service can push to the limit a policy whose aim is openly restrictive and divorced from any great concern for human rights. The Meijers committee of Dutch legal experts describes the resolution as 'not only unsound and inadequate, but even counter-productive'.[19] It is seen as an extreme example of 'downward harmonisation', with all national variations in restriction incorporated into one policy. Like the resolution on employment, it is denounced as being incompatible with international obligations under treaties such as the European Social Charter, the European Convention on Human Rights and the Convention on the Rights of the Child. These commitments were clearly set out (and duly ignored) in a paper prepared by the Commission for the European Council meeting in June 1992, one year before the ministerial resolution was signed.[20] The same Commission document, and a later NGO report,[21] illustrates how wide is the gap between the resolution and the more generous rules applied by some countries: a number of Member States admit dependent parents or other relatives in the 'ascending line', and only in Germany is the age limit for minors set at 16 rather than 18.

States adhering to the Council of Europe's European Social Charter (Chapter 2) are committed to admitting at least the wife (not the husband) and dependent children of a 'foreign worker', but this is taken to apply only to those coming from a state that has ratified the Charter. The same age limit of 21 is applied within the Union by a 1968 Regulation covering the movement between Member States of workers who are EU nationals;[22] they are also allowed to bring in older descendants (not just children) who are dependent, together with all dependent relatives in the ascending line of the worker and his or her spouse. Other family members can also come if they are 'dependent on the worker ... or living under his roof in the country whence he comes'. The spouse and children under 21 are given the right to take up employment anywhere in the Member State, even if they are not nationals of a Member State. Subsequent Directives[23] and the new Article 8a EC have established further rights of free movement and residence for EU nationals.

The discrepancy between the rules for EU nationals and those laid down by the immigration ministers' resolution is clearly enormous. The Meijers committee feared that its main effect would be to sanction a progressive restriction of the right to family reunification for immigrants. This did indeed happen in several countries: new 'primary purpose' rules began to appear in national legislation, and stricter requirements were introduced on such matters as the financial resources of the applicant and the existence of adequate accommodation.[24] The committee also drew attention to continuing gaps in most national laws regarding the status of unmarried and same-sex partners.

Policy After Maastricht

The priorities of Member State governments were well illustrated by the recommendations of a 'conference to prevent uncontrolled migration' held in Budapest in February 1993.[25] This was attended by the ministers of justice and home affairs from 33 European countries, with observers from Canada and Argentina. The conference concentrated on criminalisation of the smuggling of illegal immigrants, and called for steps to combat the employment of all those whose immigration status does not allow them to work. It recommended the setting up of special units to track down offenders, together with mobile forces (including helicopters and patrol boats) to patrol both land and sea borders. Readmission agreements (Chapter 4) were encouraged, with emphasis on cooperation on organising the transport of illegal migrants to be readmitted to their country of origin or last stay, 'in particular into countries which are far away'. The Chicago Convention was cited (wrongly) to justify the imposition of carrier sanctions on airlines (Chapter 4) and the provision of 'advice and assistance' to all carriers in preventing the transportation of 'inadequately documented passengers'.

The Commission's 1994 contribution to the immigration debate,[26] which also dealt with asylum (Chapter 4), was notably different in tone and also departed from the stance of its 1991 paper. A new realism is apparent, coupled with an admission that 'illegal immigrants' may well include asylum-seekers who are denied the full and fair hearing of their claim that was previously available to all. There are no sweeping statements about abuses of the asylum procedure, and instead a recognition that refugees 'would normally have preferred to stay in their country of origin, had the human rights situation been better there'.

Above all, there is a new urgency about the need to tackle the 'polarisation in the attitudes of different sectors of society towards the issue of new immigration and towards established immigrant communities'. It is recognised that high unemployment has aggravated this effect, in which a perception that large numbers of people are immigrating to Europe 'is often based on feeling rather than facts'. A plea is made for governments to 'build on the public's tradition of tolerance, by putting more energetic emphasis on the benefits of immigration, both economic and social, while at the same time showing that immigration is under control by putting a coherent long-term strategy in place.'

There is also a deeper understanding than before of the limitations of trying to reduce migration pressure at source. The Commission quotes a 1992 declaration of the European Council[27] that lists important elements in such a strategy (termination of armed conflicts, respect for human rights, a liberal trade policy and development aid). It points out, however, that economic aid needs to be linked with policies on debt management, international trade and investment – a much broader approach than the inward-looking and protectionist stance that has so far characterised Union policy towards the world outside.[28] The Commission adds some further factors to the list of causes for migration pressure, including population growth and environmental degradation due to natural disasters, desertification and erosion. It warns that any new external policy will only be effective in the long run; the corollary is that it is vital meanwhile to manage migration without pretending that it can be brought to an end.

The Commission clearly hopes that before too long it will gain a more far-reaching power under Article K.9 TEU to take the initiative in matters of both immigration and asylum. Article K.1 specifically mentions, as 'matters of common interest', a number of topics relating to non-EU nationals: conditions of entry and movement within the Union, conditions of residence, family reunification and access to employment. The 1994 Communication mentions some areas in which the Commission evidently thinks it could do better than the immigration ministers have so far done. One of these is family reunification, where the Commission favours a legally binding instrument such as a Convention to give non-EU nationals a more secure basis for their rights than widely divergent national laws.

Another such area is the position of illegal immigrants. The Commission points out that they 'can be subject to exploitation and be in an extremely vulnerable position'. It recommends all Member States to sign and ratify the 1990 UN Convention on the Protection of the Rights of All Migrant Workers and Members of their Families, which aims to guarantee equal treatment of nationals and migrant workers regardless of their status. The Convention affirms that if this is achieved then 'recourse to the employment of migrant workers who are in an irregular situation will also be discouraged if the fundamental human rights of all migrant workers are more widely recognised'.[29] The Commission agrees that legal as well as illegal immigrants can be in need of such protection. It may be significant that no Member State of the Union has so far ratified this Convention. Even the European Convention on the Legal Status of Migrant Workers, which by definition applies only to legal immigrants, has attracted only five ratifications from Member States (France, the Netherlands, Portugal, Spain and Sweden) since it was signed in 1977.

A topic avoided altogether by the drafters of the TEU was that of harmonising the means by which non-EU nationals can acquire national citizenship (and hence Union citizenship as defined by the TEU) after a period of residence in a Member State. Here there are wide variations between countries in the length of residence required, in the possibility of having dual nationality, and in the status of those born of non-EU nationals during their residence in a Member State.[30] It leaves those unable to acquire national citizenship in a vulnerable position, and even liable to deportation to a 'home country' which they have never lived in. The Commission's Communication argues that there should at least be a review of national legislation to remove conditions of nationality for the exercise of rights and the granting of benefits.

A New Deal for Migrants?

As in the case of asylum-seekers, there is a broad consensus among many groups, ranging from the European Parliament to grassroots activists, that the position of non-EU nationals living and working in the Union is grossly unsatisfactory. Their second-class status becomes more and more of a handicap as the concept of Union citizenship is developed to give more rights to the nationals of Member States. Numerous proposals for reform have been put forward over the years, without having any noticeable effect on the decisions made by governments in their joint agreements.

Institutional Initiatives

The Commission has argued that the logic of the internal market should ultimately lead to 'granting access to employment in another Member State (or at least the right to reply to actual offers of employment) to certain categories of nationals from third countries admitted to take up residence in the first Member State, and *a fortiori* in the transborder regions'.[31] The Commission intends to make a concrete proposal on this in 1995.[32]

The European Parliament passed a resolution in 1990[33] that called for an urgent examination of ways to extend the rights of migrant workers and their families from third countries. It pointed out that the preamble to the Community's Social Charter (Chapter 6) stipulates that such people should be 'able to enjoy, as regards their living and working conditions, treatment comparable to that enjoyed by workers who are nationals of the Member State concerned'. This was followed over the next four years by a series of detailed reports and recommendations by the civil liberties committee of the Parliament.

The committee covered the whole field of immigration policy in 1992.[34] While taking a hard line on illegal immigrants, its report insists on the right of any legally resident non-EU national to be joined by a spouse, children and any other close relative. It calls for family members to be given a legal status independent of that of the breadwinner after a two-year period. It also demands a continued right of residence for any non-EU national whose marriage to an EU national has broken down. The report includes many other recommendations on the granting of equal rights to immigrants and the combating of racism and xenophobia.

The same committee produced two more reports in 1993 which, unusually, proved too radical to be accepted by the whole parliament.[35] A report on the status of non-EU nationals[36] recommends the introduction of a European residence permit that would allow all legal residents (not just workers, and wives independently of husbands) to travel freely within the Union, settle in another Member State and take up employment on the same terms as EU nationals. It calls for easy access to dual nationality, affirmative action to encourage integration and a ban on expulsion following conviction for a criminal offence, since this in practice amounts to double punishment for the same offence.

The second rejected report[37] goes further and calls for the recognition of non-EU nationals who are normally resident as full citizens of the Union. This would require a revision of the EC treaty to define Union citizenship in terms of a constitutional charter of civil and political rights, instead of tying it to nationality. Such a charter would include the right to vote and stand as a candidate in European elections, and the right to join the civil service in a Member State (a possibility currently restricted by national laws). One advantage of this route is that it would avoid the problem faced by non-EU nationals such as Turkish citizens, who forfeit certain rights in Turkey if they have to renounce their nationality.

Another report on the rights and duties of non-EU nationals resident in the Union was referred back to the committee,[38] and though redrafted and published[39] it never reached the full Parliament; as an 'own initiative' report it had to be withdrawn at the end of the five-year term of the Parliament in 1994. This report proposes a detailed charter of rights for non-EU nationals, balanced by obligations to respect the laws and cultural values of their host country while still preserving their own culture. There is a specific prohibition of practices which, though derived from the traditions or religion of their country of origin, 'are injurious to human dignity and/or the physical integrity of women or minors'.

A further report by the civil liberties committee,[40] also withdrawn at the end of the Parliament's term, emphasises the need to pay more attention to the integration of national, ethnic, religious, cultural and linguistic minorities. It endorses the call for a charter of rights and duties, and suggests the setting up of a Union-funded task force for coordinating action in this field.

The Migrants' Forum, a consultative body set up (but not controlled) by the Commission, has called among other things for the creation of an 'observatory' of immigrants' rights to be set up.[41] This would comprise representatives of migrants' associations, the Commission and the European Parliament. The Forum also favours the introduction of a European residence card, as suggested by the Parliament, which would entitle the holder to travel without hindrance throughout the Union.

In 1991 the Union's consultative Economic and Social Committee (ESC) exercised its right to produce an own-initiative Opinion on the status of non-EU migrants.[42] This points out that privileged treatment is already offered to non-EU nationals covered by association and cooperation agreements with particular countries. As an example it quotes the EC–Morocco agreement which includes some guarantees of non-discrimination in pay, employment and social security conditions for workers from Morocco. The European Court of Justice has ruled that such agreements form an integral part of Community law.[43] It has also given criteria under which some of their provisions apply directly to individuals, though national governments have contested the issue and it remains to be clarified.[44]

In the Council of Europe, both the Committee of Ministers and the Parliamentary Assembly have issued many recommendations relating to the rights of migrants, and there is a European Committee on Migration (CDMG) which commissions expert reports.[45] A special project, running from 1991–95, was initiated by the CDMG on the problem of achieving integration and equal opportunities for migrants; another relates to the legal protection of short-term migrants.

Of all such initiatives, that of the Commission on immigration and asylum policies (Chapter 4 and above) is likely to carry most weight in the future because of its potential for being translated into Community law under the TEU. Much will depend on the climate of opinion when the treaty comes up for revision.

NGO Proposals

The Meijers committee supplements its trenchant criticism of the 1992 and 1993 asylum and immigration agreements (Chapter 4 and above) with a strong plea that such agreements should serve only as a basis for further consultation with national parliaments and the institutions of the Union. It argues strongly for a more transparent and democratic process of decision-making on all 'third pillar' topics.[46] On family reunification, national parliaments are urged to induce their governments to draw up guidelines for a harmonised set of less restrictive legal rules for Member States to aim for. The committee also suggests a Protocol giving the ECJ jurisdiction to interpret these rules.

In 1994 a consortium of church-based bodies (Caritas Europa, the European Catholic Information and Initiative Office and the ecumenical Churches' Commission for Migrants in Europe) issued a joint call for European immigration policy to be recast on entirely new lines. This would be based on a stronger adherence to the principles of human rights and a recognition that a managed admission policy would be more practical than a fruitless attempt to stop immigration altogether.[47] The details would be worked out and coordinated at Union level and applied uniformly throughout the Union, using the powers provided for in Article K TEU.

The key proposal of the consortium is that an annual limit should be fixed for the number of new permanent residents on Union territory. This would not include refugees recognised under the Geneva Convention, non-EU spouses of EU nationals and those admitted in the context of family reunification, since they have an unconditional right of entry. The annual limit would be fixed for five years at a time, with the possibility of an annual adjustment. A broad-based committee or 'clearing house' would advise the Commission on fixing the limit. Within this limit, three categories would be defined in the following order of priority:

- category A, comprising close relatives not otherwise eligible under rules for family reunification;
- category B, consisting of those whose temporary residence permits can be changed into permanent ones; and
- category C, those whose reasons for applying are mainly economic.

After categories A and B were filled, category C candidates would be selected on a points system based on the Union's preferences (age, qualifications, etc.) and on the candidate's own reasons for applying (including the situation in the country of origin).

The hope is that this programme, combined with a coherent social policy within the Union and action to help countries which are sources of migrants, would enable existing immigrants to achieve a free choice of residence and employment in the Union. The approach is, however, somewhat gradualist compared with that of other reformers; the document accepts a need for immigrants to initially be restricted to the territory of a single Member State. A plea is made for Community structural funds to be used to compensate Member States that accept a relatively high number of immigrants – a valid point, as Germany has discovered when its calls for 'burden sharing' are ignored by other Member States.

Issues for the Future

The positive case for immigration has been supported by academic studies which suggest that immigration by young workers and their families will be essential in the future to offset the ageing of Europe's slowly declining population.[48] An active rather than reactive policy, in which immigration is managed rather than feared, is seen as beneficial to all concerned. Unfortunately the Member States have gone a long way down the second road, and public opinion has been allowed or encouraged to develop an entirely negative attitude to immigration. The situation has been made worse by the obsessive secrecy in which discussions between governments have been conducted:

> Precisely because the subject is such a sensitive one, the closed approach adds to the general climate of anxiety, and reinforces the suspicions of those uneasy about restrictive policies. This contributes to a further polarisation of the debate in a way that works against the development of rational policy.[49]

For this the governments of the Union have only themselves to blame. The hope must be that a change of approach will be made easier when issues like immigration are finally brought within the ambit of Community law, so that transparency is the order of the day and human rights are given more than just lip service in the measures that are agreed. The Court of Justice has shown itself to be more scrupulous in this respect than the governments of Member States, and it will be able to test the effects of Community legislation against the case-law of the Council of Europe's European Court of Human Rights (Chapter 2).

Within the Member States the debate must continue on how best to bring immigrant and minority communities into full and equal membership of society. Opinions differ widely on whether the best approach is 'integration' (preserving differences) or 'assimilation' (absorption into the national culture). Some countries have adopted the second approach either deliberately or by default, making few concessions to the cultures of minority groups. Others have gone to some lengths to encourage the preservation of minority languages and cultures, which are thus integrated to form a richer national patchwork. Although this seems more just and humane than assimilation, it carries the danger that a minority group may become isolated and inward-looking, to the extent that young people leaving school are disadvantaged through lack of practice in the majority language. Examples of both approaches will emerge in the country profiles of Chapter 8.

The task facing all concerned, particularly politicians and the media, is to undo the harm done to community relations by years of negative portrayal of the character and motives of immigrants. It would be tragic if the obsession with abolishing internal frontiers were to have as its main outcome the erection of physical barriers between the Union and most of the people outside it, combined with walls of hatred around a substantial number of its own inhabitants.

NOTES

1. For a concise discussion of this problem see 'International migration flows in selected EC countries – 1991', *Rapid Reports: Population and Social Conditions*, 1993 no. 12 (Luxembourg: Eurostat). See also D. A. Coleman, 'Europe under migration pressure: some facts on immigration', in *Immigration into Western societies: implications and policy options*, proceedings of conference: University of South Carolina, May 1994 (to be published); John Salt, Ann Singleton and Jennifer Hogarth, *Europe's international migrants: data sources, patterns and trends* (London: HMSO, 1994).
2. For data sources in the UK see Reuben Ford, 'Current and future migration flows', in Sarah Spencer (ed.), *Strangers and citizens: a positive approach to migrants and refugees* (London: Rivers Oram/Institute for Public Policy Research, 1994) pp. 44–90.
3. Ursula Mehrländer, 'The development of post-war migration and refugee policy', in Sarah Spencer (ed.), *Immigration as an economic asset: the German experience* (London: Institute for Public Policy Research/Trentham Books, 1994) pp. 1–14.
4. *Migration News Sheet*, December 1994.
5. For some rough annual estimates see Jonas Widgren, *The key to Europe: a comparative analysis of entry and asylum policies in Western countries*, Swedish Government Official Reports 1994:135 (Stockholm: Fritzes, 1994) Table 1, p. 19.
6. *Rapid Reports* (note 1).
7. *Eurostat demographic statistics 1993* (Luxembourg: Office for Official Publications of the European Communities, 1993) Table H1.
8. Widgren, *The key to Europe* (note 5) p. 66.

9. 'Guidelines for a Community policy in migration', *Bulletin of the European Communities*, Supplement 9/85 (Luxembourg: Office for Official Publications of the European Communities, 1985).

10. Commission of the European Communities, *Policies in immigration and the social integration of migrants in the European Community*, SEC(90) 1813 final (internal document, 1990).

11. Commission of the European Communities, *Commission Communication to the Council and the European Parliament on immigration*, SEC(91) 1855 final (internal document, 1990).

12. Commission of the European Communities, *Communication from the Commission to the Council and the European Parliament on immigration and asylum policies*, COM(94) 23 final (Luxembourg: Office for Official Publications of the European Communities, 1994).

13. Joint Council for the Welfare of Immigrants, in House of Lords Select Committee on the European Communities, *Community policy on migration*, Session 1992–93, 10th Report (London: HMSO, 1992) evidence pp. 17–18; Doris Meissner, in *Migration and development: new partnerships for co-operation*, proceedings of a conference in Madrid, March 1993 (Paris: OECD, 1994) pp. 299–301.

14. *Resolution on limitations on admissions of third-country nationals to the Member States for employment*, 7705/94; for analysis see *ILPA Update*, July 1994 (London: Immigration Law Practitioners' Association).

15. Ad Hoc Working Group on Immigration, *Harmonisation of national policies on family reunification*, WGI 1497 (1993). For text see P. Boeles, R. Fernhout, C.A. Groenendijk, E. Guild, A. Kuijer, H. Meijers, Th. de Roos, J.D.M. Steenbergen and A.H.J. Swart, *A new immigration law for Europe?* (Utrecht: Dutch Centre for Immigrants, 1993) pp. 78–82.

16. For the twelve Member States prior to 1995 see Commission of the European Communities, *Family reunification in the light of international law, Community law and Member States' laws and/or practice*, V/384/92 (internal document, 1992); for ten of these excluding Denmark and Greece see *The right to family life for immigrants in Europe* (Paris: Groupe d'Information et de Soutien des Travailleurs Immigrés [French version] and London: Joint Council for the Welfare of Immigrants, 1994); for Denmark, Greece and the UK see *Family reunification for refugees in Europe* (Copenhagen: Danish Refugee Council/European Council on Refugees and Exiles, 1994). See also Widgren (note 5) Table 7, p. 68 for Austria, Denmark, France, Germany, the Netherlands, Norway, Sweden, Switzerland and the UK.

17. Joint Council for the Welfare of Immigrants, in House of Lords, *Community policy on migration* (note 13) evidence pp. 28–30, QQ 157–67.
18. Children's Legal Centre, *ibid.* evidence pp. 94–5.
19. P. Boeles and A. Kuijer, *'Harmonisation of family reunification'*, in Boeles *et al.*, *A new immigration law for Europe?* (note 15) pp. 25–34.
20. Commission of the European Communities, *Family reunification* (note 16).
21. *The right to family life* (note 16).
22. Regulation (EEC) no. 1612/68 of the Council, *Official Journal of the European Communities*, L257 (15 October 1968). See also Directive 73/148/EEC, *ibid.* L172 (1973) regarding self-employed people and providers or recipients of services.
23. Directive 90/366/EEC, *Official Journal of the European Communities*, L180 (1990) p. 30 (later revised as Directive 93/96/EEC) for students; Directive 90/365/EEC, *ibid.* L180 (1990) p. 28 for retired persons; Directive 90/364/EEC, *ibid.* L180 (1990) p. 26 for other 'non-economically active persons'.
24. *Family reunion policies in six European countries*, EuroBriefing no. 1 (London: Joint Council for the Welfare of Immigrants, 1994).
25. *Financial Times*, 17 February 1993; *Platform Fortress Europe?*, March 1993. The recommendations were reproduced in an annex to the European Parliament document PE 203.656.
26. *Communication from the Commission*, COM(94) 23 final (note 12).
27. *Declaration on principles of governing external aspects of migration policy*, Conclusions of the Presidency, Edinburgh, 12 December 1992.
28. See also Jan Niessen and Roger Zegers de Beijl, *International migration, economic development and human rights*, Briefing Paper no. 18 (Brussels: Churches' Committee for Migrants in Europe, 1994).
29. For commentary and a summary of the text of the Convention see *Proclaiming migrants' rights: the new international Convention on the protection of the rights of all migrant workers and members of their families*, Briefing Paper no. 3 (Brussels: Churches' Committee for Migrants in Europe/Geneva: World Council of Churches, 1991).
30. Rainer Bauböck (ed.), *From aliens to citizens: redefining the status of immigrants in Europe* (Aldershot: Avebury, 1994); Rainer Bauböck, *Transnational citizenship: membership and rights in international migration* (Cheltenham: Edward Elgar, 1994). See also Widgren (note 5) Table 8, p. 70; Liz Fekete and Frances Webber, *Inside racist Europe* (London: Institute of Race Relations, 1994) pp. 39–66.
31. Commission of the European Communities, *Immigration and employment*, SEC(92) 955 (internal document, 1992).
32. *Migration News Sheet*, December 1994.

33. *Official Journal of the European Communities*, C175 (16 July 1990) pp. 180–1.
34. Committee on Civil Liberties and Internal Affairs (rapporteur: M. van den Brink), *Report on European immigration policy*, A3–0280/92 (European Parliament, 1992).
35. *Migration News Sheet*, February 1994.
36. Committee on Civil Liberties and Internal Affairs (rapporteur: D. Tazdait), *Report on the status of nationals of non-member countries in the European Union*, A3–0332/93 (European Parliament, 1993).
37. Committee on Civil Liberties and Internal Affairs (rapporteur: R. Imbeni), *Report on citizenship of the Union*, A3–0437/93 (European Parliament, 1993).
38. *Migration News Sheet*, February 1994.
39. Committee on Civil Liberties and Internal Affairs (rapporteur: M. Magnani Noya), *Report on a draft Charter of the Rights and Duties of Third-Country Nationals Living in the European Union*; first report A3–0437/93, second report A3–0144/94 (European Parliament, 1993 and 1994).
40. Committee on Civil Liberties and Internal Affairs (rapporteur: K. Tsimas), *Report on a new policy for integration in Europe*, A3–0073/94 (European Parliament, 1994).
41. *For a joint action for tolerance in Europe (PACT)* (Brussels: European Community Migrants' Forum, 1993).
42. Economic and Social Committee, *Own-initiative Opinion on the status of migrant workers from third countries*, SOC/215 (24 April 1991); Section for Social, Family, Educational and Cultural Affairs of the Economic and Social Committee, *Additional Opinion on the status of migrant workers from third countries*, SOC/217 (16 May 1991).
43. Elspeth Guild, *Protecting migrants' rights: application of EC agreements with third countries*, Briefing Paper no. 10 (Brussels: Churches' Committee for Migrants in Europe, Geneva: World Council of Churches, 1992).
44. *JCWI Bulletin* (London: Joint Council for the Welfare of Immigrants), vol. 5 (1993) no. 1; see also *European migration policies for the nineties after the Maastricht Summit*, Briefing Paper no. 7 (Brussels: Churches' Committee for Migrants in Europe, 1992) pp. 13–15.
45. *The Council of Europe and the protection of the rights of migrants, refugees and minorities*, Briefing Paper no. 13 (Brussels: Churches' Committee for Migrants in Europe, 1993). This is an updated version of the 1991 Briefing Paper no. 6.
46. See also Deirdre Curtin, 'The constitutional structure of the Union: a Europe of bits and pieces', *Common Market Law Review*, vol. 30 (1993) pp. 17–69.

47. *Europe: the new, legal immigration destination* (Brussels: Caritas Europa, 1994); also *The making of European immigration policies*, Briefing Paper no. 15 (Brussels: Churches' Committee for Migrants in Europe, 1994).
48. Sarah Spencer (ed.), *Immigration as an economic asset* (note 3); Werner Weidenfeld and Olaf Hillebrand, *European Brief*, December 1994, pp. 25–7; also Sarah Spencer (ed.), *Strangers & citizens* (note 2) for a UK perspective. For an opposing view see David A. Coleman, 'Does Europe need immigrants? Population and workforce projections', *International Migration Review*, vol. 26 (1992) pp. 413–61.
49. Sarah Collinson, *Beyond borders: West European migration policy towards the 21st century* (London: Royal Institute of International Affairs/Wyndham Place Trust, 1993) p. 91.

6

Racism, Discrimination and Social Rights

PROBLEMS NEGLECTED AND PROBLEMS FACED

This is a chapter of contrasts: between social ills which governments tend to ignore or dismiss as not susceptible to legislation, and other problems where legal regulation is widely accepted. An extreme case in the first category is the phenomenon of racism, always present under the surface in Europe but increasingly expressing itself in ugly mani- festations. National laws against racial discrimination are mostly limited in scope and poorly enforced, and no Union-wide legislation exists. Campaigns to get the issue tackled seriously by governments acting together have produced little more than ringing exhortations and dec- larations of intent, despite every indication that the problem is getting worse. At the other end of the scale are social problems like the lack of equality of pay and opportunity between women and men; this is so widely accepted as being open to treatment that a specific Article was included in the original Treaty of Rome to bring the matter at least partly under Community law.

Other issues involving disadvantage or discrimination lie somewhere in between. Since the health of the internal market depends on its workers, they are offered the promise of Union-wide minimum standards of working conditions and treatment by their employers. The Social Charter (see below) laid down non-binding targets which are gradually being achieved. Most of the disputes in this area relate not to the general principle but to how far and how quickly it should be imple- mented by mandatory legal instruments. Only the UK government has so far resisted the whole idea of going down this path.

People with disabilities are not treated separately in the EC treaty, but by common consent their needs are accepted as a valid subject for joint action and financial support from the EC budget. This does not, however, extend to legislation outlawing discrimination against them. Other groups experiencing discrimination or worse, such as national minorities or lesbians and gay men, are given no specific support.

The various topics mentioned are grouped together here in order to illustrate what might be achieved in the unregulated areas if they were firmly under Community law. At the same time its limitations are brought out by describing just what has been achieved and what remains lacking in those areas where it does apply.

RACISM AND XENOPHOBIA

The addition of the uncommon word 'xenophobia' to 'racism' illustrates the sensitivity of the topic; it derives in part from the reluctance of some politicians to admit that the people they represent could still harbour the kind of attitude associated in living memory with fascism and the Holocaust. Xenophobia, defined as a fear of all things foreign, implies an irrational but more excusable sentiment, capable of being expressed as much by jokes about foreigners as by violent expressions of hatred. The term is not used in international law, and even 'racism' is not a legal term in the UK. In practice the two words express aspects of the same thing: a mistrust and fear of any person whose language, culture or appearance is different to that of the majority, allied with a conviction that one's own 'race',[1] nation or culture is superior to any other. Racism can also mean discriminatory acts based on such attitudes. A 1989 public opinion survey by the Commission of the EC found that one European in three believed that there were too many people of another nationality or race in his or her country.[2]

Matters like racist violence and institutional discrimination (as in the allocation of public housing) are difficult to quantify in statistical terms, since only the more extreme instances are reported. There is, however, no shortage of examples. Apart from national press reports of racist attacks, numerous cases appear in the reports on European countries by Amnesty International, in the columns of the monthly *Migration News Sheet*, in the regular *European Race Audit* of the London-based Institute of Race Relations, and in a book published in 1994 by the same institute.[3] The violent incidents reported range from random attacks in the street to deliberate attempts to burn down buildings containing immigrants or asylum-seekers.

Underlying attitudes are recorded in the form of derogatory remarks by politicians and public officials including police officers, who tend to make sweeping statements associating criminal activity with immigrants, asylum-seekers, or simply the non-white population of the country concerned. Europe's ancient disease of anti-Semitism reappears from time to time in the form of vandalism in Jewish cemeteries or arson attacks on synagogues. Gypsies and other minority groups face new levels of hostility and harassment. Even people with disabilities have suffered. To some observers, the whole alarming scenario is a logical outcome of the restrictive regime of entry controls associated with the abolition of internal frontiers. To others, it has its roots in the rising levels of unemployment and alienation from society that arise from world recession and bear particularly hard on young people. Whatever the cause, few would now deny that more needs to be done if the Union is to preserve its claim to uphold the fundamental principles of human rights.

International Protection

A number of international Conventions on human rights and the protection of different groups in society contain non-discrimination clauses.[4] An example is the International Labour Organisation's Discrimination (Employment and Occupation) Convention, which defines discrimination as 'any distinction, exclusion or preference made on the basis of race, colour, sex, religion, political opinion, national extraction or social origin'.[5] Only one Convention, however, relates directly to racial discrimination: the UN's International Convention on the Elimination of All Forms of Racial Discrimination.[6] All Member States of the Union except Ireland have ratified this. It forbids any form of discrimination based on 'race, colour, descent, or national or ethnic origin'. However, distinctions between citizens and non-citizens are still allowed. Immigration restrictions are thus exempt, though it is often argued that they are racist both in intent and in their effects. There is an important requirement that signatory states must penalise 'all dissemination of ideas based on racial superiority or hatred' as well as incitement to racial discrimination, acts of racist violence and incitement to violence; racist organisations must be outlawed and participation in their activities punished. The evidence suggests that few Member States take this sufficiently seriously; indeed, the dearth of specific legislation in some of them (see below) appears to actually contravene the Convention.

Implementation is monitored by a Committee on the Elimination of Racial Discrimination to which each country must report every two years or whenever the Committee so requests. However, the Committee has no power to make binding judgments. It relies only on moral pressure to rectify abuses which come to its notice, and it can only consider individual complaints if the state concerned has declared that it accepts this right under Article 14 of the Convention. Only five EU countries (Denmark, France, Italy, the Netherlands and Sweden) have done so, and only three complaints were decided upon in the years to 1993. Most people have not even heard of the Convention.

There is thus no comparison with the complaints mechanism of the European Convention on Human Rights (ECHR). Unfortunately the ECHR is notably weak where racism is concerned. Article 14 says that enjoyment of the rights and freedoms listed in the Convention shall be secured without discrimination on any ground, and 'race' is given as one of many examples. However, this is not a general protection against discrimination since it only applies to certain rights; furthermore, the Convention is only in principle available to protect the individual against the actions of the state, rather than those of other individuals or private institutions. In practice no case of race discrimination contrary to Article 14 has actually been established.[7] The only positive effect of the ECHR is that its judicial interpreters have consistently recognised that freedom of expression should be upheld for those who criticise racism, but can be restricted by law for those who advocate racist ideas.

There is thus no effective international mechanism for combating racism or protecting its victims. There is an obvious need for the Union to fill this gap so far as its own Member States are concerned, and the proposals made will be discussed later in this chapter.

National Legislation

The disparate nature of national laws on racism has been brought out in a number of recent studies. At the beginning of 1992 a survey commissioned by the UK government's Department of Employment was published.[8] Although focused on discrimination in employment, this includes a useful general discussion of international Conventions and national legislation in the twelve Member States of that time. At the end of 1992 the Commission of the EC published a somewhat condensed summary of country reports from the same Member States.[9] Brief details of the position in 22 European countries (including all current members of the Union) were given in a 1994 report by a UK-based NGO.[10]

Despite the commitment of all but one Member State to the UN Convention on racial discrimination (see above), few have adopted anything like a comprehensive set of laws on the subject. All except the UK have written Constitutions in which discrimination is forbidden in general terms, often including discrimination on the grounds of race as a specific example. However, in most cases this has to be implemented by specific laws or decrees, and provision of this kind is often deficient. The constitutional prohibition may in any case be limited to acts committed by organs of the state. Legislation is similarly patchy in coverage; it may apply, for instance, to the provision of goods and services but not to employment. There is a marked contrast with the approach to sex discrimination, though this is always grouped with race discrimination in the Constitutions that prohibit it. The excuses offered for this by governments are revealing:

> When asked why similar legislation has not been introduced covering race discrimination, governments are prone to reply that race discrimination is covered by the Constitution. The fact that the same is true of sex discrimination makes one wonder why it was necessary to introduce sex discrimination legislation at all. The response to that is that it was necessary both in order to comply with the EC Directive, and to make more specific the provisions on equal treatment as between men and women.[11]

Even where criminal sanctions exist to deal with the more extreme cases of racism, they are not strongly enforced:

> In general, reports indicate that few cases are brought, and penalties imposed are generally light although the severity is increasing as judges take cases more seriously and legislatures increase the applicable sanctions. Imprisonment is almost never imposed unless it is a case of violent attack against the victim ... Fines vary enormously in the amounts imposed ... A significant number of countries report no cases of prosecution for racist offences.[12]

Civil remedies are preferred by many states, and some have an appropriate ombudsman who can take up a case. The UK is unique in having a dedicated agency, the Commission for Racial Equality (CRE), backed by legislation to define its powers and a substantial budget mostly devoted to law enforcement.[13] Other countries lack any enforcement agency and rely on NGOs to take up cases. The CRE helps individuals in lodging formal complaints; it may also conduct formal investigations on its own initiative. It has certain powers to require a named person to produce information or give oral evidence. If the CRE believes that the Race Relations Act has been contravened it may serve a 'non-discrimination notice' on the person concerned. Industrial tribunals have similar powers in cases relating to employment, together with the power to order compensation. If a warning notice seems to be having no effect and any appeal against it has failed, the CRE can apply to the courts for an injunction to order compliance at any time in the next five years. In addition to this, the CRE has the duty of keeping the Act under review and recommending amendments to the government.

Although the British system is held up by the UK government as a shining example for other states, it is not without its critics.[14] The CRE itself called in 1992 for a strengthening of the Act to deal with a persistently high level of racial discrimination.[15] Its report stated that 'undoubtedly the worst feature of race relations in this country in recent years is the terrifying scale of racial harassment'. It complained that although there was a criminal offence of incitement to racial hatred, few prosecutions were being sanctioned by the government's Attorney-General. The CRE recommended (among other things) that racial harassment should become a ground for eviction under housing legislation, and that consideration should be given to specifically criminalising racial violence. This proposal was supported by many members of the UK parliament but consistently rejected by the government.[16]

The situation across the Union at national level may be summed up in the words of EC Commissioner Padraig Flynn: 'Even existing legislation is in very many cases not in fact implemented, and actual use of national tools already to hand would do much to lift the burden of shameful discrimination borne by the residents of migrant origin'.[17] It would appear that despite their protestations of good intent, the governments of Member States are unable or unwilling to change this situation on their own.

Reports, Recommendations and Resolutions

There is no shortage of comparative studies of racism in Europe. The European Parliament commissioned a special committee report in 1985[18] whose terms of reference included the growth of fascist and racialist groups in Europe (not only the EC), the links between such groups, their effect on racism in Member States, the effects of economic and social conditions, the machinery used by governments to deal with racist organisations, and possible ways of combating them. All the present Member States except Finland were considered separately, together with Norway, Switzerland and Turkey.

The conclusions drawn were sombre: that although openly fascist or racist groups were small and fragmented into warring factions, they had increasingly turned to violent action in 'a general climate of thoughtless toleration towards violence, extremism and depreciation of constitutionality'. The committee also found serious cause for concern over the rise of a more widespread xenophobia: 'It has a distressing effect on the immigrant communities which are daily subject to displays of distrust and hostility, to continuous discrimination which legislative measures have failed to prevent ... these minorities have little confidence in the institutions on which they should be able to call to uphold their rights and to offer them protection'. Such a sentence could easily have been written ten years later, with the rider that far-right parties no longer have a monopoly of racist policies; recent electoral campaigns in

Member States have shown an increasing tendency for some mainstream politicians to tacitly or explicitly support similar ideas.

The committee made numerous recommendations, together with a call to make more use of the powers implicit in the EC treaty under Article 235. This empowers the Council (acting unanimously on a proposal from the Commission) to 'take appropriate measures' to attain an objective of the common market not provided for in the treaty. It has, for instance, been freely used to justify measures to help people with disabilities (see below). As an alternative, the committee suggested appropriate revision of the treaty – a call which went unheeded at the Maastricht conference on that topic some years later.

The report was followed in 1986 by a joint declaration of the Community institutions against racism and xenophobia.[19] This was the first of several equally sonorous but largely meaningless pronouncements that appeared in subsequent years. The institutions 'vigorously condemn' all forms of intolerance, hostility and violence against minority groups; 'affirm their resolve' to protect all individuals in society; and 'look upon it as indispensable' that all necessary steps are taken. The idea of using the EC treaty to make binding decisions is not, however, mentioned.

In 1988 the Parliament showed its impatience with the lack of action on its 1985 report and called on the Commission to come up with some concrete proposals.[20] Among the suggestions were a wide-ranging educational campaign, the creation of a forum for migrant workers, and the collection of information on anti-racist legislation in Member States. The Commission incorporated some of these into a proposal for a Council Resolution.[21] This also called on all Member States to ratify existing international legal instruments relating directly or indirectly to racism, and for all states that had not done so to bring in rigorous laws punishing discrimination or xenophobic acts.

The draft Resolution was never adopted by the Council, but the Commission later went ahead with the less controversial measures involving education, the collection of information and the setting up of a body comprising representatives of migrant associations (the Migrants' Forum). The Economic and Social Committee had already expressed 'deep disappointment' that the Commission suggested only a non-binding Resolution rather than 'an effective policy displaying a real political commitment to combat racism', and suggested the appointment of a Commissioner against Racism to monitor discrimination across the Community and supervise effective counter-measures.[22]

The Parliament returned to the attack in 1989 with a demand that the draft Resolution be adopted and put into effect by means of an action programme.[23] It noted with alarm that there had been an increase in racism and xenophobia, and in electoral support for political organisations advocating discrimination against immigrants and ethnic minorities. The Council finally produced its own 'Resolution on the fight against racism and xenophobia' in May 1990.[24] However, this was so watered down from the original proposal that the Commissioner responsible for social affairs refused to be associated with it. The Parliament was similarly outraged. The most glaring omission was the deletion from the draft (at the insistence of the UK delegation) of a sentence stating that any measures taken must protect both EU and non-EU nationals, including 'nationals who are perceived or who perceive themselves as belonging to a foreign minority'.

Meanwhile the European Parliament had set up a new committee of inquiry on the subject, and this reported in June 1990.[25] It noted that only a few of the 40 recommendations of the 1985 report had been fully implemented, and none had led to significant changes in anti-racist legislation. The Commission was exonerated from the charge of not trying hard enough to initiate action, but Member States were castigated for their inaction: 'these recommendations have virtually fallen on deaf ears in most Member States with the resulting virulent upsurge of racism and xenophobia in several of them'.

The report gives detailed backing to its arguments with country reports on all the present members of the Union together with Norway and Switzerland. Eastern Europe is also covered briefly, with a prophetic warning about the prevalence of racism in what was then the German Democratic Republic. The rise of extreme-right parties is reported and the deficiencies in anti-racist legislation documented. The report ends with 77 wide-ranging recommendations for immediate action by the Parliament, the Commission, the Council, the Member States, and the foreign ministers dealing with external relations in what was then European Political Cooperation forum (now covered by the TEU).

The only response from the Member States was the issuing of yet another declaration, produced at the Maastricht meeting of the European Council in December 1991. The heads of state noted 'with concern' the growth of racism and xenophobia, and stressed 'the undiminished validity of international obligations with regard to discrimination and racism'. After expressing more sentiments of this kind the Council requested more effort from Ministers and the Commission, to which it still denied the competence to act effectively in this field. Ritual statements of concern were repeated in the conclusions of European Council meetings in December 1992[26] and June 1993.[27]

A further report by the Parliament's civil liberties committee in 1993[28] again argued strongly for the adoption of a Directive under Article 235 EC to compel the introduction in all Member States of stringent anti-racist legislation. The Council did not take up the suggestion. Instead, the Corfu summit meeting of the European Council in June 1994 seized eagerly on a Franco-German plan to set up a Consultative Committee on the problem.[29] This was charged with setting up various subcommittees with a view to making recommendations on ways of 'encouraging tolerance and understanding of foreigners'.[30] An interim report was presented in November 1994 and a final version promised for March 1995; the Justice and Home Affairs Council was then expected to produce an overall strategy of the Union for adoption by the European Council in June.[31]

The Member States had nominated one person each to sit on the Consultative Committee; meetings were also to be attended by one MEP and one representative of the Commission. However, the Migrants' Forum – the self-governing body set up by the Commission and which claims to represent the 15 million people most affected by racism – was denied a seat, leading to suspicions that the whole thing was no more than a public relations exercise. The Forum had been campaigning since 1992 for the appointment of a Commissioner for Racial Affairs, charged with promoting Community legislation against racism and penalising Member States for non-observance.[32] It had also launched a 14-point European Manifesto Against Racism which left no doubt about its interest in the matter.

Over these years the Council of Europe contributed its own reports to the growing pile of documents detailing problems that were all too clear to those experiencing them at local level. In 1991 the Committee of Experts on Community Relations published the results of a project that had been running since 1987.[33] Their report calls for 'a legislative basis for action to ensure equality of opportunity and to combat discrimination'. Immigration control should be exercised 'so as to ensure that immigrants receive fair and courteous treatment irrespective of nationality or ethnic origin'. Authorities providing services are encouraged to recruit staff from migrant and ethnic minority groups. Practical measures are suggested such as the provision of adequate low-cost housing and the prevention of discrimination in this area. To agree on even these rather obvious recommendations took a long time, apparently because some governments were reluctant to admit the gravity of the problem.

On the particular issue of racial violence, another Council of Europe report offers a thoughtful historical analysis of the roots of racism in Europe together with country surveys of France, Germany, Italy, the Netherlands, Sweden and the UK (excluding Scotland and Northern Ireland).[34] The problem is seen as having intensified in all European countries over the previous decade. The report ends with a detailed checklist of recommended actions for governments, the police, other public agencies and anti-racist groups in the community.

The Council of Europe sponsored a summit meeting of European heads of state in 1993 whose Vienna Declaration included a plan of action on combating racism, xenophobia, anti-Semitism and intolerance.[35] This issued the usual appeal to Member States to improve their legislation and develop work in the fields of education and social policy. It also authorised the creation of a committee of government experts with a mandate to recommend national and international action. The committee was set up at the beginning of 1994 under the chairmanship of Sweden's Ombudsman Against Ethnic Discrimination, and styled itself the European Commission Against Racism and Intolerance.

From the non-governmental sector, many organisations have (as mentioned earlier) documented the rise of far-right political parties and the increase in racist violence across Europe. A 1991 report[36] commissioned by International Alert and the Netherlands Institute of Human Rights (SIM) includes reports on the twelve Member States of that time, based on visits to national NGOs concerned with migrants and racism. Each country report documents the main concerns, the position of non-EU nationals, integration policy (if any) and proposals for national legislation, together with an overview of the government agencies and NGOs involved.

In 1993 Amnesty International published details of cases of racist torture and ill-treatment by the police of Austria, France, Germany, Greece, Italy, Portugal, Spain and the UK.[37] The case-studies follow a depressingly similar pattern of racist abuse, beating and judicial inaction following complaints. Amnesty International calls for a stronger moral lead from governments and a fully independent investigation of complaints. It followed this in 1994 with a report devoted only to France;[38] this details cases of killings and violence by law enforcement officers, directed mostly against victims of non-European origin.

The Starting Line

In 1993 a joint initiative called The Starting Line was launched by the Churches' Committee for Migrants in Europe, the UK Commission for Racial Equality, the Dutch National Bureau Against Racism and the Commissioner for Foreigners' Affairs of the Senate of Berlin.[39] This is prefaced by some sobering information about the upsurge in racist attacks in many Member States during 1992; in the first three months of that year, 600 attacks on foreigners were recorded in Germany alone. Most of the attackers were under 20 years of age.

The essence of the proposal, which is complemented by declarations from other church-based bodies,[40] is a Directive modelled on the one issued in 1976 on the principle of equal treatment for women and men.[41]

This would oblige Member States to ensure that their laws, regulations and administrative provisions were adequate to prevent discrimination in a wide range of fields including employment, social security, health and welfare benefits, education and training, housing, the provision of goods, facilities and services, and participation in social, cultural, religious and public life. Direct or indirect discrimination would be forbidden on grounds of race, colour, descent, nationality, national or ethnic origin.

Governments would also have to provide legal sanctions against racist or xenophobic propaganda and insult, and against incitement to racial discrimination, hatred or violence. Judicial remedies and compensation would have to be made available to persons alleging discrimination against them, with appropriate support for the victims in bringing complaints. Once a presumption of discrimination was established, the burden of proof that it did not occur would lie with the respondent, the complainant having the benefit of any doubt that remained. Other requirements of the draft relate to measures in education, training and information to discourage all forms of racism. Like other Directives, this one would include a requirement for Member States to adopt the necessary provisions by a fixed deadline (two years is proposed), and to submit regular reports on their compliance with it.

The draft Directive provides a refreshing contrast to the empty declarations of governments, and also to the less focused demands of other reports and recommendations. The inclusion of a clause on the burden of proof is guided by experience in the field of sex discrimination, where this is still a contentious issue. The proposal is backed by a reasoned argument that, contrary to the assertion of Member States, there is already Union competence to issue legally binding instruments in this field; it is also argued that the case-law of the European Court of Justice supports the application of the same principles to non-EU nationals. On the question of Union competence, there is certainly support for its existence under the current treaties among legal experts[42] and within the Commission.[43]

In any case the draft serves as a model for what could be pushed forward after a definitive revision of the EC treaty. As its title indicates, it would serve as a framework for future legislation covering specific aspects of the problem and particular fields of application, just as the equal treatment Directive laid the ground for further measures relating to the position of women. The sponsors of The Starting Line have also made a concrete suggestion for amending the treaty; called The Starting Point, it is in two parts.[44] The first is an addition to the list of 'activities of the Community' in Article 3 EC. This would read

... the elimination of discrimination against persons or groups of persons whether citizens of the European Union or not, on the grounds of race, colour, religion, or national, social or ethnic origin, and the promotion of harmonious relations between such persons or groups of persons.

In addition there would be a new Part 1A (Non-discrimination) between Part 1 (Principles) and Part 2 (Citizenship of the Union). This would give the Council the power to issue binding Directives and Regulations on the elimination of discrimination as defined above. These would be approved under the codecision procedure of Article 189b.

The case for treaty revision was officially espoused by the Commission in its 1993 White Paper on social policy.[45] The lack of clear competence for introducing legislation is described as 'increasingly hard to justify in today's Europe', and a call is made for specific reference in the treaty to combating discrimination on the grounds of race, religion, age and disability. The sorry saga of prevarication by the Member States is evidence that such action is long overdue.

UNPROTECTED MINORITIES

Hostility and discrimination can affect many groups in society regardless of race or skin colour. Some have suffered persecution or social exclusion for centuries because of their lifestyle, beliefs or physical attributes. Their problems do not derive from recent immigration from elsewhere but from long-standing attitudes in national cultures. Even if the major evil of racism is effectively tackled by the Union, other problems will remain to be addressed by those who hope to eliminate intolerance against minority groups from European society. Some examples are given here to illustrate this fact; for reasons of space the list is far from exhaustive and the discussion limited in scope. There is, however, much that could be repeated from the conclusions drawn above in connection with racism.

A common factor is the wide variation in national policies and laws relating to minority groups, ranging from institutionalised discrimination to tolerance or positive action to guarantee their rights. This variation can hardly be justified on the grounds of 'subsidiarity' (Chapter 1) and national sovereignty alone; if the declarations attached to successive Union treaties are to be taken seriously, no group in society should be at a disadvantage where human rights and civil liberties are concerned.

National Minorities

Many European countries have long-established ethnic, linguistic and religious minorities whose presence derives from historical changes in national borders or long-past migratory movements.[46] Others have substantial but scattered communities whose traditional lifestyle is nomadic. They receive little attention from the institutions of the Union, though in some cases they suffer discrimination and hostility of a racist nature at least as severe as those experienced by recent immigrants and their descendants. The OSCE (formerly CSCE, Chapter 2) and the Council of Europe have devoted the most concern to the problems faced by such people. Within the Union, many of whose states have a Constitution guaranteeing equal rights to all, there is still a reluctance to admit that ethnic minorities should be treated in any way differently to the majority of citizens. Article 27 of the UN's International Covenant on Civil and Political Rights (ICCPR, Chapter 2) offers all minorities a general right to 'enjoy their own culture, to profess and practice their own religion, or to use their own language'. However, few cases have been brought under this Article; France had in any case declined to accept its application to the Republic.[47]

The UN Commission on Human Rights established a Sub-Commission on Prevention of Discrimination and Protection of Minorities in 1978, but it was not until 1992 that a draft declaration on the subject was finally adopted by the General Assembly.[48] This laid down some general principles derived from other UN Conventions, but avoided giving minorities any new form of redress against abuses. In 1994 the Sub-Commission recommended the establishment of a broadly-based working group to include NGOs and representatives of minority groups.

The CSCE as it then was (see above) had meanwhile given increased attention to the question of minorities, though the need to achieve a consensus among its more than 50 member countries limited the scope of its decisions.[49] A 1990 meeting of the Conference on the Human Dimension endorsed a list of rights which anticipated many features of later proposals including the UN declaration, such as the right of minorities to use their own language and 'establish and maintain unimpeded contacts among themselves within their own country as well as across frontiers with citizens of other states with whom they share a common ethnic or national origin, cultural heritage or religious beliefs'. This was followed in 1992 by the decision to appoint a High Commissioner on National Minorities. The powers of this functionary were, however, to be somewhat limited; although mandated to provide early warning of tensions involving national minority issues, this would not include 'issues in situations involving organised acts of terrorism'. The extreme sensitivity of some states to the issue of minorities was apparent in the numerous caveats entered by national delegations to the Helsinki conference at which the matter was discussed. Nevertheless, the High Commissioner was able to arrange visits in 1993 to the Baltic states and Slovakia, and was authorised to undertake a study of the situation of Roma (Gypsies) throughout Europe.[50]

The European Commission for Democracy through Law, a consultative body of the Council of Europe, made a proposal in 1991 for a European Convention for the Protection of Minorities.[51] This was intended to complement existing international protection for individual members of minority groups with a Convention that included clauses relating to the groups as such. Although limited to nationals of the state concerned, the Convention would cover any minority group having 'ethnical, religious or linguistic features different from those of the rest of the population'. It would cover their right to be protected against forced assimilation and 'any activity capable of threatening their existence'.

The Council of Europe's Parliamentary Assembly came out in favour of an alternative proposal which other experts had already put forward: an additional Protocol to the European Convention on Human Rights (ECHR).[52] The proposed text covered much the same ground as the draft Convention, and (unlike both the ECHR and the ICCPR) was again restricted to citizens of the state concerned. Though mostly limited to the protection of individual rights, it included a statement that 'deliberate changes to the demographic composition of the region in which a national minority is settled, to the detriment of that minority, shall be prohibited'. The explanatory report emphasised that Roma and other nomadic groups were to be covered by the Protocol.

The Council of Europe summit meeting in October 1993 included in its Vienna Declaration[53] an instruction to the Committee of Ministers to begin work on both a framework Convention on the protection of national minorities and a Protocol to the ECHR. The Convention would be open for signature by non-Member States. The reference to a Protocol mentions only individual rather than group rights, which suggests a reluctance to concede the principle involved.

The European Parliament took up the issue of Roma groups in 1994 – an appropriate if ironic choice, since travelling communities personify the freedom of movement which is so central to Union policy. A resolution drafted by its civil liberties committee[54] points out that 'the Rom people constitute one of the largest minorities in the European Union'. It expresses the fear that such people will be less able than most to assert their basic rights in the face of a general upsurge in racism and xenophobia. The resolution deplores an agreement signed in 1992 with Romania which led to the forcible repatriation from Germany of 30,000 Roma who had sought asylum; in return the Romanian government was given a DM 1,000 million loan. Among other recommendations, the report endorses the idea of a Protocol to the ECHR that would specifically mention such people as a landless minority.

The issue of national minorities, highlighted by the terrible events in the former Yugoslavia, is here to stay on the agenda of matters to be tackled by the Union. No amount of early warning of potential conflicts will suffice unless a firmer system of legal protection is in place, backed by a political will among governments which has so far been notably lacking.

Lesbians and Gay Men

The Union's drive for harmonisation in other areas of policy has scrupulously avoided the issue of legislation on homosexuality, where disparities between Member States are particularly striking. The assertion that there is no competence under the treaties to tackle the matter has always been questionable, and a strong case for intervention has been made on several grounds. The first argument is that discrimination for any reason is contrary to the broad principles of human rights affirmed by the treaties. The second is that freedom of movement between Member States is not assured, even for citizens of the Union, when laws on homosexuality can render a couple whose position is legally recognised in one country liable to criminal prosecution in another. Such laws can also deny them benefits in some Member States for which they are eligible in others.

The variation between Member States is less now than it was some decades ago, when in some countries any form of homosexuality between men was punishable by law. The slowness of progress towards more open attitudes is reflected in continuing differences between Member States in the age of consent. This can vary between 12 and 18 in a complex manner depending on the sex of the couple and many other factors. There has been a slow trend towards equalising the age for all categories (lesbian, gay and heterosexual), but official attitudes vary widely: in a few cases it is still illegal for certain bodies such as local authorities to 'advocate or promote' homosexuality. On the other hand there is legal recognition in other Member States (Denmark and Sweden, and to a lesser extent the Netherlands) that a homosexual couple can enjoy virtually all the rights assigned to married couples of opposite sex. Discrimination against homosexuals is forbidden in only a few Member States.

The European Parliament took an early interest in the issue. In 1984, following a report on sexual discrimination against homosexuals in the workplace,[55] it urged Member States to abolish laws against homosexual acts between consenting adults; to introduce a common age of consent;

to ban the keeping of special records on homosexuals by the police; and to reject the classification of homosexuality as a mental illness (a reference to the World Health Organisation, which later deleted the relevant entry). The report also called on the Commission to report on all forms of discrimination against homosexuals in Member States regarding employment, housing and other problem areas. When the 1989 Social Charter (see below) was under discussion, the Parliament amended the report of one of its committees to call for equal protection of all workers regardless of 'nationality, race, religion, age, sex, sexual preference or legal status'.[56] Most recently, a 1994 report of the civil liberties committee reiterated the demands of the 1984 resolution and added other calls for action against discrimination.[57] It specifically asked the Commission to draft a Directive on combating discrimination on the basis of sexual orientation.

Before this, the Commission had set up a unit to study the issue and commissioned a detailed report which was published in 1993.[58] This examined all the legal, social and economic aspects of the problem in the framework of international human rights and Community law. The report ended with a call for a Community action plan to combat discrimination. This covered nine areas:

- official recognition of a role for the Commission in combating homophobia and protecting the fundamental rights of lesbians and gay men;
- the setting up of an *ad hoc* task force to prepare and monitor a detailed plan of action to include the items listed below;
- preparation of a Community Declaration analogous to those issued on racism and xenophobia;
- eradication of discrimination in the workplace against lesbians and gay men working for institutions of the Community;
- amendment of the equal treatment Directive to prohibit discrimination based on sexual orientation;
- a review of other existing and planned Community legislation to include wording that ensures the protection of equal rights in the areas of employment, social policy and the internal market;
- a review of ways in which the Commission could encourage Member States and private institutions to combat discrimination;
- further study and monitoring of discrimination by the Commission, particularly in the sphere of economic activity, with a view to enhancing awareness and taking action; and
- inclusion of a prohibition against discrimination on grounds of sexual orientation in any future Community Bill of Rights or treaty.

Among the many other issues raised in the report is that of asylum for those persecuted because of their homosexuality; only limited recognition of the principle has so far been achieved in a very few Member States.[59] The problems facing non-EU nationals applying to enter the Union as partners of EU nationals are also discussed.[60] There is detailed discussion of the applicability of the European Convention on Human Rights[61] and the proposal for an amending Protocol to the ECHR; the latter idea is discouraged on the grounds that Community law provides a better avenue of attack on discrimination.[62]

The Commission evidently decided that the issue was one in which it was fruitless to draw up proposals for legislation that would be rejected outright by the Council. Its reluctance to do so has already been remarked in the area of racism, though in both cases there are strong arguments for Community competence. Some of the contributors to the report were also hesitant: 'Independently of the merits, it is our view that specific legislation to cover anti-homosexual discrimination will be perceived, and touted, as an example of Community legislative excess.'[63] One of the few cases to date in which the Commission has felt confident enough to mention the issue is in the context of sexual harassment in the workplace; in a recommended code of practice published in 1992 it states that lesbians and gay men are among those groups that are particularly vulnerable to sexual harassment.[64]

The report includes a concrete suggestion for extending the protection available to lesbians and gay men under the existing regime of Community law, particularly the equal treatment Directive.[65] It is argued that there is scope for bringing more test cases before the European Court of Justice in order to challenge the exclusion of lesbians and gay men from the scope of anti-discrimination legislation. In the developing case-law of the ECJ there is increasing reference to principles of human rights that are not necessarily spelt out in the treaties, together with a readiness to take into account non-binding Recommendations; this could well include the one on sexual harassment.

This might render it unnecessary to put forward an amendment to the Directive as advocated in the nine-point plan described above. In parallel with this there could, of course, be an attempt to get the principle established once and for all in the next revision of the EC treaty. The report emphasises the principle at issue: 'If ... a Common European Market is to be created in which human dignity, personal freedom and social justice are essential aspects, EC action to abolish any form of discrimination against lesbians and gay men is a dire necessity and the political will must be found.'[66]

People with Disabilities

There is no disagreement about the need to enable people with disabilities to lead a normal and independent life, and most Member States have acted to progressively remove some of the physical barriers to achieving that goal. Although this group of people is not specifically mentioned in the EC treaty, the Commission has been able to set up Community-funded programmes to assist their training and employment (HORIZON), integration into society (HELIOS), access to information (HANDYNET) and use of special technology (TIDE). This action was mostly approved under Article 235 EC, which (as mentioned above) can be applied to certain matters not specified in the treaty. However, while most governments are happy to see Community finance used in this way, they dislike the idea of being obliged under Community law to do more themselves. Their resistance to proposals to outlaw discrimination is stronger still.

The European Parliament has called for the Union to treat the question of equal treatment for people with disabilities as a matter of human rights, and to incorporate this into an amendment to the EC treaty that would outlaw all forms of discrimination.[67] Meanwhile, it recommends the creation of a special Directorate within Directorate-General V of the Commission to develop policy initiatives for people with disabilities, in consultation with organisations representing their interests. There should also be a monitoring of all legislative proposals with regard to their implications for this group of people. The Commission's subsequent White Paper shows a broad sympathy with these aims, and declares that for disabled people there is 'a need to build the fundamental right to equal opportunities into Union policies'.[68]

Black and Ethnic Minority Women

While women in general are assumed to be slowly on the way to achieving equal treatment with men under the protection of Community law, it has long been recognised that black and ethnic minority women (especially the wives of immigrants) are disadvantaged in special ways. They are liable to discrimination in the labour market because of both their sex and their colour, and the poverty in which many of them live make them further liable to exploitation. The insecure jobs they are able to get carry little legal protection, and they find it harder to get access to opportunities for training. Their contribution to the economies of the countries in which they live goes largely unrecognised.

All this was acknowledged in a 1988 report by the Commission.[69] This quoted the warning given in 1981 in the first Action Programme on the Promotion of Equal Opportunities for Women, to the effect that the 1976 equal treatment Directive had had 'little or no impact on women immigrants'. The problem was referred to at intervals by the Commission and by the European Parliament, without anything much being done about it.

The creation in 1990 of the European Women's Lobby was followed by its decision to make the position of this group of women the subject of a special project. A team led by the European Forum of Left Feminists conducted a country-by-country survey based on interviews with grassroots organisations involved in the issue. Its report was later published by the European Parliament.[70] Although it was criticised in some countries for bias in its choice of the organisations consulted, the report gives a graphic picture of the double burden of racism and sexism borne by many black and ethnic minority women. Some groups, such as Filipino women, are imported as domestic workers in more than one Member State under conditions little short of slavery; they are tied to one employer on pain of deportation and widely ill-treated and exploited.[71] Action at European Union level to rectify this kind of abuse is long overdue, and could easily be initiated under the existing treaties.

Social Policy under Community Law

Treaty Provisions and the Social Charter

The 'social chapter' of the EC treaty comprises Articles 117–22. The most unequivocal statement of policy is made in Article 119, establishing the principle that men and women should receive equal pay for equal work. Other Articles lay down general aims, such as Article 118a on the harmonisation of conditions affecting health and safety at work (see Chapter 1). On matters relating to employment, labour relations and most aspects of social security the treaty is cautious, enjoining the Commission to do no more than promote 'close cooperation between Member States in the social field'.

The limited range of topics specified in the treaty led to the formulation in 1989 of a Community Charter of the Fundamental Social Rights of Workers,[72] usually called the Social Charter (not to be confused with the Council of Europe's European Social Charter of 1961). Although not binding on the Member States, the Charter was regarded as symbolic of the Community's determination to avoid being seen as a purely commercial institution, remote from the lives of ordinary citizens.

The Charter listed a wide range of social rights to be developed within the framework of Community law; apart from freedom of movement and health and safety in the workplace (already accepted as priority areas in the treaty) the headings covered employment and pay, living and working conditions, social protection, freedom of association and collective bargaining, vocational training, equal treatment and equal opportunities for men and women, consultation and participation of workers, the protection of young people at work, the elderly, and people with disabilities. The associated Action Programme[73] listed a wide range of measures to be taken, ranging from Directives and Regulations to Recommendations and other non-binding measures.

Three years later the Commission reported that of 47 items in the Action Programme, 28 had been presented to the Council and 15 adopted by it.[74] However, there were significant failures to achieve the necessary agreement between Member States, nearly all of them relating to the rights of workers: Directives on the organisation of working time, 'atypical' (part-time and temporary) work and works councils were all blocked. In each case the principal objector was the UK, which under the Thatcher government had refused to join the other eleven Member States in signing the Charter. Even the deletion of a reference to the desirability of a minimum wage did not soften its stance.[75]

The UK government's main argument at the time was that the measures proposed would 'hamper job creation, hinder competition within the market, damage competitiveness in world markets and put at risk all the benefits of the Single Market itself.'[76] This profoundly negative view was reiterated many times over subsequent years. The issues were as diverse as the burden of proof in sex discrimination cases, the duration of paid maternity leave, retirement ages, short-term contracts, the protection of young people at work, limits to working hours, and parental leave for men as well as women.[77]

The Maastricht Protocol

Frustration with the UK's readiness to veto or delay proposals led to a determination among other Member States to get something more concrete on social policy into the EC treaty. The opportunity arose at Maastricht in 1991, and a new social chapter was drafted. This led to one of the recurrent battles of will between the UK and the majority of other Member States. The outcome was a peculiar compromise with uncertain implications for the future: a Protocol on Social Policy including an Agreement on Social Policy, signed by eleven Member States without the UK.[78] It was agreed that where unanimity on an issue covered by the Protocol could not be reached by the full twelve, the eleven signatories could proceed without the participation of the UK in discussions and in Council votes (see Chapter 1). The Protocol included a requirement for the Commission to consult both management and labour before submitting a proposal, and to give the two sides the opportunity to work out an agreement between themselves during a renewable period of nine months. Only if that failed would the Commission proceed on its own.

There was little new about the topics listed in the Protocol, but the UK government objected to the fact that unanimity in the Council would no longer be longer required for decisions on some of them. The European Parliament, which was never fully satisfied with the Social Charter,[79] complained that the Union had missed a golden opportunity to expand its social policy and had left the Parliament with little more influence than before.[80] However, the importance of the Protocol was that it enabled the log-jam of blocked measures to be freed, in the expectation that sooner or later the UK would abandon its isolated position.

The first use of the procedure came in 1994, when the Commission presented the third version of a proposal for European works councils in multinational corporations. This was aimed at giving workers the right to information and consultation over corporate decisions taken outside the country in which they were employed. The proposal had been held up since 1990, despite numerous meetings and successive revisions of the draft.[81] Under Article 2(2) of the Protocol its adoption required only a qualified majority of the eleven voting states, and the proposal was duly adopted. Although it did not strictly apply to multinational subsidiaries in the UK, it was expected to strongly influence them all the same.

Other candidates for treatment under the Protocol emerged as time passed. The first was the draft Directive on parental leave and leave for family reasons, stalled for a record ten years.[82] This would allow both fathers and mothers three months of parental leave each, without loss of job security or social security rights; there would also be a right to annual leave for urgent family matters. At present there is wide variation between the provisions in the 15 Member States, with some offering no rights at all.[83] Another favourite for application of the Protocol was a draft Directive on the burden of proof in cases of sex discrimination which had been stalled since 1988.[84]

Extending Protection

The examples given above serve to show that although social policy has been slow to develop under Community law, progress is ultimately made in areas where legal competence cannot be denied. Periodic initiatives like the Commission's 1994 White Paper[85] serve to restate the agenda, even if this involves no more than a catalogue of unfinished business. The contrast with areas in which the legal base is absent or disputed is clear, and the conclusion obvious: that in the absence of a perceived threat to political or economic stability, Member States are not likely to act in a concerted manner on any outstanding social problem. They will only do so if faced with a Commission proposal firmly based on the Union treaties. For problems not so covered, the only answer is a clearly-drafted revision of those treaties.

Notes

1. In some circles the term 'race' is treated as suspect, since it can imply a 'social construct' rather than a physical reality.
2. *Eurobarometer*, November 1989.
3. Liz Fekete and Frances Webber, *Inside racist Europe* (London: Institute of Race Relations, 1994). See also the special European issue of its journal *Race & Class*, vol. 32 (1991) no. 3, and the journal *Race and Immigration* of the London-based Runnymede Trust.
4. Jan Niessen, *International instruments to combat racial discrimination in Europe*, Briefing Paper no. 8 (Brussels: Churches' Committee for Migrants in Europe, 1992).
5. International Labour Organisation Convention No. 111 (1958): United Nations, *Treaty Series*, vol. 362, p. 31. Ratified by all Member States except Ireland, Luxembourg and the UK.
6. See Chapter 2 and Aleidus Woltjer, 'The United Nations International Convention on the Elimination of All Forms of Racial Discrimination', in Julie Cator and Jan Niessen (eds), *The use of international Conventions to protect the rights of migrants and ethnic minorities*, proceedings of seminar: Strasbourg, November 1993 (Brussels: Churches' Committee for Migrants in Europe, 1994) pp. 9–18.
7. Hans Christian Krüger and Wolfgang Strasser, 'Combating racial discrimination: the European Convention on the Protection of Human Rights and Fundamental Freedoms', *ibid.* pp. 19–25; also Donna Gomien, 'The rights of minorities under the European Convention on Human Rights and the European Charter on Regional and Minority Languages', *ibid.* p. 52, footnote 14 on a case brought by East African Asians.
8. Ian Forbes and Geoffrey Mead, *Measure for measure: a comparative analysis of measures to combat racial discrimination in the member*

countries of the European Community (London: Racial Equality Section, Department of Employment, 1992).

9. Commission of the European Communities, *Legal instruments to combat racism and xenophobia* (Luxembourg: Office for Official Publications of the European Communities, 1992).

10. Fekete and Webber, *Inside racist Europe* (note 3).

11. Forbes and Mead, *Measure for measure* (note 8) p. 13.

12. Commission of the EC, *Legal instruments to combat racism* (note 9) p. 56.

13. *Racial discrimination: a guide to the Race Relations Act 1976* (London: Home Office, 1977).

14. *Racism: the destruction of civil and political liberties* (London: National Council for Civil Liberties/Anti-Racist Alliance, 1993).

15. *Second review of the Race Relations Act 1976* (London: Commission for Racial Equality, 1992).

16. *Migration News Sheet*, May 1994.

17. *Ibid.*, May 1993.

18. Committee of Inquiry into the Rise of Fascism and Racism in Europe (rapporteur: D. Evrigenis), *Report on the findings of the inquiry* (European Parliament, 1985). For the Parliament's subsequent resolution see *Official Journal of the European Communities*, C36 (17 February 1986) pp. 142–3.

19. European Parliament, Council and Commission, 'Declaration against racism and xenophobia', *Official Journal of the European Communities*, C158 (25 June 1986) pp. 1–3.

20. *Ibid.* C68 (14 March 1988) pp. 29–30.

21. 'Communication from the Commission to the Council on the fight against racism and xenophobia', *ibid.* C214 (16 August 1988) pp. 32–6.

22. Economic and Social Committee, *Opinion on the proposal for a Council Resolution on the rights against racism and xenophobia*, SOC/164 (23 November 1988); *Official Journal of the European Communities*, C23 (30 January 1989) p. 33.

23. Political Affairs Committee (rapporteur: B. van der Lek), *Report on the Joint Declaration against racism and xenophobia and an action programme by the Council of Ministers*, A2–261/88 (European Parliament, 1998); *Official Journal of the European Communities*, C69 (20 March 1989) pp. 40–4.

24. *Official Journal of the European Communities*, C157 (27 June 1990) p. 1.

25. Committee of Inquiry into Racism and Xenophobia (rapporteur: G. Ford), *Report on the findings of the Committee of Inquiry*, A3–0195/90 (European Parliament, 1990).

26. *Migration News Sheet*, January 1993.

27. *Ibid.*, July 1993.

28. Committee on Civil Liberties and Internal Affairs (rapporteur: C. de Piccoli), *Report on the resurgence of racism and xenophobia in Europe and the danger of right-wing extremist violence*, A3–0127/93 (European Parliament, 1993).

29. *Migration News Sheet*, July 1994.

30. *Ibid.*, October 1994.

31. *Ibid.*, December 1994 and January 1995.

32. *Forum* (Brussels: Migrants' Forum), 1992, no. 2.

33. *Community and ethnic relations in Europe*, MG–CR (91) 1 final (Strasbourg: Council of Europe, 1991).

34. Robin Oakley, *Racial violence and harassment in Europe*, MG–CR (91) 3 rev. 2 (Strasbourg: Council of Europe, 1992).

35. *Netherlands Quarterly of Human Rights*, vol. 11 (1993) pp. 513–20; *Combating racism in Europe*, Briefing Paper no. 16 (Brussels: Churches' Commission for Migrants in Europe, 1994) pp. 20–2.

36. Deny de Jong and Marcel Zwamborn, *Equal treatment and discrimination in Europe* (London: International Alert, 1991).

37. 'Racism: torture and ill-treatment in Western Europe', *AI Newsletter* (London: Amnesty International) February 1993, pp. 3–6.

38. *France: shootings, killings and alleged ill-treatment by law enforcement officers*, AI Index EUR 21/02/94 (London: Amnesty International, 1994).

39. *The Starting Line: a proposal for a draft Council Directive concerning the elimination of racial discrimination* (Brussels: Churches' Committee for Migrants in Europe, 1993).

40. *Combating racism in Europe* (note 35).

41. Directive 76/207/EEC (9 February 1976).

42. Richard Plender, in House of Lords Select Committee on the European Communities, *Community policy on migration*, Session 1992–93, 10th Report (London: HMSO, 1992) evidence pp. 63–4; Elspeth Guild, 'Race discrimination and Community law', *Migrantenrecht*, vol. 93, no. 1 (1993) pp. 6–12.

43. Denis Martin, 'Race discrimination and Community law', paper presented at a JCWI/RDLDF/ILPA seminar on legal remedies against racial discrimination and racial attacks, London, 19 November 1993, organised by the Joint Council for the Welfare of Immigrants.

44. Available from the Churches' Commission for Migrants in Europe, Brussels (see Appendix) or the Commission for Racial Equality, London.

45. Commission of the European Communities, *European social policy – a way forward for the Union*, COM(94) 333 final (Luxembourg: Office

for Official Publications of the European Communities, 1994) part VI, para. 27.

46. See various reports of the London-based Minority Rights Group, for instance *The Southern Balkans* (1994) on Albania, Greece and the Former Yugoslav Republic of Macedonia.

47. Rachel Brett, 'The International Covenant on Civil and Political Rights and minorities', in Cator and Niessen, *The use of international Conventions* (note 6) pp. 32–40.

48. Patrick Thornberry, 'Draft UN declaration on minority rights', *Interights Bulletin*, vol. 6 (1991) pp. 80–1; *Declaration on the rights of persons belonging to national or ethnic, religious and linguistic minorities*, General Assembly Resolution 47/135 (18 December 1992).

49. Rachel Brett, (a) *The development of the Human Dimension Mechanism of the CSCE*, (b) *The challenges of change: report on the Helsinki Follow-up Meeting of the CSCE* (Colchester: University of Essex Human Rights Centre, 1992); (c) *Is more better? An exploration of the CSCE Human Dimension Mechanism and its relationship to other systems for the promotion and protection of human rights* (Colchester: University of Essex, Human Rights Centre, 1994); Urban Gibson and Jan Niessen, *The CSCE and the protection of the rights of migrants, refugees and minorities*, Briefing Paper no. 11 (Brussels: Churches' Committee for Migrants in Europe, 1993).

50. Brett, *Is more better?* (note 49) pp. 45–8.

51. *Human Rights Law Journal*, vol. 12 (1991) pp. 270–3; *Explanatory report on the proposal for a European Convention for the Protection of Minorities*, CDL (91) 8 (Strasbourg: Council of Europe, 1991).

52. Parliamentary Assembly of the Council of Europe (rapporteur: Mr Worms), *Report on an additional Protocol on the rights of minorities to the European Convention on Human Rights*, doc. 6742 (Strasbourg: Council of Europe, 1993); Parliamentary Assembly, Recommendation 1201 (1993). The latter includes a text in French as well as English.

53. *Netherlands Quarterly* (note 35).

54. Committee on Civil Liberties and Internal Affairs (rapporteur: J. de D. Ramírez Hereida), *Report on the situation of Gypsies in the Community*, A3–0124/94 (European Parliament, 1994).

55. Committee on Social Affairs and Employment (rapporteur: V. Squarcialupi), *Report on sexual discrimination in the workplace*, 1–1358/83 (European Parliament, 1984).

56. *Official Journal of the European Communities*, C323 (22 November 1989) pp. 44–8.

57. Committee on Civil Liberties and Internal Affairs (rapporteur: C. Roth), *Report on equal rights for homosexuals and lesbians in the EC*, A3–0028/94 (European Parliament, 1994).

58. Kees Waaldijk and Andrew Clapham (eds), *Homosexuality: a European Community issue* (Dordrecht: Nijhoff/Brussels: European Human Rights Foundation, 1993).
59. Kees Waaldijk, *ibid.* pp. 126–7; Antonia Tanca, *ibid.* pp. 281–3.
60. Kees Waaldijk, *ibid.* pp. 100–1.
61. Pieter van Dijk, *ibid.* pp. 180–206.
62. Andrew Clapham and J.H.H. Weiler, *ibid.* pp. 61–5.
63. *Ibid.* p. 29.
64. Angela Byre, *ibid.* pp. 214–5.
65. *Ibid.* pp. 215–7.
66. *Ibid.* p. 359.
67. Committee on Social Affairs, Employment and the Working Environment (rapporteur: R. Oomen-Ruijten), *Report on the Green Paper entitled 'European social policy – options for the Union'*, A3–0270/94/Part A (European Parliament, 1994).
68. Commission of the EC, *European social policy* (note 45) part VI, paras 22–4.
69. Commission of the European Communities, *Communication on the social situation and employment of migrant women*, COM(88) 743 final (Luxembourg: Office for Official Publications of the European Communities, 1988).
70. *Confronting the fortress: black and migrant women in the European Union*, Women's Rights Series E-2 (Brussels: European Women's Lobby and Luxembourg: European Parliament, 1995).
71. See for example *Britain's secret slaves: an investigation into the plight of overseas domestic workers* (London: Anti-Slavery International/Kalayaan, 1993).
72. For the text of this and the associated Action Programme, together with articles written from different points of view, see *Social Europe* 1/90 (Luxembourg: Office for Official Publications of the European Communities, 1990).
73. *Ibid.* pp. 51–77.
74. Commission of the European Communities, *Second report on the application of the Community Charter of the Fundamental Social Rights of Workers*, COM(92) 562 final (Luxembourg: Office for Official Publications of the European Communities, 1992). This includes detailed country reports on implementation.
75. See *Social Europe* (note 72) pp. 97–101 for the earlier draft.
76. House of Lords Select Committee on the European Communities, *A Community Social Charter*, Session 1989–90, 3rd Report (London: HMSO, 1989) report p. 9, para. 16.

77. For more details of these and other social issues see Michael Spencer, *1992 And All That: civil liberties in the balance* (London: Civil Liberties Trust, 1990) pp. 104–19.
78. Paul Beaumont and Gordon Moir, *The European Communities (Amendment) Act 1993* (London: Sweet and Maxwell, 1994) pp. 260–4.
79. Committee on Social Affairs, Employment and the Working Environment (rapporteur: M. Buron), *Report on the Community Charter of Fundamental Social Rights*, A3–69/89 (European Parliament, 1989).
80. Committee on Social Affairs, Employment and the Working Environment (rapporteur: V. Reding), *Second report on the new social dimension of the Treaty on European Union*, A3–0091/94 (European Parliament, 1994). The first report (A3–0274/93) had been referred back by the full parliament. See also (from the same committee and rapporteur) *Report on the application of the Agreement on Social Policy*, A3–0269/94 (European Parliament, 1994).
81. Commission of the European Communities, *Proposal for a Council Directive on the establishment of European Committees or procedures in Community-scale undertakings and Community-scale groups of undertakings for the purposes of informing and consulting employees*, COM(94) 0134 final (Luxembourg: Office for Official Publications of the European Communities, 1994). Earlier versions were COM(90) 581 and COM(91) 345.
82. Commission of the European Communities, *Amended proposal for a Council Directive on parental leave and leave for family reasons*, COM(84) 631 final (Luxembourg: Office for Official Publications of the European Communities, 1984); *Official Journal of the European Communities*, C336 (9 December 1993) pp. 6–8 and C316 (27 November 1984) pp. 7–9.
83. Equal Opportunities Unit, *Leave arrangements for workers with children*, V/773/94 (Brussels: Commission of the European Communities, 1993).
84. Spencer, *1992 And All That* (note 77) pp. 108–10; Commission of the European Communities, *Proposal for a Council Directive on the burden of proof in the area of equal treatment for women and men*, COM(88) 269 final (Luxembourg: Office for Official Publications of the European Communities, 1988); *Official Journal of the European Communities*, C176 (5 July 1988) p. 5.
85. Commission of the EC, *European social policy* (note 45).

7

Policing, Data Protection and State Control

PERSONAL DATA AND THE STATE

Like the previous chapter, this one offers a contrast between areas of policy that are excluded from Community law, and other related areas that are accepted as being subject to it. In the first category, matters of national policing are jealously guarded by Member States under the doctrine of subsidiarity, while cooperation between the police forces of different states is confined to secret intergovernmental discussions. Cooperation between the various security services is even less open, with all but a few ministers in each government knowing nothing of their activities.

Such cooperation involves above all the exchange of information, both 'hard' (factual) and 'soft' (speculative, or classified as intelligence that would not be used in a court of law). As shown in earlier chapters, the exchange of such information increasingly involves the use of computer networks and the automated storage of vast amounts of data. Intelligence exchange takes place in various additional ways, including verbal communication that is difficult or impossible to regulate. Yet the dangers to the individual of false or inaccurate personal data being circulated throughout the Union have only recently attracted official concern, and the safeguards so far proposed are of doubtful validity.

This contrasts strongly with the attitude to personal data that circulate in other spheres. The Council of Europe drew up in 1981 a definitive Convention on the protection of computerised personal data. This has served as a model for later proposals for Union-wide legislation and inter-governmental agreements. However, as will be seen below, the Convention is subject to exceptions which leave the individual inadequately protected in relation to agencies of the state in general and the police in particular. This dichotomy persists in the proposals for Union legislation on data protection; although privacy protection is stated as an important principle, the driving force is the need to allay misgivings about a free flow of commercial and other non-governmental information in the operation of the internal market. Uses of personal data by the state are subject to the same kinds of exemption as in the 1981 Convention, and in some cases their regulation is left to agreements between governments or further Conventions drawn up outside the scope of Community law.

There is therefore a prospect of increasing regulation of commercial uses of personal data, to the point where some industries claim (with varying plausibility) that their operations will actually be hindered by it; in contrast, inadequately controlled exchanges of data between police and other state bodies may lead to the individual losing rather more than personal privacy. Cases of wrongful and violent arrest, detention and deportation have already cropped up from time to time as illustrations of what can go wrong.[1]

In parallel with the growth in exchanges of information between states, governments have eagerly embraced new technologies with the aim of documenting and keeping track of every person within their borders. Sophisticated new forms of identity card are being introduced, on which much more than the name and address of the person can be stored. There are commercial pressures to do this as well; the operators of credit card systems would be happy to see a Union-wide database established in which every citizen had a unique identification number. Such moves are also promoted as the answer to increasing levels of crime, not to mention illegal immigration and undocumented labour.

The discrepancy between the levels of protection in the two areas of policy is thus likely to get worse, and the need for an extension of Union competence to cover both of them will become more and more urgent.

POLICE COOPERATION IN THE UNION

Police and security forces in the different Member States vary greatly in the way they are organised.[2] In some countries the rivalries between various fiefdoms are so strong that they do not cooperate readily with each other. Cooperation with the forces of other countries has tended to be cautious and in any case informal rather than structured, with *ad hoc* collaboration across joint frontiers or in special cases like the Channel Tunnel.

A central argument for improving police cooperation has been that freedom of movement within the Union would release a flood of cross-border crime. Some police experts always doubted the assumption. Even now, when the process of dismantling border controls is well advanced, there is still a basic lack of information about the extent of such crime. A lengthy programme of research into police cooperation among the twelve Member States existing in 1993 concluded that 'very little data are available about the extent of cross-border crime in Europe ... The concern about crime is real enough as is the fear of crime but these appear to be inversely related to the knowledge of the scale of the problem.'[3] Another worker in the same field has warned against fostering cooperation for the wrong reasons:

> The shallow nature of the arguments for further improvements in the quality of police cooperation, often proposed by ministers and police agencies with their own agendas, is a particular illustration of the necessity of new conceptions of the European Community. Creating fantasies and fears about potential threats to internal security concerning a flood of illegal immigrants bringing with them drugs, arms dealing, organised crime and racketeering may have a certain populist appeal but it is not an adequate substitute for ethical arguments on which to base new obligations.[4]

Unfortunately those two statements represent a fair description of the atmosphere in which police cooperation in the Union has been allowed to develop. It has acquired a momentum of its own, and real but temporary threats to internal security (such as a series of terrorist outrages) have been enough to maintain the drive towards closer cooperation and ultimately a supranational police force.

Two parallel paths were initially followed: that of the Trevi structure of cooperation between EC Member States and that of the Schengen countries (Chapter 3). The Trevi group was set up in 1976 and formed a number of subsidiary working groups comprising government officials, policemen, immigration and customs officers, and representatives of the security services; they dealt with such matters as terrorism, police training, organised crime and drug trafficking.[5] Under its aegis there is daily contact between European police and security forces through secure telecommunications and facsimile links. Under the TEU the Trevi working groups were transmuted into satellites of the 'K4 Committee' (Chapter 1); they included an *ad hoc* group charged with preparing the ground for the creation of Europol (see below). Few details of their work are ever revealed, though occasional declarations of the Trevi ministers have repeatedly justified it in terms of a fight against terrorism, international crime, narcotics and other illegal trafficking.

The Schengen Convention introduced an altogether more ambitious system of police cooperation that also embraced external border controls and the admission or exclusion of immigrants. Parts of it were copied with little modification in drafting the Union-wide external frontiers Convention and plans for a European Information System (Chapter 3). The principle of the Schengen Information System for exchanging basic information on crimes and criminals was also adopted in setting up Europol, though as shown below this went much further than the mere exchange of factual information. Europol also proved to be far more ambitious (and less restricted) in its aims than Interpol, its only predecessor in the field of international police cooperation.

Interpol

The International Criminal Police Organisation (Interpol) traces its origin to 1923, when a differently titled predecessor was set up in Vienna. By 1963 it was comprised of police forces from 78 countries, rising to 174 in 1993 (80 per cent of those in the world). There is no international Convention to govern its operation, so its Constitution is interpreted or amended by a General Assembly of the constituent members. Its original concerns were with policing in Europe, and even now most of its work relates to that continent: of the 1 million messages handled in 1992, 800,000 were European and of these 400,000 were sent by EU members states.[6] Although it was not chosen as a basis for Europol, it clearly served as a model in many respects. What remains unclear is whether the overlap in their respective activities will ultimately lead to a withering of Interpol's role in Europe. There would undoubtedly be strong resistance to this idea.

Like the nascent Europol, Interpol has a central office for passing messages between the National Central Bureaux (NCBs) of the subscribing states. These often concern descriptions of wanted persons who may be liable to extradition; an Interpol 'red notice' is a request for arrest of a suspect with the assurance that an extradition warrant will follow. Some 60 per cent of Interpol's work is concerned with drug-related offences. Until 1984 (when new guidelines were adopted) its Constitution was often interpreted as excluding cooperation over the arrest of terrorists who claimed a political motive. The present rule allows a distinction to be made between criminal terrorist offences and politically legitimate actions.

Liaison officers from the member countries work with the General Secretariat at Interpol's headquarters in Lyon, and intelligence analysis is included in its work. In view of all these similarities with the EU ministers' plans for Europol one may ask why they did not turn to Interpol, which already had a European Secretariat. The reasons for not doing so are partly related to past criticisms of Interpol on the grounds of inefficiency and poor security, defects which it has striven to correct.[7] A more basic problem for the architects of Europol was that it would not be under their exclusive control, and plans to give it a new operational role would require the approval of the General Assembly (unlikely to be forthcoming) for a change in its Constitution.

The multiplicity of member countries, some of which have little respect for human rights, creates a dilemma where data protection is concerned. It is far from clear that Europol can avoid the same problem in its dealings with non-EU states. As a senior Interpol official told a conference on the Schengen Convention in 1992, 'The great majority of member countries of Interpol do not have arrangements for data protection. For them, the very idea of data protection does not have the cultural roots that caused it to blossom in Europe'.[8] He went on to point out that for countries suffering from more pressing economic and social problems, data protection could seem a luxury; they also lacked the practical means to set up such a system. If Interpol was to maintain world-wide cooperation between police forces, it had to accept this fact and do what it could to reassure those who were more worried about the protection of data. Rules could not legally be imposed on the NCBs by Interpol; they had to be trusted to ensure the reliability of their data. He ended with a warning that if the Schengen countries took a stricter view of such matters and operated a closed system of data exchange, they would risk losing the cooperation of countries denied access to it.

Europol

The idea of a 'European FBI' with investigative powers was raised in the late 1980s and adopted with particular fervour by Germany's Chancellor Kohl, who continued to press for it in the 1990s; in 1994 he was quoted as saying *'Wir brauchen eine schlagkräftige europäische Polizeitruppe, die quer durch unseren Kontinent Verbrecher verfolgen darf'* (We need a powerful European police force which can pursue criminals across our continent).[9] The response from other Member States was mixed, with some of them determined to accept nothing more than a passive information exchange system of the kind operated by Interpol; indeed some (especially France, which hosts the headquarters of Interpol) preferred the idea of expanding the activities of Interpol within Europe. Nevertheless, the June 1991 meeting of the European Council agreed in principle to incorporate the basic idea into the TEU.

Article K.1(9) TEU duly refers to 'the organisation of a Union-wide system for exchanging information within a European Police Office (Europol)'. The wording appears carefully chosen not to restrict Europol to that task alone, and the Council's lawyers later gave confidential advice that it would be legally possible to assign operational duties to the organisation.[10] The Declaration on Police Cooperation appended to the TEU states that 'Member States agree to consider on the basis of a report, during 1994 at the latest, whether the scope of such cooperation should be extended'.

The European Parliament approved of the idea of ultimately giving Europol further powers, but insisted that its creation and control should be entirely within the scope of Community law.[11] To this end it called for the Commission to submit a proposal for setting up Europol under the all-purpose Article 235 EC. This demand was ruled out of order by the Council's legal advisers, and preparatory work went ahead in secret under the direction of the intergovernmental Trevi group.

Although the TEU did not come into force until November 1993, a nucleus for Europol had already emerged in April of that year in the form of the Europol Drugs Unit (EDU). At the end of November 1993 it was finally agreed, after intense competition between Member States, to base Europol (incorporating the EDU) in The Hague. In the absence of a Convention ratified by Member States it still lacked a legal existence. Jürgen Storbeck, formerly of the German BKA (the federal office of criminal investigation) was officially confirmed by the Justice and Home Affairs Council as 'coordinator' of the EDU in June 1994, with a budget of 3.7 million ECU to start work in 1995.[12] Well before this he had talked openly to a Swiss newspaper of his belief that even before a Convention was set up, Europol should expand its activities 'prag-matically' beyond its official remit of working on drug trafficking.[13]

The first draft of a Convention was produced in November 1993,[14] and later released with no publicity whatever to the parliaments of some at least of the Member States for scrutiny (though not for open debate and approval). It attracted surprisingly little attention even within those bodies, and only reached the public domain in the middle of 1994.[15] Other more detailed drafts leaked out later in the year; their existence was officially made known only to a few bodies such as a committee of the German Bundesrat (upper house), which made some recom-mendations to the German government. The parliaments of the Länder were also involved. The UK House of Lords instituted a public enquiry on the basis of one of these drafts,[16] though the UK government could not be bound by its recommendations.[17]

It was clear throughout that the German government, which held the presidency of the Council in the second half of 1994, was extremely keen to get agreement during its term of office. There were, however, strong differences of opinion between Member States that made this impossible to achieve. The European Council then made the extraor-dinary decision in December 1994 to simply extend the role of the EDU to cover all the main types of crime reserved for Europol (see below). This was done in advance of the formal adoption of 'joint action' required under Article K.3(2)(b) TEU, revealing a cavalier attitude to even this token process of legitimising the decision.[18] The secondment of liaison officers from the Member States to the non-existent Europol had already taken place.[19] The upgraded EDU would apparently lack only Europol's capacity to create a central store of personal data. President Mitterand promised that France (which had been one of the principal objectors) would do its best to finalise the Europol Convention during its presidency in the first half of 1995.

The later drafts of the Convention have many features in common. The objective of Europol is broadly stated as that of aiding Member States in preventing and combating organised forms of 'terrorism, unlawful drug trafficking and other serious forms of international crime'. Continuing differences over how much priority to give to terrorism (a preoccupation of the Spanish and Greek governments) and what else to classify as 'serious international crime' led to a compromise draft under which Europol's primary tasks are stated in the main text, and other possible options are listed in an annex to the Convention. The main targets are listed as

- drug trafficking,
- crimes connected with nuclear and radioactive substances,
- illegal immigrant smuggling,
- motor vehicle crimes such as illegal sale in other states and theft of goods in transit, and
- associated money laundering operations.

The annex lists a further 22 items, any of which the Council may add to the list on a unanimous vote. The first is 'terrorism', and 19 other types of crime are grouped under three headings:

- *Crimes against life, freedom from bodily harm and personal freedom:* homicide, grievous bodily harm, kidnapping and hostage-taking, unlawful traffic in human organs, exploitation of prostitution.
- *Crimes against the state:* illegal trafficking in arms, munitions and explosives; illegal technology transfer, traffic in human beings, unlawful supply of labour, forging official documents, environmental crime, illegal trafficking in works of art and antiques (particularly in connection with burglary and receiving stolen property).
- *Crimes against the property of others:* robbery and blackmail (especially protection rackets); forgery of money, cheques and securities and passing off such forgeries; credit card crime, product piracy, investment

fraud, computer crime, international fraud as defined in Article K.1(5) TEU (this appears to exclude customs fraud).

The final two items, which can be associated with any of the above crimes, are 'money laundering' and 'membership of a criminal organisation'.

This comprehensive catalogue will give the Council a free hand to direct Europol in almost any direction. The items involving illegal labour and document forgery, like the reference in the main text to 'illegal immigrant smuggling', are clearly designed to allow the involvement of Europol in matters relating to immigration. While the agencies implementing the external frontiers Convention will use the European Information System to deal with the exclusion of unwanted immigrants, Europol will be able to target those who are suspected of helping them to slip through the net or obtain work after they arrive.

Europol and its computer system will be connected to national units run by a single agency in each Member State (a subject of fierce competition between the police and security forces of certain countries). Europol is to facilitate information exchange between Member States and is also to collect, collate and analyse both factual information and intelligence. This is to be shared with the national units to keep them informed of links established between criminal offences. Europol will also help national units with research, 'strategic intelligence', training and general support for their investigations. In return, national units are to supply all necessary information to Europol.

Each national unit will provide liaison officers to work at Europol headquarters. They will have access to data from Europol's information system that concern their country of origin, and can transmit both personal data and intelligence to their national units; they thus provide a channel of communication that is less restricted than the automated system (and almost impossible to regulate).

Europol's computerised information system, which can be supplied with data and interrogated directly by national units, will contain basic personal data on suspects, persons already liable to imprisonment, and 'persons concerning whom the facts provide justified grounds for presuming that they will commit criminal offences'. Other data will relate to the facts of their alleged offences.

Europol will also maintain its own system of files (not necessarily computerised) for intelligence and analysis. These will contain data on persons other than those described above: potential witnesses, possible future victims, contacts and escorts of suspects, informers and other sources of information. Member States failed to agree in 1994 on the extent of national access to these files. Information can be requested from 'third units' defined as other interstate and supranational organisations (including Interpol) and non-EU states; automatic information exchange with their computerised systems will also be allowed where this is covered by other agreements.

Rules are laid down to order compliance with standards based on the Council of Europe Convention on data protection (see below); national units and Europol are responsible for applying these rules to the data that they themselves collect or transmit. The Council of Europe's Recommendation R (87) 15 on sensitive data is to be 'taken into account'. Supervision of data protection is divided between national authorities (which have the power to inspect the offices and documents of their country's liaison officers) and a joint authority made up of two representatives of each national authority; this has the task of monitoring Europol's own adherence to the rules.

Individuals who have cause for complaint about the use of their personal data have certain rights. They can ask for details of the data held about them, though this is subject to the usual exceptions for subject access to police data. Where access is refused, the joint data protection authority can be asked to check the data on the person's behalf but may not be allowed to reveal the contents to the applicant. There is a distinctly parsimonious right of compensation (no more than 100,000 ECU, some £80,000 in the UK) for financial loss or 'serious infringement of personal rights'.

There will be a Management Board comprising one representative of each Member State. The Commission of the EC can attend but has no voting rights. The Council retains control over all major decisions, and is given the power to decide various matters (usually by unanimity) relating to rules of procedure and data protection that are not detailed in the Convention. The servants of Europol may be subject to security vetting and have a lifelong duty of confidentiality. They will have privileges and immunities that remain to be specified in a later Protocol to the Convention. An earlier proposal to give them the blanket immunity from prosecution accorded to all EC employees (a little-known feature of a Protocol to the Brussels Treaty of 1965) was evidently thought to be too sweeping to apply to police officers, though a similar immunity applies to Interpol headquarters staff in France.[20]

Member States still disagreed at the end of 1994 over the very limited procedure proposed for keeping the European Parliament informed and listening to its views, without giving it any real control over Europol. The Council's Legal Service had advised that to do any less than this would constitute a clear violation of Article K.6 TEU. Since this Article makes no mention of consulting national parliaments, they are simply assured that all this is 'without prejudice to the rights of national parliaments'.

An even more intractable issue was the possible involvement of the European Court of Justice, to which France and the UK were implacably opposed while most others (particularly the Netherlands) regarded it as essential. The ECJ could have a key role in ruling on the interpretation of the Convention by national courts when considering claims by individuals for misuse of their personal data by Europol or any of its national units. One draft of the Convention (but not others) incorporates a remarkable concession to the objecting states: an option that on acceding to the Convention, any state may decline to be bound on this point and this point alone. Citizens of such a state would thus be left to the vagaries of their national courts in the interpretation of an international Convention which was not incorporated into domestic law, and whose detailed provisions had never previously been tested.

This is perhaps the most surprising defect of a drafting process that shows other signs of having been muddled through without due consideration of the implications for individuals. The lack of any meaningful democratic control is, of course, a danger in this as in all the intergovernmental agreements going through under Title VI of the TEU. There are also far too many items left for later decision by the Council, and in all but one case (the Protocol on privileges and immunities) there will be no need for even token approval by national parliaments.

The provisions on data protection are comprehensive in theory, but fatally undermined by the difficulty that is likely to arise in enforcing them. According to the drafts so far proposed, Europol may use personal data supplied by non-EU countries and is responsible for ensuring that the data were collected and transmitted according to the standards of data protection laid down in the Convention. This seems an impossible task when one considers the total absence of data protection laws in most non-EU states. Europol may also transmit personal data to non-EU states after seeking assurances on data protection from the recipients and assessing their value 'taking into account all the circumstances'. The pressure to exchange data with such countries in the interests of mutual assistance might well in practice outweigh considerations of strict data protection.[21] As illustrated above in relation to Interpol, this is probably why (among other reasons) that body, with its wide range of subscribing states, was not considered to be a suitable vehicle for the development of European police cooperation.

One other problem in data protection arises from the creation of yet another joint supervisory body, drawn from the data protection authorities of all the Member States. The data protection commissioners of the Union are beginning to wonder how much time will be spent by their senior staff in travelling round Europe to attend the meetings of the different joint bodies, and how effective their supervision will be in practice. The more rational idea of a general data protection Convention for all Title VI agreements appears to have been set aside.

An even more serious question that is left unresolved by the Convention is the possible extension of Europol's powers at some time in the future to a more operational role. The trend has already been set by allowing Europol, on its own initiative, to collect and analyse data from anywhere in the world. A logical development would be the power to send investigating officers to Member States and non-EU countries; within Member States they could also be given powers of arrest, in a manner already introduced in the Schengen Convention for 'hot pursuit' across internal frontiers by national police officers. The Convention rules none of this out, though presumably a Protocol or amendment would have to be brought in to legitimate it. The pressure on Member States to approve this might prove to be irresistible.

Had a powerful organisation like this been set up under the rules of the EC treaty it would have been the subject of much open discussion, consultation at all levels and detailed consideration by the European Parliament. National parliaments would have had a say, however limited, through their normal procedures for scrutiny of EC legislation.[22] It remains deeply disturbing to many observers that in the present case the matter will be agreed in secret between the executives of Member States, with very little chance for any other body to influence the outcome.

STANDARDS OF DATA PROTECTION

'Third pillar' fields of intergovernmental cooperation are not only outside the ambit of Community law; they are also less bound by the constraints accepted by Member States in their domestic legislation. This is illustrated most clearly in the case of data protection, where most Member States adhere to the norms laid down by the Council of Europe and all will soon be subject to Union-wide Directives. However, these will not for instance apply to Europol, which unlike Schengen and the European Information System (Chapter 3) will collect and analyse its own data in addition to passing messages between national units. So far as its own data are concerned, Europol will follow its internal rules and there is no obligation to do more than use the Council of Europe's standards of protection as a model. This unsatisfactory situation arises from the fact that Europol will not be a nation state capable of acceding to the relevant Convention. This Convention, together with related Recommendations and draft Directives, is described below to indicate the minimum standards that should apply to intergovernmental activities. They are also important in protecting the privacy of individuals in other areas of data processing.

The Council of Europe Convention

The 1981 Council of Europe Convention,[23] now ratified by all EU Member States except Greece and Italy, recognises the need to 'extend the safeguards for everyone's rights and freedoms, and in particular the right to the respect for privacy, taking account of the increasing flow across frontiers of personal data undergoing automatic processing'. At the same time the Convention defines the essential compromise that has to be made between privacy protection and 'freedom of information regardless of frontiers'. It also allows exceptions to be made in the interests of 'protecting state security, public safety, the monetary interests of the state or the suppression of criminal offences'. This removes protection for the individual from some of the areas where it is most needed, especially that of files held by the security services.[24]

The Convention lays down principles that have been followed in all subsequent measures. Article 5 says that personal data shall be

- obtained and processed fairly and lawfully;
- stored for specified and legitimate purposes and not used in a way incompatible with those purposes;
- adequate, relevant and not excessive in relation to the purposes for which they are stored;
- accurate and, where necessary, kept up to date; and
- preserved in a form which permits identification of the data subjects for no longer than is required for the purpose for which those data are stored.

Article 6 adds an important restriction on the use of 'sensitive' data revealing racial origin, political opinions or other beliefs, and data concerning health or sexual life; such data, like those concerning criminal convictions, 'may not be processed unless domestic law provides appropriate safeguards'. The option of applying the Convention to data that are not processed automatically ('manual data' such as paper records) is left open; conversely, states may declare that certain categories of data will not be subject to the Convention. Another option is to extend the Convention to cover groups and 'legal persons' (corporate bodies) as well as individuals.

Other Articles relate to data security, the right of a person to know what information is held and to have errors corrected, enactment of implementing laws, sanctions and remedies for violations, safeguards for transborder data flows, and cooperation between signatory states. This last requires the designation of a national authority for each state; in practice this has resulted in the creation of a specialised agency in each country, headed by a data protection commissioner or registrar who also supervises compliance with the domestic law and considers complaints and requests for help from individuals. There is no international body to oversee the Convention apart from a consultative committee to advise on interpretation and consider possible amendments to it.

Signing of the Convention was followed over the years by a number of Recommendations by the Council of Europe's Committee of Ministers.[25] These cover various fields of activity such as R (81) 1 on medical data banks, R (83) 10 on statistical and research data, R (85) 20 on direct marketing, R (86) 1 on social security, R (89) 2 on employment, R (89) 14 on HIV data, R (90) 19 on payment operations and R (91) 10 on data held by public bodies (the figures in brackets indicate the year of issue). The most influential, however, has been R (87) 15 on the use of personal data in the police sector; it is cited as a standard to be taken account of in several of the intergovernmental Conventions discussed in this book, though detailed compliance is not implied. It is considered separately below.

The Recommendation on Police Data

The Council of Europe's non-binding Recommendation R (87) 15 was drafted to counteract the possibility that states would use their powers of derogation under the 1981 Convention to exclude data held by bodies with police powers.[26] It reiterates in a stricter and more detailed manner the principles of the Convention. Manual processing of data 'should not take place if the aim is to avoid the provisions of this Recommendation'. Factual data should be categorised separately from 'data based on opinions or personal assessments'. The nature of permanent computer files should be notified to an independent supervisory authority. The collection of personal data 'should be limited to such as is necessary for the prevention of a real danger or the suppression of a specific criminal offence'. Where data are stored without the subject's knowledge, the person should be informed 'wherever practicable ... as soon as the object of the police activities is no longer likely to be prejudiced'. Perhaps most importantly, there is a stricter rule on sensitive data:

The collection of data on individuals solely on the basis that they have a particular racial origin, particular religious convictions, sexual behaviour or political opinions or belong to particular movements or organisations which are not proscribed by law should be prohibited. The collection of data concerning these factors may only be carried out if absolutely necessary for the purposes of a particular enquiry.

The adherence of states to R (87) 15 is patchy. Although its adoption by the Committee of Ministers implied acceptance by all members states of the Council of Europe, there was allowance in the text for reservations. The UK, for instance, reserved the right 'to comply or not' with two crucial requirements: notification of the data subject, and storage of sensitive data. This was reflected in the absence of any reference to R (87) 15 in the official code of practice for police computer systems. Germany declined to accept the limitation on collection of data to that 'necessary for the prevention of a real danger ...'. To some observers it seemed that R (87) 15 was in any case unrealistic in what it expected from working policemen, more accustomed to the idea that the ends justify the means where catching criminals is concerned.

The Parliamentary Assembly of the Council of Europe felt that in view of developments in police cooperation like Europol (see above) there was a need to replace the Recommendation by a binding Convention.[27] This idea was rejected by the Committee of Ministers, who asked their expert advisers to consider alternatives such as a revision of R (87) 15.[28] The experts were believed to feel, however, that in the present political climate any move of this kind might lead to a weakening of the provisions rather than the desired reinforcement, and they decided not to suggest any changes. The only alternative might be an optional Protocol to the basic Convention. All this must have been a disappointment to the drafters of both the Convention and the Recommendation, since in each case they envisaged the rules as minimum standards on which a higher level of protection could be based.

The Draft General Directive

If all Member States of the Union had adopted the 1981 Convention immediately and without reservation, there might have been little need for further action at Union level. However, despite a strong recommendation to do this from the Commission of the EC, progress was slow and a number of states entered the 1990s with no domestic law on the subject.[29] The laws that had been enacted were also not uniform between countries: some but not others covered manual data, and only a minority protected legal persons (see above). Not all states took the

Convention seriously regarding sensitive data; UK law left it to the discretion of a government minister to rule on the matter, and this was never done.

In 1990, following pressure from the data protection commissioners of Europe to do something about the variation in standards between Member States, the Commission issued a package of five proposals[30] for

- a general or 'framework' Directive embodying the principles of the Council of Europe Convention, but going into much more detail and eliminating most of the existing variations between the data protection laws of Member States;
- a Council Resolution in which the Member States would pledge themselves to apply the same principles to files held by those parts of the public sector to which the Directive did not apply (meaning agencies outside the scope of Community law such as the immigration and security services);
- a Directive governing data protection in the rapidly expanding field of public digital telecommunications networks, particularly integrated services digital networks (ISDNs) and public mobile networks;
- a Council Decision on negotiating for the EC as a body to accede to the Council of Europe Convention; and
- a Council Decision on information security.

Also included was a declaration of intent by the Commission that, although the EC was not yet a signatory to the Convention, the same principles would be applied to the institutions and other bodies of the Community.

Even before the proposals appeared in print, intense lobbying by commercial interests (including those based in the USA, which has no general data protection laws) had got under way with the aim of weakening various provisions in the proposed general Directive. The draft reflected the relatively high levels of protection afforded by the relevant laws in France and Germany. However, it was seen as imposing an unnecessary financial and administrative burden on companies handling data, particularly in the rules for obtaining a person's consent to inclusion in a data file. The proposed application to manual data also led to objections. Governments faced with raising standards above those of their existing laws were notably unenthusiastic. Those with no laws at all saw less of a problem, since they were in a position to draft appropriate legislation from scratch; indeed they were anxious to see a Directive agreed so that they could get on with the task.

The European Parliament approved the draft in principle but suggested amendments. These were so numerous that in 1992 the Commission withdrew the proposal and issued a new one.[31] This also took account of other criticisms and was generally felt to be an improvement; there was still, however, strong opposition from commercial lobbies and from Member States like the UK.[32] A slow process of bargaining in the working parties of the Council then followed throughout 1993 and 1994,[33] during which the other proposals in the original package were largely put aside. It was already clear, however, that the proposed Council Resolution on activities outside Community law would meet stiff opposition; in answer to a House of Lords recommendation to support it,[34] the UK government declared that it should be left for each Member State to decide 'whether and to what extent to apply data protection legislation to activities outside the scope of Community law'.[35]

The revised draft Directive, as detailed in the Council's Common Position of February 1995, contains a number of important features not included in many existing national laws, though the exemptions attached to them rather weaken the effect:

- Article 3 makes it clear that manual as well as automated data are included. However, the Final Provisions (Article 32) include a derogation clause under which Member States may take as long as twelve years to apply the full rigours of the Directive to data already held in manual filing systems when the corresponding national provisions come into force. The rest of the Directive is to be implemented within three years of its adoption.
- Article 7 starts with the general principle that the 'data subject' has to consent to the processing of his or her personal data (meaning all the operations from data collection onwards). However, the various exceptions include processing that is necessary 'for compliance with a legal obligation to which the controller is subject' and 'the performance of a task carried out in the public interest or in the exercise of official authority ...'. This would exclude most government activities (see below).
- Article 8 rules that sensitive data are normally to be processed only with the explicit consent of the person concerned. The exceptions include processing done for legitimate purposes by certain foundations or non-profit-seeking bodies in relation to their own members or regular contacts. There is also a broad reference to regulating the processing of data relating to offences and criminal convictions. However, the restrictions in the Commission's earlier draft of the practice known as 'enforced subject access' have been deleted. This is a device used, for instance, by employers to make job applicants

request and hand over police records of all past convictions and cautions, however old, as a condition of being interviewed.

- Although Article 13 allows a person to be denied subject access (or even confirmation of the existence of a file) for reasons such as national security, the supervisory authority (Article 28) is to have the power to verify the lawfulness of processing.
- Article 14 gives the data subject a right to object to processing and disclosure of data in certain cases, particularly where direct marketing is concerned (a source of loud complaint by the industry).
- With some exceptions, Article 15 lays down that nobody is to be subject to 'a decision which produces legal effects concerning him or significantly affects him and which is based solely on automated processing of data intended to evaluate certain personal aspects relating to him, such as his performance at work, creditworthiness, reliability, conduct, etc.'
- Under Article 28 the national supervisory authority has a right of access to any data covered by the Directive, effective powers of intervention (such as ordering the erasure of data) and the power to bring an action before the courts.

For all its attention to detail, the draft Directive fails to regulate at least two areas of government activity which are within its scope and capable of adversely affecting the rights of the individual. The first is the sharing of data between government departments and agencies. This is increasingly facilitated by the growth of government data networks. By 'data matching' between files it is then possible to build up personality profiles of the kind mentioned above. A government with repressive tendencies could use such profiles to categorise certain groups of people as 'undesirables', and data protection commissioners have warned against this possibility.

Although Article 6 includes a restatement of the principle of using data only in a way compatible with the original purpose of collection, the exemption noted above to the requirement for consent by the data subject ('performance of a task carried out in the public interest ... ') would make it very hard to tell whether the principle was being adhered to in practice by government agencies and whether data matching was taking place. The national supervisory authorities are not given a specific mandate to conduct data protection audits of government departments, as is done for instance by Australia's Privacy Commissioner under its 1989 Privacy Act.

The second and related problem with the proposal is its failure to set any limits to the use of unique personal identification numbers (PINs), which facilitate both the data matching process and the introduction of universal identity cards. Article 8(7) simply leaves it to Member States to 'determine the conditions under which a national identification number or any other general identifier of general application may be processed'. In Germany the use of an all-purpose PIN has been declared unconstitutional. In Sweden, where PINs were introduced in 1947 and widely employed since then in all areas of public and private administration, some restrictions on their use were introduced in 1992.[36] The need for further legislation to limit their application to legally authorised purposes was recognised by an official commission two years later.[37] Outside Europe, Canada started in 1989 a process of de-linking government files in departments making common use of the Social Insurance Number to identify individuals.[38]

Since a Directive, however detailed, is no more than a statement of principles which have to be transposed into national law, there is still likely to be variation between states in its interpretation. This is likely to be greatest in the area of government data. While some Member States have a long tradition of secrecy and no general right of access even to one's personal data, Sweden in particular follows an equally strong and legally guaranteed principle of open access to all files and documents concerned with public administration (Chapter 8). Data in government files relating to such matters as a person's employer, taxed income and ownership of a car or house are freely available to third parties. Only matters specifically covered by the Secrecy Act are excluded.[39]

Overall, the draft Directive is capable of raising the current standard of data protection in the Union, but its impact will be mostly on the commercial sector. In the field of government activities, where the individual may stand to suffer serious harm from improper or erroneous uses of personal data, the protection is either entirely absent (for matters not covered by Community law) or so hedged about with exceptions that the dangers are almost as great.

SURVEILLANCE AND NEW TECHNOLOGIES

In 1989, a year before the Commission issued its first data protection proposals, an experts' report for the Council of Europe considered the implications of the rapid changes in telecommunications technology.[40] Apparently innocuous current or potential developments like telemetry (remote meter reading), itemised recording of telephone calls, teleshopping, telebanking and electronic polling have one thing in common: they give the provider of the service a highly detailed record of the subject's day-to-day actions, preferences and decisions. The experts could have added only a few years later that credit card, automatic debiting and cash dispenser records now offer information about a person's movements as well, since the time and place of the transaction are noted. If machine-readable identity cards become universal and used for routine purposes in daily life, they will offer another opportunity to monitor the activities of the individual.

If the holder of the information is a commercial concern, the 'profile' that it can provide of an individual is a marketable commodity. If the state is involved, the implications are more serious:

> In fact, there is from now on the possibility of total surveillance of the individual. In addition, information is today being circulated, disseminated and dispersed in conditions which make it more and more difficult to protect.[41]

The draft general Directive attempted to deal with one application of profiling (that of automated vetting), and its general rules on disclosure of stored personal data apply in principle to the misapplication of any data linked with an identifiable individual. This is, however, only part of the problem. The rest of this chapter discusses the problems posed by new technologies that have grown up alongside the ever more powerful computer systems, and what dangers they may pose to the privacy and basic rights of individuals. With the exception of only certain aspects of telecommunications (see below), few of these matters currently come within the scope of Union policy or law.

The ISDN Directive

The second draft Directive in the 1990 package issued by the Commission[42] attempted to deal with the expanding area of telecommunications which depends on the 'digitisation' of all information – voice, text and image – in the form of binary digits. These can then be stored and processed by computers, opening up a whole new range of operations that were not possible with the older 'analogue' systems. An integrated services digital network (ISDN) allows the transmission of a mixture of all three types of data through a single subscriber line.

Apart from privacy protection, a principal motive for introducing the Directive was the uneven and uncoordinated growth in services offered by telephone companies, particularly itemised billing and calling-line identification in which the caller's number appears on a display at the recipient's end of the line.[43] There was an increasing risk of Member States adopting divergent technical standards for the capabilities of the equipment. The draft Directive cited the general argument that guarantees of privacy are necessary if the internal market is to function efficiently. It aimed to limit the use of subscriber-linked data stored by the service providers, and to impose some duties on them in relation to unsolicited calls and unauthorised surveillance (telephone tapping). It actually contained nothing specific to ISDN networks alone.

After criticisms from the European Parliament and heavy lobbying from the industry, a second draft was produced in 1992.[44] This then fell foul of a new enthusiasm for the dogma of subsidiarity as being too detailed, and a third slimmed-down version was produced two years later.[45] This included a new statement making clear that parts of the Directive would apply also to service providers other than telecommunications organisations, and to other telecommunications services provided via the public network.

On itemised billing the revised draft does no more than demand preservation of the privacy of both callers and called subscribers, effectively leaving the present variation between countries untouched. On calling-line identification there are more specific rules on the options that must be offered for callers to eliminate identification, or for recipients to refuse unidentified calls. There must be an override facility for tracing malicious calls and calls to the emergency services. Tracing must also be possible 'upon specific court order, in order to prevent or pursue serious criminal offences'.

Deliberate telephone tapping and other surveillance must only occur with suitable authorisation, a provision that will not reassure those who already suspect state agencies of government-sanctioned addiction to such practices. However, Article 4 lays down a general rule that where security is easily breached (as in mobile telephony) the service provider is supposed to offer encryption facilities. As shown below, this issue has revealed a conflict between the right to privacy and the trend towards increasing surveillance of the individual.

State Surveillance of Telecommunications

Digital systems can easily incorporate encryption, and with the spread of electronic mail networks there is an obvious demand for it. It is an integral feature of advanced forms of communication through ISDNs, fibre optics systems, packet-switched networks and personal satellite links. State agencies in a number of countries soon realised that this posed a threat to their ability to conduct surveillance. In the USA, the FBI proposed that all forms of communication should by law have a built-in capacity for surveillance. This led to an ongoing controversy, with another government agency pointing out that the same requirement would make it easier for criminals, spies and computer hackers to penetrate government networks.[46]

In Europe, state agencies were equally alarmed when it emerged that the agreed operating standard for mobile phones included a degree of encryption for the radio-transmitted part of a telephone call. In 1993 the German security services demanded that computer software to overcome this feature should be produced, and that there should be restrictions on the export of equipment embodying encryption.[47] In the Netherlands, the Minister of Justice tabled a bill in 1994 requiring users to deposit a key to the encryption facility of their equipment with the authorities.[48] The Dutch government also persuaded the Enfopol working group of the K4 Committee to draft a Council Recommendation to the effect that 'in the development and standardisation of telecommunications early consideration should be given to the integration of technical facilities for interception'.[49]

All this demonstrates the high importance attached by governments to their ability to conduct surveillance at will.[50] Other developments in technology will enhance this ability; for instance, the digitisation of ordinary telephone networks means that telephone tapping no longer requires a physical connection to be made to the telephone line. Tapping can be performed remotely by sending signals to the exchange switching system, and this can even in principle be done from another country. The UK's British Telecom assists the security services and other agencies in this activity.[51]

Video Surveillance and Digitised Images

Developments in closed-circuit television (CCTV) systems mean that high-quality images of individuals can be recorded in poor illumination with small, unobtrusive cameras. Only some data protection laws (such as those of Germany) classify pictures as personal data, though digitisation and computer storage would bring them under the draft general Directive. In practice CCTV has been in use for some time in many countries in the form of security cameras for commercial premises, and (more controversially) to monitor the activities of employees in the workplace.

The French data protection authority CNIL was sufficiently concerned about the matter to produce a special report on the matter.[52] It subsequently came into conflict with the French government, which proposed in a Public Security Bill to exclude CNIL from jurisdiction over video surveillance unless the images were used in a name-linked file.[53] CNIL's report, which also includes information about the relevant laws in

Denmark, Luxembourg, the Netherlands, Norway and Sweden, brings out the general lack of information (and of legislation) on this potentially intrusive technique. Evidence for its effectiveness is largely anecdotal, and privacy considerations tend to be discounted. The UK seems to be the video surveillance capital of Europe, with a booming industry supplying equipment to increasing numbers of local authorities for the continuous surveillance of public places.[54]

The attraction of such systems for law enforcement and general surveillance is obvious, particularly as it is now possible to automatically compare digitised video recordings with stored images to identify an individual. The ability to digitise pictures has other applications: photographs supplied by individuals for attachment to driving licences, identity cards and passports can be scanned and stored in a data bank. In the absence of specific restraints, such data can then be shared with other agencies and used for quite different purposes to the original one.

Identity Cards and 'Big Brother'

Contrary to widespread belief, national identity (ID) cards are not used in quite a few Member States and the Commission does not hold that they constitute an essential feature of a Union without internal frontiers.[55] Of the 15 Member States, only six (Belgium, Germany, Greece, Luxembourg, Portugal and Spain) have, or soon will have, a compulsory ID card system; in all of these except Germany it must legally be carried at all times. Four Member States (Austria, Finland, France and Italy) have a voluntary system, though in the last two some means of identification must be produced on a demand by the police. The remaining five (Denmark, Ireland, the Netherlands, Sweden and the UK) have no universal system.[56]

Some of the last group of states have shown signs of moving in the direction of ID cards. In 1992 Ireland introduced a card for adults as part of a 'national ID system for state services'.[57] In the Netherlands, where ID cards had long been rejected through their association with wartime Nazi occupation, a 1994 law made it obligatory to produce a means of identification on demand in many everyday situations such as travelling on public transport or attending a football match.[58] A voluntary European identity card was offered to Dutch citizens in 1995.[59] The government of the UK, where the National Insurance Number is already becoming a de facto personal identification number (PIN),[60] indicated support for a voluntary system for the first time in 1994.[61] On the other hand countries like Sweden, though familiar with the use of universal PINs, show no signs of linking them with ID cards.

The arguments for and against ID cards are various. Politicians and policemen who favour them assert that innocent individuals have nothing to fear, though in some countries there is plenty of anecdotal evidence that non-white people are much more likely to be harassed with demands to identify themselves. At the same time, others call for a Union ID card that would enable third-country nationals to readily prove that they are not illegal immigrants. The claim that ID cards help to reduce crime lacks supporting evidence, and professional criminals have always found ways of forging them.

What is certain is that with the advent of machine-readable cards and 'smart cards' incorporating a miniature computer chip, their potential for the control and tracking of citizens by the state is greatly enhanced. They can carry digitised photographs (as in the new UK driving licences[62]) which are also stored in a central computer and can be transmitted anywhere in the world. The draft general Directive on data protection has nothing to say on such matters, and leaves it to Member States to regulate the use of personal identification numbers. Proposals to make either PINs or ID cards universal throughout the Union will need to be treated with extreme reservation.

Finally, new technologies are constantly being developed and carry their own potential dangers to individual rights. A new system for rapid identity checks on air passengers involves the checking of finger or palm prints on a glass screen against computerised records;[63] a natural extension of this would be to take such records for the entire population. Some policemen have advocated universal DNA testing of men as a means of tracing rapists. The yardstick for judging all new techniques needs to be the principle that underlies data protection law: that although recording data for a limited purpose may be valid, this does not justify applying the same process to every person or every situation on the assumption that the information might one day come in useful. That way lies the totalitarian state.

NOTES

1. See for example House of Lords Select Committee on the European Communities, *Protection of personal data*, Session 1992–93, 20th Report (London: HMSO, 1993) evidence p. 56, QQ 238–43; *Statewatch*, September–October 1994, p.6.
2. For a historical overview and analysis of the issues, together with data on police forces and security services in 17 EU and EFTA states, see Tony Bunyan (ed.), *Statewatching the new Europe* (London: Statewatch, 1993). Detailed comparative information is given in two

1993 reports from the Domestic Security Research Foundation (Postbus 11178, 1001 GD Amsterdam): (i) *The state of Europe: a digest of European police systems, prison conditions, private security, human rights and civil liberties and the internal security situation in the 1990s;* (ii) *An inventory of European intelligence services.* For a comparison (in French) of Belgium, France, Germany, Italy, Spain and the UK see J.M. Erbes, J.C. Monet, A. Funk, H. Reinke, P. Ponsaers, C. Janssens, Y. Cartuyvels, M. Dauge, J.J. Gleizal, C. Journes amd S. Palidda, *Polices d'Europe* (Paris: Institut des Hautes Études de la Sécurité Intérieure, 1992). For data on the twelve signatories of the TEU see John Benyon, Lynne Turnbull, Andrew Willis, Rachel Woodward and Adrian Beck, *Police co-operation in Europe: an investigation* (Leicester: University of Leicester Centre for the Study of Public Order, 1993); also Patrice Meyzonnier, *Les forces de police dans l'Union Européenne* (Paris: l'Harmattan, 1994). For a historical and legal study of security services in Denmark, France, Germany, the Netherlands, Sweden, Switzerland and the UK see Barbara Forbes, *Under surveillance: critical citizenship and the internal security services in Western Europe* (Brussels: Quaker Council for European Affairs, 1994).

3. Benyon *et al.*, *Police co-operation in Europe* (note 2) p. 19.

4. Malcolm Anderson, 'The agenda for police cooperation', in Malcolm Anderson and Monica den Boer (eds), *Policing across national boundaries* (London: Pinter, 1994) p. 9.

5. Tony Bunyan, 'Trevi, Europol and the European state', in Bunyan, *Statewatching the new Europe* (note 2) pp. 15–25.

6. For more on its history and current role see Malcolm Anderson, *Policing the world: Interpol and the politics of international police co-operation* (Oxford: Clarendon Press, 1989); also Benyon *et al.*, *Police co-operation in Europe* (note 2) pp. 121–33.

7. Parliamentary Assembly of the Council of Europe, *Report on police cooperation and protection of personal data in the police sector* (rapporteur: Mr Stoffelen), doc. 6557 (Strasbourg: Council of Europe, 1992).

8. Egon Schlanitz, 'L'échange international d'informations de police dans le cadre des systèmes d'information d'Interpol et de Schengen', in Alexis Pauly (ed.), *Les accords de Schengen: abolition des frontières ou menace pour les libertés publiques?* (Maastricht: Institut européen d'administration publique, 1993) pp. 39–52 (author's translation).

9. *Focus*, 22 August 1994.

10. Advice from the Legal Service of the Council, 5527/93 (19 March 1993).

11. Committee on Civil Liberties and Internal Affairs (rapporteur: L. van Outrive), *Report on the setting up of Europol*, A3–0383/92 (European Parliament, 1992).

12. *The Week in Europe* (London: Commission of the European Communities) 23 June 1994.
13. *Platform Fortress Europe?*, December 1993–January 1994.
14. Communication 9757/93 (8 November 1993) from the Presidency to Steering Group II of the K4 Committee.
15. *Platform Fortress Europe?*, May 1994; *Statewatch*, May–June 1994.
16. Council document 10324/94 (27 October 1994).
17. House of Lords Select Committee on the European Communities, *Europol*, Session 1994–95 (London: HMSO) in preparation.
18. *Statewatch*, November–December 1994; *Fortress Europe?*, November 1994.
19. Jürgen Storbeck, 'A Single Market for the world's gangsters', *European Brief* (December 1994) pp. 34–7.
20. Anderson, *Policing the world* (note 6) p. 64.
21. Charles D. Raab, 'Police cooperation: the prospects for privacy', in Anderson and den Boer, *Policing across national boundaries* (note 4) pp. 121–36.
22. Madeleine Colvin and Michael Spencer, 'Bringing Europol into the open', *European Brief* (December 1994) pp. 43–4.
23. *Convention for the protection of individuals with regard to automatic processing of personal data*, Convention no. 108 (Strasbourg: Council of Europe, 1981).
24. Forbes, *Under surveillance* (note 2) pp. 29–40.
25. See also Michael Spencer, *1992 And All That: civil liberties in the balance* (London: Civil Liberties Trust, 1990) pp. 62–3.
26. *Regulating the use of personal data in the police sector: Recommendation No. R (87) 15 and Explanatory Memorandum* (Strasbourg: Council of Europe, 1988).
27. Parliamentary Assembly, *Report on police cooperation* (note 7); Parliamentary Assembly of the Council of Europe, Recommendation 1181 (1992).
28. *Interim reply by the Committee of Ministers to Recommendation 1181 (1992)*, AS/Jur (44) 15 (30 June 1992).
29. Spencer, *1992 And All That* (note 25) pp. 53–9; *Privacy Laws & Business*, no. 23 (June 1993) pp. 26–7.
30. Commission of the European Communities, *Communication on the protection of individuals in relation to the processing of personal data in the Community and information security*, COM(90) 314 final – SYN 287 and 288 (Luxembourg: Office for Official Publications of the European Communities, 1990).
31. Commission of the European Communities, *Amended proposal for a Council Directive on the protection of individuals with regard to the processing of personal data and on the free movement of such data*,

COM(92) 422 final (Luxembourg: Office for Official Publications of the European Communities, 1992). For a simplified version see *Privacy Laws & Business*, no. 22 (December 1992) pp. 6–12.

32. For a general discussion of the issues see Charles D. Raab and Colin J. Bennett, 'Protecting privacy across borders: European policies and prospects', *Public Administration*, vol. 72 (Spring 1994) pp. 95–112.

33. *Privacy Laws & Business*, no. 25 (September 1994) pp. 2–7. The Council finally adopted a Common Position in February 1995, and the draft went to the European Parliament for its Second Reading (Chapter 1).

34. House of Lords, *Protection of personal data* (note 1) report p. 34.

35. House of Lords Select Committee on the European Communities, *Correspondence with Ministers*, Session 1993–94, 2nd Report (London: HMSO, 1993) pp. 22–6.

36. For a comparison of policies in 19 Council of Europe states and a general discussion see *The introduction and use of personal identification numbers: the data protection issues* (Strasbourg: Council of Europe Directorate of Legal Affairs, 1990).

37. *Statens offentliga utredningar (SOU)*, 1994:63, pp. 549–51.

38. *Privacy Laws & Business*, no. 9 (February 1989) p. 4; David H. Flaherty, *Protecting privacy in surveillance societies* (Chapel Hill: University of North Carolina Press, 1989) pp. 281–4.

39. *Platform Fortress Europe?*, May 1993.

40. *Computers and law. Study on new technologies: a challenge to privacy protection?* (Strasbourg: Council of Europe Directorate of Legal Affairs, 1989).

41. *Ibid.*, p. 11.

42. Commission of the European Communities, *Proposal for a Council Directive concerning the protection of personal data and privacy in the context of public digital telecommunications networks, in particular the integrated services digital network (ISDN) and public digital mobile networks*, COM(90) 314 final (Luxembourg: Office for Official Publications of the European Communities, 1990); *Official Journal of the European Communities*, C277(5 November 1990) p.12.

43. For a comparison of the situation in France, Germany, the Netherlands, the UK and the USA see Robert Bradgate, Cosmo Graham and Tony Prosser (eds), *Privacy and telecommunications: a comparative study* (Sheffield, UK: Sheffield University Centre for Socio-Legal Studies, 1991).

44. *Official Journal of the European Communities*, C311 (27 November 1992) p. 30.

45. Commission of the European Communities, *Amended proposal for a European Parliament and Council Directive concerning the protection*

of personal data and privacy in the context of digital telecommunications networks, in particular the integrated services digital network (ISDN) and digital mobile networks, COM(94) 128 final–COD 288 (Luxembourg: Office for Official Publications of the European Communities, 1994); *Privacy Laws & Business*, no. 26 (October 1994) pp. 11–14 .

46. David Banisar, 'Cryptography, the FBI, and wire surveillance', *International Privacy Bulletin*, vol. 1, no. 2 (1993) pp. 14–16. For arguments from both points of view see *Communications of the Association for Computing Machinery*, vol. 36, no. 3 (1993) pp. 25–41.

47. *Platform Fortress Europe?*, March 1993.

48. *Statewatch*, May–June 1994.

49. *Platform Fortress Europe?*, October 1994.

50. For more on telephone tapping in different countries see Forbes, *Under surveillance* (note 2) pp. 23–8.

51. Patrick Fitzgerald, 'All about eavesdropping', *New Statesman & Society*, 29 July 1994, pp. 30–1.

52. Louise Cadoux, *Vidéo-surveillance et protection de la vie privée et des libertés fondamentales* (Paris: Commission nationale de l'Informatique et des Libertés, 1993).

53. *Privacy Laws & Business*, no. 26 (October 1994) pp. 17–18 and No. 27 (December 1994) p. 10.

54. Simon Davies, 'They've got an eye on you', *Independent*, 2 November 1994.

55. House of Lords Select Committee on the European Communities, *Community policy on migration*, Session 1992–93, 10th Report (London: HMSO, 1992) evidence p. 11, Q 98.

56. Information collected in September 1994 by Liberty (the National Council for Civil Liberties, London).

57. *Statewatch*, September–October 1992.

58. *Platform Fortress Europe?*, February 1993.

59. *ESMV List of Events* (Utrecht), December 1994.

60. *Tenth report of the Data Protection Registrar* (London: HMSO, 1994) pp. 7–8.

61. *Statewatch*, September–October 1994; *Guardian*, 14 October 1994.

62. Simon Davies, 'Watching every single move we make', *Independent*, 15 September 1994.

63. *Statewatch*, September–October 1994.

8

National Variations

The Member States of the Union differ not only in their experience of the problems discussed in this book, but also in their history, traditions, democratic structure and popular culture. These differences affect the attitudes of ordinary people towards all the main topics considered. Such attitudes influence in turn the formulation of national policies and government responses to harmonisation measures at Union level. Some understanding of these national differences is essential if the future prospects of the Union are to be assessed.

A book of this size cannot hope to cover such variations in a comprehensive manner. The time and resources available for the research were also far too limited to make a full comparison possible. Instead a limited series of visits was made to six carefully selected countries (other than the UK), during which experts were consulted and relevant documents collected. As explained in the Introduction, the countries were chosen so as to compare certain broad 'types': old and new Member States, those with and those without a history of immigration, South and North European states, and so on. The omission of so many other countries does not imply that they were thought to be in any way of lesser importance. Some of those that are included are given relatively more space because their more serious problems are well documented and typify, to a greater or lesser degree, those that affect all Member States.

The findings reported here are therefore mainly summarised impressions, gained from conversations with people having direct experience in each of the fields mentioned and supplemented by following current events. With a few exceptions the people consulted were not government officials but rather lawyers (both academic and practising), NGO staff, research workers and grassroots activists. Without their insights the whole of this book would have been the poorer.

FRANCE

The self-image of France is well summed up in a recent newspaper article by the current Prime Minister, Edouard Balladur: 'France is the oldest nation in Europe, its state is one of the longest established and best organised, and it is France which gave the rest of the world the concept of nationhood and liberty which together founded our concept of democracy'.[1] He goes on to express his ideas on the future of the Union, starting with 'one obvious fact: the organisation of Europe is an extra source of power and influence for France'. The direction taken by French policy after the 1995 presidential election may have a crucial effect on the 1996 intergovernmental conference.

Though Balladur's historical claims for France may be disputed in some quarters, there is no doubt that the 1789 and 1793 Declarations of the Rights of Man and of the Citizen have served as models for many other national Constitutions and international treaties on human rights.[2] France's written Constitution is protected by a *Conseil constitutionnel* which examines all new laws and has the power to delete any provisions that breach its basic principles. There is also a broadly based advisory committee on human rights, the *Commission nationale consultative des Droits de l'Homme*. Some laws make specific reference to human rights: the comprehensive data protection act of 1978 starts by declaring that data processing 'shall infringe neither human identity, nor the rights of man, nor privacy, nor individual or public liberties'.

At the same time, it has always been clear from the experience of many countries that declarations and legal guarantees are not enough; as proof of this, the current French government has been quite ready to push through an amendment to the Constitution rather than change its policy. France therefore also has a long tradition of independent monitoring of the state's respect for human rights: the *Ligue des Droits de l'Homme* was founded in 1898 at the height of the Dreyfus affair, and set up an international federation of comparable bodies in 1921. It has been active in criticising French policies in all the sensitive areas covered by this book.

Such monitoring is particularly necessary because another feature of the French state is its centralised system of government. Although there is a degree of devolution to regional and municipal authorities, the government retains tight control over the instruments of social control or persuasion: the police, education and to a lesser extent television. Allied with this is a degree of government secrecy that probably exceeds even that of the UK. As in the UK, the government has been accused of flouting its own laws in order to monitor the activities of its opponents. In response to complaints about telephone tapping by the state an official commission was set up, but this had no real power.

Immigration Old and New

Racist views and policy proposals have attracted more open and electoral support, and equally strong opposition backed up by mass demonstrations, than in any other Member State with the possible exception of Germany. It was taken sufficiently seriously for a law of 1990 to specify that the government's human rights advisory body (see above) should publish an annual report on the problem and the measures taken to deal with it. These reports are extremely detailed and include contributions from a wide range of NGOs active in the field; different aspects are covered each year.[3]

The roots of racism in France, as in the UK, lie in its past experience of colonialism and immigration from former possessions; it also stems (paradoxically) from the strong emphasis placed on the unifying force of French culture and attachment to fundamental rights. French is a first or second language in some 25 Third World countries, quite apart from the remaining relics of empire. Long before they achieved independence, several of the colonies were granted metropolitan status and democratic representation as being politically part of France. Immigration has a long history, and from the 1950s to the mid-1970s large numbers of immigrants (mainly men) came to take up work, especially in the car factories. Many came from North Africa, but in the early years they also came from poorer European countries that are now Member States of the Union.

This did not mean, however, that immigrant workers were ever treated as equal in all respects to native French citizens; their pay was inferior, their living conditions sub-standard, and they were liable to instant deportation if they got into trouble with the authorities or could not renew their work permits through lack of employment. For Arabs in particular, police harassment and racist abuse were a part of their lives, a pattern that unfortunately is still not eradicated.[4] The war of independence in Algeria left a bitterness towards them that persists in a current suspicion that Islamic fundamentalists from that country are bent on subverting French culture. At the same time, black people feel rather more welcome than in many other European countries; history rather than colour is the dominant factor.

Gradual settlement of immigrant workers and subsequent family reunion led to new tensions, exacerbated (as in other countries) by rising unemployment. Another factor then emerged, as the growing Islamic communities showed every sign of wishing to preserve their culture and practice their religion in France. This was highlighted by a long-running controversy over whether girls should be allowed to wear the Islamic

headscarf in school classrooms.[5] The official policy of assimilation into
French society, implying no concessions for minorities attached to
different cultures, appeared no longer to be working. This made it easier
for right-wing politicians to arouse hostility to immigrants; they
competed to produce the most hard-line policy on immigration and
asylum, and leaders of the left failed to resist a wave of popular support
for such ideas.

The Pasqua Laws

The 1992 and 1993 intergovernmental agreements on immigration
and asylum (Chapters 4 and 5) fell on fertile ground in France. Charles
Pasqua, the Interior Minister of a newly formed right-wing government,
soon announced a policy of 'zero immigration' coupled with increased
powers for the police; he defended it as 'a new chance, perhaps the last,
for the French model of integration'.[6] His package of measures included
three draft laws, all of which were passed after some moderation at the
insistence of the *Conseil constitutionnel*:

- A nationality law depriving children born in France of foreign
  parents of an automatic right of citizenship at 18; their parents
  would also be denied the right to apply on their behalf at an earlier
  age. Children between 16 and 21 would be able to apply for citizenship, but this could be refused on the basis of certain criminal
  convictions.[7]
- An extension of the right of the police to carry out random identity
  checks, ostensibly aimed at detecting illegal immigrants.[8]
- A comprehensive Aliens Law embracing restrictions on the rights of
  asylum and family reunification; residence rights would also be
  harder to obtain and subject to withdrawal on various grounds,
  while instant deportation would be made easier. Other measures were
  aimed at denying welfare benefits to illegal residents and preventing
  'marriages of convenience' with French citizens.[9]

The Aliens Law produced the most widespread objections from all sides:
the *Conseil constitutionnel* rejected large parts of the initial draft and it
was denounced by the *Commission nationale consultative des Droits de
l'Homme*, church bodies, lawyers and NGOs.[10] The restrictions on
asylum (brought in to comply with the Dublin and Schengen
Conventions) required an amendment of the Constitution.[11] In the
course of the controversy over all three laws, three prominent NGOs
withdrew their support from the human rights advisory committee

because they felt it had not been vigorous enough in its protests.[12] The government had in any case shown little respect for the committee, allowing it only one day to discuss the 40 Articles of the draft Aliens Law. The committee later made up for this by devoting much of its next annual report to the subsequent effects of the legislation.[13]

Passage of these laws was followed by the creation of a new police department to combine border control (formerly the task of a separate force) with combating the employment of clandestine immigrants and carrying out their expulsion.[14] A further law was passed in 1994, aimed at facilitating the detention of aliens in 'waiting zones' in certain railway stations as well as airports.[15] Police operations involving pre-dawn raids and widespread identity checks became more common, and aroused increasing alarm among anti-racist groups.[16] There were more reports of arbitrary arrest and expulsion on minor technicalities of the residence laws. To some, the advent of a police state seemed uncomfortably close, but the government continued to feel that it had broad popular support. The effect of all this on many non-white residents of France (particularly the younger generation) can well be imagined, and the bitterness engendered will remain a problem for all future governments to face.

GERMANY

Germany's history made it an ideal candidate for leading membership of the 'ever closer union' envisaged by the original EC treaty. Its federal structure, abolished by Hitler but restored in a strengthened form after the Second World War, demonstrated the feasibility of setting up a decentralised system in which states retained their independence in many areas without weakening the central control of broad policy issues. Each of the 16 *Länder* of the reunified Federal Republic has its own parliament, ministries, judiciary, education system and even customs officers (at external borders), and cultural variations are strongly maintained. All this is not matched anywhere outside North America, though Belgium has moved in that direction and regional autonomy is on the increase in some other states.

At the same time there has been a determination, shared with France, to avoid any accusation that the largest Member State of the Union could ever again entertain ambitions of dominating Europe on its own – though this very closeness with France, underlined by a bilateral treaty in 1963, has led historically-minded politicians of other countries to talk darkly of a new hegemony recalling the era of Charlemagne. These fears have been offset by the evident desire of both governments to extend membership of the Union to other states and, at least in Germany's case, to move towards a more democratic structure for its institutions. In a controversial policy paper released in September 1994, Chancellor Kohl's Christian Democrat (CDU) party supported the idea of the European Parliament becoming a genuine law-making body with the same rights as the Council.

Human rights in Germany are protected by the 1949 *Grundgesetz* (Basic Law), overseen by a Constitutional Court. The very liberality of the Basic Law in two key areas – asylum for refugees and citizenship for non-residents of German descent – has led to unexpected problems and bitter controversy over how to solve them. NGOs in the field of human rights tend to be more regionally oriented than in other countries, though there is a small but effective Berlin-based *Internationale Liga für Menschenrechte* (founded in 1922 and suppressed by Hitler); also, as in other countries, a national section of Amnesty International which includes the domestic treatment of refugees in its remit. A leading role in educational campaigns on everything from asylum to racism has been taken by the national trade union federation *Deutscher Gewerkschaftsbund* (DGB).[17] Awareness of the importance of civil liberties is perhaps more widespread than in some European countries; in Germany there is even a radical association of dissenting police officers which has criticised Europol (Chapter 7) as a dangerous precedent for a European secret police force.[18]

Foreigners, Refugees and Ethnic Germans

Like France, Germany has experienced extensive immigration by foreign workers whose presence was originally assumed to be temporary. By the end of 1993 there were nearly 7 million foreigners living in Germany, accounting for 8.5 per cent of the population.[19] Of these the largest group was some 2 million Turks, including many who were born in Germany as children of earlier arrivals; yet few of them have achieved citizenship and the majority live as second-class citizens with no guarantee of permanent residence. Although the DGB insisted from the beginning on equal pay and treatment for foreign workers, this has not prevented extensive exploitation of underpaid recruits to non-unionised employment. This lack of protection stems from two factors. The first is a continuing insistence among many politicians that, despite all the evidence to the contrary, Germany is not a country of immigration. As a consequence there has never been legislation to regulate immigration, nor an official policy of integration and guaranteed residence; yet the economic role of immigrants is indisputable (see Chapter 5).[20]

The second factor preventing integration has been a restrictive concept of nationality, assumed (with limited exceptions) to be reserved for those descended from German parents, even after generations of residence abroad. Under a law dating from 1913, immigrants of other nationalities and their descendants are in most cases denied the possibility of dual nationality, so that Turks in particular stand to lose inheritance rights in Turkey if they give up Turkish nationality. In November 1994 the new coalition government proposed a curious kind of second-class citizenship for children whose parents (at least one of whom was born in Germany) had lived there for at least ten years. At the age of 18 these 'foreigners with German child nationality' (the official description) would revert to being foreigners unless they renounced their original nationality within a year.[21]

A second major source of net immigration has been the unprecedented number of asylum seekers accepted by Germany, well in excess of those received by other Member States (Chapter 4). This arose partly for geographical reasons but also because Article 16(2) of the Basic Law, unlike the Geneva Convention, offered an absolute guarantee of asylum to anyone subjected to political persecution. Apart from those accepted under this heading, many other remained with a 'tolerated' status (*Duldung*).[22] Demands to change the Basic Law were resisted until 1993, when the main political parties agreed on an amendment to bring it into line with the laws in other Member States.[23] The right of asylum remains in principle, but will no longer be granted to applicants from 'safe third countries' (Chapter 4). Rapid deportation of rejected asylum seekers is provided for, and the right of appeal restricted.

The changes threw the legal system into some confusion, with courts in the *Länder* issuing contradictory rulings and the Federal Constitutional Court overturning some deportation decisions;[24] a final decision on whether the change in the Basic Law was in fact constitutional was not expected until early 1995.[25] In the meantime the application of the new law resulted in many deportations and a large decrease in asylum applications: over the first year of its operation, the number fell to a third of the previous year's total.[26] Human rights activists expressed alarm at the methods used to discourage applicants from filing applications on arrival,[27] and at the conditions under which they were detained in airports.[28] There was also controversy over the deportation of Kurds to Turkey and former contract workers to Vietnam, and over the return of refugees to parts of the former Yugoslavia. Germany's refugee policies now seemed all too 'harmonised' with those of other Member States.

An extra motive for the hardening of refugee policy was the impact of a purely German phenomenon arising from reunification in 1990 and the collapse of the Soviet bloc. Huge numbers of immigrants arrived in the former West Germany from the impoverished eastern part, followed by even greater numbers of *Aussiedler* of German origin from the countries of Eastern Europe (Chapter 5). All were guaranteed recognition as German citizens, but their arrival induced severe economic and cultural stress in existing communities, where the existence of large camps containing asylum-seekers was already arousing hostility. In the former German Democratic Republic (DDR) an immediate consequence of reunification was the collapse of state-supported full employment. A recession was beginning everywhere to bite, and the search for scapegoats led to an upsurge in racism which found politicians unable or unwilling to respond in time.

Warnings and Reactions

Racism is a term which still stirs uncomfortable memories in Germany, and politicians have preferred to characterise it as hostility to foreigners (*Fremdenfeindlichkeit*). As in France, the idea of recognising ethnic minorities as such has also been avoided in case they then demanded special treatment. At local level such semantic distinctions have been irrelevant. In the early 1990s a succession of violent attacks on foreigners erupted, most seriously in the former DDR where the relatively small population of Vietnamese contract workers was singled out. Observers noted that violence was perpetrated not only by unemployed working-class youths but also by the sons of some middle-class parents. An opinion poll later found that students in the former DDR were far more xenophobic than those in the western *Länder*.[29]

The federal Commissioner for Aliens, Liselotte Funcke, warned of what was building up in March 1991 and complained bitterly of lack of support from Chancellor Kohl.[30] In July she resigned in protest.[31] Official statistics for the month of October 1991 recorded 904 criminal offences against foreigners, including 54 assaults and 167 cases of arson.[32] The total for June 1993 was 1307.[33] In the interim there had been two horrific arson attacks, one on an asylum-seekers' hostel at Rostock in August 1992 and the other at Solingen in May 1993, when five Turks were burned to death. The police and the authorities were heavily criticised for failing to prevent the outrages.

Public opinion (at least in the western *Länder*) changed from indifference to alarm at these developments. In December 1992, following the murder of three Turks in Mölln, there were mass demonstrations against racist violence in several cities, and 'human chains' were formed to protect refugee hostels from attack. Major industrialists called for greater tolerance towards foreigners.[34] Opinion polls revealed a growing fear of right-wing extremism.[35] In September 1993, Chancellor Kohl finally joined the chorus of condemnation of racist attacks; he also pointed out that foreign immigrants contributed more to the state than they took in benefits.[36] By the end of 1993 the rate of attacks on foreigners seemed to be decreasing, but in May 1994 there was a prolonged racist riot in Magdeburg which the police did little to control; 50 or more neo-Nazis were arrested but released the same night, to the open disgust of President von Weizsäcker.[37]

All this led to much soul-searching and analysis.[38] One conclusion was that it would take a generation for attitudes in the former DDR to change: the system had made its policemen unused to the idea of protecting rather than harassing ordinary citizens, while people in the street were reluctant to report incidents or intervene themselves because of an ingrained fear of the authorities. Racist behaviour by the police, a recurrent problem,[39] was also highlighted. In December 1994 the German Penal Code was amended to include as punishable acts certain forms of racism including incitement to hatred. The record of events served as an awful warning, not just to Germany but to other Member States, that racism can easily get out of control if public figures and the authorities do not move quickly to condemn it publicly and prevent a recurrence. In the longer term, educational campaigns need to go hand in hand with addressing the needs of both 'immigrants' (whether new or long-standing) and those who, through their own deprivation, feel threatened by them.

ITALY

In becoming a founder member of the EC, Italy made a quantum leap into a future role for which its previous history left it somewhat ill prepared. Although unification of its independent city states was completed in 1871, Italy never achieved a widely obeyed system of central government; centuries of past experience ensured that most administrations were regarded by Italians with suspicion, and their laws and taxation demands treated with contempt. Even Mussolini's dictatorship has been described as a 'tyranny tempered by the complete disobedience of all laws'.[40] Governments were also regarded as inevitably corruptible, a view that current events continue to illustrate. The family remained the only real centre of loyalty. The disciplines of a centrally directed common market did not therefore easily take root, though membership of the EC helped Italy to move from being one of the poorer countries in Europe to overtaking the UK in the league table of Gross Domestic Product.

Italy's politicians have been readier than most to accept that an effective European Parliament and a supranational judicial authority (in the shape of the European Court of Justice) would offered a measure of stability that has been lacking in their own system, in which there were 50 changes of government between 1947 and 1992. This showed itself in a willingness to accept ECJ jurisdiction over intergovernmental agreements such as the Schengen Convention (Chapter 3). In this respect Italy is more sympathetic to the federal school of thought than more ancient nation states like France and the UK. It sees no reason to be left out of any scheme for closer integration involving those Member States that are ready for it.

From Emigration to Immigration

A major difference between Italy and the two countries so far considered has been its relatively short experience of large-scale immigration. In the early years of the EC, Italy was still a country of emigration and many workers left to take up offers of work abroad; Italians were among the first 'guest workers' recruited by Germany. This was also true of the other southern European nations of Greece, Portugal and Spain. The situation changed rapidly from the late 1970s onwards, as the more northern 'immigration countries' drastically reduced their intakes of foreign workers. Italy then became the first southern EC state to receive large numbers of immigrants, mainly from northern and central Africa. Their initial aim was to use Italy as a transit country, in the hope of moving on to other countries where they had previously been recruited for work.[41]

At that time it was very easy for them to enter Italy as tourists, and many of them in the event stayed on as members of the flourishing hidden economy of undocumented workers; they filled the seasonal and low-paid jobs that the increasingly affluent Italian workers were unwilling to take. Their numbers became so large that successive governments made two attempts (in 1987 and 1990) to regularise the situation by offering an amnesty for illegal workers, who would then be able to apply for renewable residence and work permits. The schemes were only partly successful because workers in rural areas did not always get to hear of them, and some employers preferred to keep the workers in an illegal and insecure situation.

Meanwhile, Italy's new partners in the Schengen Agreement (Chapter 3) were exerting pressure on the government to restrict further entries and set up a rigorous system of border controls; they feared that otherwise there would be nothing to stop illegal immigrants from spreading through Italy to other countries as soon as the internal frontiers were abolished. The response was the wide-ranging Law No. 39 of 1990 (called the 'Martelli law' after its proponent). This recognised the need for at least some further immigration by allowing for an annual decree determining which broad categories would be admitted. These have so far covered asylum seekers, those eligible for family reunification, workers, and (since 1993) those allowed in on humanitarian grounds (especially former Yugoslavs). Apart from offering an amnesty of the kind mentioned above, the law also laid down new rules for political asylum (see below), visa requirements, and the expulsion for life of many categories of offender including anyone violating the regulations on entry and residence.

The other countries expressed satisfaction at the new law and Italy was allowed to accede to the 1990 Schengen Convention in November of that year. However, they had reckoned without the more relaxed Italian approach to the implementation of legislation. Article 7(7) of the Martelli law stated that all those served with a notice of expulsion must leave the country within 15 days, or alternatively 'report to the Police Headquarters to be escorted to the frontier by the same date'. The result in practice was that many of those served with such notices quietly melted into the underground economy and were never seen again; others exercised their right to stay during a lengthy appeal process. While some 30,000 deportation orders were issued annually, few were ever executed.

This could be regarded as a justifiable response to an intractable human problem. However, the wide scope of the law criminalised large numbers of people whose offence might be as slight as a failure to apply for a residence permit within eight days of arrival. Lawyers attempting to help them were greatly hindered by the fact that many regulations were specified in government circulars that were not always made public and could not be challenged directly in court; they also felt that the law put far too much arbitrary power into the hands of officials and policemen charged with applying it. In 1993 the government attempted to reduce the right of appeal by proposing instant deportation for alleged offenders even before their trials, but the parliament refused to pass a law to put the government decree into effect.[42] Meanwhile clandestine immigration continued, mainly by boat along Italy's extensive coastline.[43] An expert committee set up in 1993 to consider the reform of immigration and asylum law produced a comprehensive draft, but in 1994 the newly elected Berlusconi government decided not to put it to the parliament. Instead a new and stricter law to replace the Martelli law was considered, including deportation with no appeal for those attempting to enter illegally.[44]

The effect of putting so many immigrants outside the law over a long period had an obvious effect on public opinion; their poverty and squalid living conditions, and the recourse of some of them to activities such as selling contraband cigarettes, led to their being regarded as a horde of petty criminals and a threat to the stability of society. Italians had previously prided themselves on being free of racism, more associated in the public mind with the USA and its treatment of the black community. In the 1990s racism began to emerge in Italy too, and there were some ugly incidents in which Africans in particular were attacked.[45] Gypsies, always regarded with suspicion and subject to discrimination,[46] also experienced increasing harassment by police and vigilante groups.[47] In July 1993, a new law against propagating racist ideas was passed[48] but there were complaints that the police took little action to enforce it. The government was blamed by many people for allowing this situation to develop, and the three Italian trade union federations jointly supported a platform of equal rights, proper contracts, training and representation for all immigrant workers.[49]

Refugees and the Constitution

Like other post-fascist Constitutions, that of Italy (approved in 1947) went well beyond the Geneva Convention in its definition of a refugee; Article 10(3) states that 'A foreigner to whom the practical exercise in his own country of democratic freedoms, guaranteed by the Italian Constitution, is precluded, is entitled to the right of asylum within the territory of the Republic, under conditions laid down by law'.[50] However, until 1990 the only laws on this subject were those implementing the Geneva Convention and its 1967 Protocol; there was also a 'geographical limitation' to refugees from within Europe. The 1990 Martelli law removed this limitation but still kept to the Geneva definition of a refugee. The frontier police were also given the power to turn away various categories of asylum-seeker without further consideration of their case. Official recognition rates were very low, and the bureaucratic obstacles meant that most asylum-seekers were not even registered as such; in practice an unknown but large proportion stayed on with an uncertain *de facto* status.

The system was therefore unprepared for the unprecedented waves of asylum-seekers arriving from Albania, Somalia and the former Yugoslavia in the early 1990s. The government responses were variable and inconsistent. Albanians were at first accepted as refugees but later, as the numbers increased, they were turned away as illegal immigrants.[51] Former Yugoslavs were, however, given temporary residence permits on a generous scale; at the end of 1994 there were some 55,000 permits in force, though it was not known how many of the holders had by then left the country again.[52] In an attempt to bring Italian refugee law firmly into line with the Constitution, the main NGO in this field proposed a comprehensive draft law in 1994.[53] By the end of the year this had secured enough support to guarantee a debate in the Italian parliament, and hopes were high that at least some of its provisions would become law in spite of the change in political climate.

The draft law starts with the broad definition of a refugee in the Italian Constitution, with special mention of the categories of persecution listed in the Geneva Convention. A further provision extends the same rights on a more short-term basis to individuals or even whole groups fleeing from war, civil strife, serious breakdown of public order or extensive violations of human rights – the categories of people covered by the Cartagena Declaration (Chapter 4). Finally, the law would allow an application for asylum to be submitted outside Italy to a diplomatic representative or to the captain of an Italian ship or aircraft. The definition of a 'manifestly unfounded' application is limited to cases such as prior recognition elsewhere or residence of at least three months in a safe third country. Various legal and social rights for asylum-seekers and refugees are specified in detail.

It is clear that a law of this kind would set an unusual example to other Member States, whose policies have so far been moving in an opposite and more restrictive direction. Its approval would represent a rare victory for those calling for a more humane policy on asylum, and could have a profound influence on the future trend of Union policy.

The Netherlands

Dutch history has been regularly punctuated by periods of oppression by other European powers. This, and its long mercantile tradition, made the Netherlands[54] a ready candidate for EC membership as a new trading opportunity combined with a chance to put an end to destructive European wars. As a relatively small Member State without delusions of grandeur, the Netherlands brought with it a readiness to accept joint decision-making, together with a long tradition of respect for human rights (particularly freedom of beliefs) and sturdy independence among its parliamentarians.

This last quality proved invaluable in the monitoring of treaty proposals outside the scope of Community law. Before the Schengen Convention (Chapter 3) could be incorporated into Dutch law, MPs insisted on a right to see the documents relating to a proposal for executive action by the signatory states. The responsible minister could be forbidden to agree to such action if the parliament objected; a failure to comply could in the last resort lead to a vote of no confidence and the fall of the government. A similar right was obtained with regard to action under the TEU. There was in any case a long-standing rule that no international treaty such as a Title VI Convention could be ratified unless the parliament passed a Bill of Approval (Chapter 1).

This insistence upon direct accountability compares favourably with the routine acceptance of intergovernmental agreements by the parliaments of most other Member States, despite much rhetoric being expended on the virtues of national sovereignty and subsidiarity. The Dutch proposals for reform of the EC treaty, though rejected at Maastricht, may yet influence the development of a more democratic Union. There is also a strong tradition of independent monitoring by academic jurists; the Meijers committee of legal experts has been influential in analysing and communicating to the parliament the defects of the Schengen Convention and other agreements affecting refugees and immigrants (Chapters 3, 4 and 5).

New Stresses

Although there is a tradition of tolerance towards minority groups, the Netherlands has not escaped the tensions arising from increases in the numbers of asylum-seekers and potential immigrants. The rate of asylum applications began to rise in 1986 and even more steeply in mid-1993, following the application of stricter rules in Germany; some of those rejected there simply travelled across the border in the hope of a second chance in the Netherlands. There were increasingly severe problems in housing the people concerned. Since then the Dutch government has brought in a series of restrictive measures that in some respects are harsher than those enacted in other Member States. Their effects have been partially mitigated by the existence of a number of officially funded but independent agencies charged with protecting the interests of those most at risk; the trend, however, is not encouraging and the agencies themselves are now under financial pressure.

Proposals for amending the 1965 Aliens Law, initiated in November 1992 and put to the parliament in 1993, were finally approved in December 1993.[55] For potential refugees they made up the familiar package of accelerated asylum procedures, carrier sanctions, reduced appeal rights, and detention and expulsion provisions; there were also new restrictions on family reunification (Chapters 4 and 5). Lawyers were disturbed to note a departure from the previous Dutch policy of according equal rights to aliens and Dutch citizens. Under the new law, aliens in general and asylum-seekers in particular would have fewer opportunities to contest government decisions in the courts.[56] There was particular concern over the absence of a statutory limit to the time during which asylum-seekers whose applications were inadmissible or 'manifestly unfounded' could be detained while their expulsion was considered. It was pointed out that this was a potential violation of the European Convention on Human Rights; the detention was not a consequence of committing a criminal act, but simply a result of having applied for asylum.

More was to come in 1994. Controversial legislation was proposed to define 'safe third countries' whose nationals would be refused asylum, or to which asylum-seekers could be sent if they had passed through them;[57] at first there was to be no right of appeal in such cases, but MPs forced a change on this point before the measure was approved.[58] Special mobile posts, manned by the paramilitary *marechausee* force, were set up near to the Belgian and German borders with the aim of carrying out identity checks. Under new legislation, everyone seeking asylum would have to report to one of two registration centres, where an initial decision would be made within 24 hours; however, most Dutch lawyers refused to participate in the arrangement because they felt it would be impossible to give adequate legal advice in the time allotted.[59] At the end of the year a strict new law on marriages of convenience was introduced.[60]

As an indication of how far the Netherlands had changed, 1994 also saw a move towards identity cards[61] – something that a few years earlier would have been unthinkable, since many people associated them with the years of Nazi occupation. The law specified the occasions on which people could be required to identify themselves to the police. These were, however, widely drawn and included attendance at a football match and the use of public transport. Perhaps more significantly, the criteria included 'the control of illegal labour' and 'enforcement of the surveillance on aliens or for the control on illegal border crossings'.[62] After protests that this would lead to random checks in the street and harassment of non-white residents, instructions to the police were issued to reduce this danger but there were fears that they did not go far enough.

Positive Responses

The restrictions on asylum need to be seen in the light of the fact that the Netherlands is the most densely populated country in Europe; it has nevertheless absorbed more asylum-seekers than many Member States of the Union. Racism has appeared as the internal strains have intensified, and (as elsewhere) it is argued that official policies have made it more socially acceptable to make racist remarks. However, there has until recently been a general acceptance of the need to do everything possible to welcome those who choose to settle in the Netherlands; the official policy on minorities was stated in 1983 as 'the achievement of a society in which the members of minority groups ... have identically adequate chances of development, either individually or as a group'.[63] Though integration was encouraged, ethnic minorities were not expected to abandon their traditional culture or language. In former years all identifiable groups were encouraged to set up a 'pillar' of associations to foster and maintain their own traditions and language. More recently, however, this has changed with the realisation that a failure to become fluent in the Dutch language is an obvious handicap when seeking employment or training. There was even talk of requiring new arrivals to sign an undertaking to learn Dutch and integrate as soon as possible.[64]

With rising unemployment in which ethnic minorities fared particularly badly, a new law was proposed in 1993 (with some hesitation) to oblige firms with more than 35 employees to report on the number of people they employed from specified minority groups.[65] They would also have to show what positive measures they were taking to ensure equal opportunities for such groups. The law was approved in 1994, though there were some objections on the grounds of privacy and data protection. In September 1994 a new General Law on equal treatment came into force.[66] This elaborated Article 1 of the amended 1983 Constitution by prohibiting both direct and indirect discrimination on grounds of religious or other convictions, political tendencies, race, sex, nationality, sexual orientation or civil status. An independent commission was to be set up to ensure compliance and receive complaints. Observers feared that for racial discrimination in particular, an agency with stronger legal powers on the UK model would be needed. The activities of the existing *Landelijk Bureau Racismebestrijding* (LBR) are mainly limited to advice, legal aid and research.[67]

In the future, the most positive contribution of the Netherlands to the debate on Union immigration policy may come be seen as its championship of the principle of giving all third-country nationals equal rights with EU citizens after a qualifying period of residence. This gained little support (except from Spain) in the negotiations leading up to the TEU, so the Netherlands took its own steps to make Dutch nationality more readily available to its own non-Dutch residents.[68] There was an enormous response to this offer. However, as shown above in Chapter 5, there is a growing feeling that equality of rights must ultimately come; when this happens, it will demonstrate that a Member State does not have to be large or powerful to have a long-term influence on Union policy.

SPAIN

During the past two decades, Spain underwent some remarkable trans-
formations: a peaceful transition from dictatorship to democracy in 1977,
admission to the EC in 1986 (nearly 30 years after its founding), a
rapid increase in prosperity, and a change from being a country of
emigration to one of immigration. Spain began to look forward to an
international status that it had never achieved since the loss of its main
colonial possessions in earlier centuries and the consequent decline into
relative poverty.

The country's history may contribute to the preoccupation of the
Spanish government with avoiding a new relegation to second-class
standing in the Union. This could follow from the accession of richer
new members from Scandinavia, and also from funds for development
being diverted to another wave of poorer candidates from Eastern
Europe. Spanish national pride remains strong, giving rise to a reluctance
to yield in a long-standing dispute over the status of Gibraltar – a topic
on which the UK, which seized the territory in 1704, is equally obstinate.
The two powers have successfully blocked a treaty affecting the entire
Union on that issue alone (Chapter 3), an illustration of the hold that
past history still has in certain areas. At the same time Spain has actively
promoted the concept of Union citizenship as a symbolic means of inte-
grating a previously divided continent. Its quasi-federal structure, with
17 regions having various degrees of autonomy (especially the Basque
country, Cataluña and Galicia, which also maintain their own languages),
offers an example to governments that are reluctant to follow this path
at the European level.

Refugee Law Under Attack

Spain's recent experience illustrates with particular clarity the way in
which immigration and asylum policies can soon become inextricably
entangled, with all the usual problems for the individuals concerned.
Their difficulties have been compounded by a shortage of practising
lawyers with experience of the field.

Spain's transition to becoming a new country of immigration followed
that of Italy; emigration virtually stopped in 1974, while immigration
(mainly from Africa, but also from Spanish-speaking countries like the
Dominican Republic) later rose considerably.[69] Following the passage
of a new Aliens Law in 1985,[70] there was an attempt to regularise immigration at a level consistent with the continuing needs of the labour

market. A system of annual quotas was introduced, together with an amnesty in 1991 for clandestine immigrants; by the end of that year more than 80,000 applications had been accepted.[71] This was expected to bring the total number of legal immigrants in Spain to some 700,000 with up to 300,000 still trying to achieve this status;[72] in contrast with Italy, a promise of work for at least six months was a precondition for acceptance and this presented a particular problem for seasonal workers.

All this generated social and political tensions in a country that had no recent experience of immigration, and there was a sharp increase in attempts to enter Spain illegally. This mostly involved hazardous journeys in small boats from North Africa, despite the efforts of the Moroccan government to discourage it at source.[73] Those detained in Spain were held under harsh conditions which led in 1994 to a highly adverse report by a group of judges on the internment centre at Malaga;[74] there was later a hunger strike by the inmates, who claimed that conditions were worse than in a prison.[75] The government also announced its intention to expel some 3000 foreign inmates of Spanish prisons in an attempt to reduce overcrowding, a decision condemned by human rights groups as inciting xenophobia.[76] There was already evidence for an increase in racist attitudes, though the government claimed that extreme-right groups were insignificant in comparison with many other Member States.[77]

An unfortunate side-effect of these changes was a departure from what had previously been a model refugee law, based on the 1978 Constitution.[78] This recognised two categories: *refugiados* who satisfied the criteria of the Geneva Convention, and *asilados* who were allowed to stay on humanitarian grounds or as *de facto* refugees (Chapter 4). These constituted only a minority of those accepted, but the official recognition of their status was important in principle; they were protected against *refoulement* and guaranteed residence and other rights. The new law passed in 1994,[79] only ten years after its predecessor, eliminated the second category altogether.

Another change was a dilution of the basic rights of an asylum-seeker: to ask for asylum, to have the application properly examined, and to stay in the country while it was being considered. Under the newly proposed law, like those being introduced in other Member States, only the first right was guaranteed. Applications deemed to be 'manifestly unfounded' could be rejected out of hand at the border. After protests by MPs and by the refugee NGO *Comisión Española de Ayuda al Refugiado* (CEAR), an amendment was added to suspend an expulsion order if the representative of UNHCR expressed disagreement within three days.[80]

A regulation subsequently issued under the new law was severely criticised by the *Consejo de Estado*, a consultative body which examines whether laws are compatible with the Constitution; the regulation would have restricted the freedom of movement of displaced persons from areas of conflict who did not satisfy the Geneva criteria.[81] The *Tribunal Constitucional* (Constitutional Court) had already been sent an opinion by the *Defensor del Pueblo* (see below) that the law itself was contrary to the Constitution in allowing detention without judicial control for more than 72 hours. The new law changed this to seven days, and the period was sometimes extended by up to three weeks in the case of detention at Madrid airport.[82] Thus although the Constitution itself was not yet under threat as in France or Germany (Chapter 4), there was increasing disquiet at the way in which it was being undermined in practice.

Defending the People

One reform introduced with the return of democracy to Spain is worth a special mention, because it could provide a model for better protection of individual rights throughout the Union. Following the example of Sweden's system of Ombudsmen, now copied in some form in nearly all Member States of the Union, Spain set up the independent office of *Defensor del Pueblo*.[83] The *Defensor* is a non-party official elected for a five-year term by the parliament on a three-fifths majority in both houses, and probably has wider powers than in any other state; the 1992 annual report to the parliament was more than 1000 pages long, and a further volume detailed the 69 official recommendations made in that year.

The powers of the *Defensor* include investigating the usual complaints by individuals about maladministration by officials at each level from national to local. Every person (including minors, prisoners and members of the armed forces) has a right to make a complaint. Only certain court matters and military decisions affecting 'the command of national defence' are excluded from consideration.

The *Defensor* can also consider whether new laws are constitutional, either independently or on being approached (for instance) by NGOs; thus in the case of the new refugee law mentioned above, the initiative came from CEAR and the human rights NGO *Asociación pro Derechos Humanos de España*. The *Defensor* then made a formal submission to the *Tribunal Constitucional*. The latter can also be petitioned by the President, any group of 50 MPs or senators, or by a regional government or parliament.

In another case, after the lobbying of several bodies by the privacy protection NGO *Comisión de Libertades e Informatica*, four separate sub-

. missions against Spain's first data protection law of 1992 were sent in 1993 to the *Tribunal Constitucional* by the *Defensor del Pueblo*, the national opposition *Partido Popular*, and the regional government and parliament of Cataluña. They claimed that it gave too much licence to the police and other public authorities and thereby contravened the Constitution, which is modern enough to specify that 'The law shall limit the use of data processing in order to guarantee the honour and personal and family privacy of citizens and the full exercise of their rights' (Article 18(4)). The only problem with this procedure for questioning a law is that it remains in force until disallowed by the *Tribunal Constitucional*, a process that can take about two years.

There are thus several ways in which new laws can be challenged. From time to time the *Defensor* also issues a special report on a particular issue; one of particular relevance here concerned a conference held in 1993 (in conjunction with NGOs) on the rights of immigrants and their many problems.[84] The report ended with a set of specific recommendations by the *Defensor* to the four government ministries involved with admitting or rejecting immigrants, and with helping those who have already been accepted.

It is obvious that all this goes well beyond the distinctly limited mandate of the Ombudsman created under the TEU. One reason is that the *Defensor* has a clear duty to protect all those individual rights that are laid down in the Spanish Constitution. Another is the freedom of NGOs to raise general issues that do not have to be tied to an individual case – an advance even on the working of the European Convention on Human Rights. The fruitful interaction of a written Constitution, a Constitutional Court, a powerful Ombudsman and active NGOs is something that is currently lacking in many Member States; an elected parliament on its own is simply not enough in our complex society.

SWEDEN

Sweden's accession to the Union in January 1995 may ultimately have an effect out of all proportion to the country's population of under 9 million. Sweden will bring with it a particularly well-developed tradition of open government in which freedom of information is an essential feature. As mentioned in Chapter 1 and elsewhere, this is an area where the Union's declared principles are not reflected in present practice. In asylum and immigration policy, too, Sweden's approach has in the past been more far-sighted and liberal than in most other European countries. Although there were signs before 1995 of a shift of its policy towards those of the more restrictive Member States, Sweden still differs in its underlying philosophy on refugees. It will have some allies in the Council when arguing for a more humane and less reactive long-term policy in this area. Sweden will also be able to support Member States calling for a more democratic structure for the Union, including increased powers for the European Parliament.

Although the public campaigns for and against membership centred (as in all candidate countries) on the possible economic effects, the factors outlined above were also brought into the argument. The need to protect Sweden's system of open government from attack and extend the principle to Union affairs became an important issue. Advocates of Sweden's membership added that the country's tradition of interna-tionalism and support of the United Nations would help to counteract the Union's tendency to become an inward-looking club with no high ideals; they also pointed out that only membership would give Sweden a say in determining common policies to protect the environment. Opponents, on the other hand, argued that Sweden's long tradition of neutrality could be lost on joining a club in which members like France were pressing for a common defence and foreign policy. They also expressed a fear that Sweden's welfare system – recently under strain, but not as seriously threatened as elsewhere – would be dragged down to a lower common level and that jobs would be lost. Now that the question of membership is settled, there is no doubt that Sweden will work hard to avoid any such effects.

Constitutional Rights

Sweden's Constitution offers a particularly instructive model for improving the transparency of decision-making at Union level, and for that matter at the national level in other Member States. It comprises four fundamental or 'organic' laws that can only be changed by the *Riksdag* (parliament) after two identically worded resolutions are passed in separate sessions, with a general election held in between; a referendum may also be called for. The Riksdag Act is partially protected in the same way. The four fundamental laws are the Instrument of Government, which lays down individual rights and freedoms and includes a ban on discriminatory laws and regulations; the Act of Succession; the Freedom of the Press Act; and a Freedom of Expression Act which extends most of the principles of the Freedom of the Press Act to the media in general.[85]

While the catalogue of rights and freedoms is similar to that in other Constitutions, the Freedom of the Press Act is a remarkable document by the standards of most other countries in the world. It originated in

1766 and was last amended and strengthened in 1949.[86] It guarantees freedom of expression in print with few restrictions, and prohibits prior censorship; perhaps more importantly, it gives both citizens and aliens the right to see most official documents at every level of government. This may even extend to the daily correspondence of the Prime Minister, and it covers material relating to proposed legislation. Access must be facilitated by the preparation of suitable lists of available documents and by access to computerised data. Exceptions to the rule are laid down in a periodically revised Secrecy Act[87] which covers information relating to such areas as international relations, defence, the prevention and prosecution of crime, medical data on individuals and so on; although the list is extensive, there is an underlying principle that secrecy must be justified by the potential harm that would result from disclosure of the information. The Secrecy Act does not imply a blanket classification of whole documents; a journalist may in principle demand to see a copy with secret information erased. There is also a right of appeal to the courts against refusal of access.

As an essential adjunct to this right of access, individuals communicating information to the press are in most cases protected from prosecution and have a legally enforceable right to remain anonymous. This even extends to civil servants, and it is a criminal offence to seek out 'whistle blowers' for exposure or punishment. Penal sanctions for abuse of the Freedom of the Press Act (under Chapter 7 of the Act) are limited to the more serious cases of disclosure of secret information, as listed in Chapter 16 of the Secrecy Act. This means that a civil servant may sometimes brief a reporter on the contents of a restricted document without handing it over. Only a court can in certain circumstances demand the name of an informant, but (in the words of one journalist) 'you are not obliged to have a good memory'.

All this is a mirror image of the situation in many states, where secrecy is the norm and those breaching government or commercial secrecy rules can suffer loss of their employment and even imprisonment. The prospect of such a situation arising in Sweden has alarmed not only journalists but all those concerned with freedom of expression and open government; they believe that any change would destroy for ever the relative degree of trust which Swedish citizens place in their governments. Sweden's rulers have periodically tried, against fierce resistance, to weaken the level of access to information. The fear associated with Union membership is that documents previously classified as 'domestic' (and therefore available) will now, if they relate to Union decisions affecting Sweden, be reclassified as secret under the heading of 'international relations'. The government has promised to amend the Secrecy Act to limit this to cases where foreign relations could be harmed.[88] There are also reservations about the effect of the draft data protection Directive (Chapter 7), which includes limitations on individual access to officially held data. It is unfortunate that Sweden was not a member of the Union during the earlier negotiations on the Directive; there will, however, be plenty of opportunities for its views to be made plain when agreements under Title VI of the TEU come up for discussion. From the point of view of opening up the decision-making process, this can only be beneficial.

Principles Under Threat

Sweden's humanitarian traditions have been exemplified by a liberal interpretation of the concept of asylum. Chapter 3 of the 1989 Aliens Act[89] defines three categories of people eligible for asylum: refugees as defined in the Geneva Convention, 'war-resisters' who have deserted a theatre of war or fled to escape war service, and *de facto* refugees who can plead strong grounds for not wishing to return home on account of the political situation there. A fourth non-asylum category is defined in Chapter 2 of the same Act, which allows a permanent residence permit to be issued to 'an alien who, for humanitarian reasons, should be allowed to settle in Sweden'. Unlike most other immigrants, people in these categories may have residence applications considered when they are already in the country. Sweden has also accepted groups of 'quota refugees' from world crisis areas on the recommendation of UNHCR.

In the early 1990s this approach led Sweden to accept far more refugees per capita than most European countries. Money and resources were put into reception facilities; by the middle of 1993 there were about 90,000 asylum-seekers, mostly from the former Yugoslavia, in some 270 clearance and residential centres.[90] Those accepted were given every encouragement to integrate into Swedish society on a basis of equal opportunities; an earlier policy of arranging instruction to children and trainees in their native language was modified when it became apparent (as in the Netherlands) that this led to disadvantage in the job market. Although interpreters were still provided where needed, there was a new emphasis on offering free Swedish lessons to all immigrants. Most municipalities in the country were given grants to enable them to offer training and education to those accepted for residence; the idea was to avoid over-concentration in a few urban areas. This was only partly successful, as newcomers tended to gravitate to towns where relatives or compatriots were already settled.[91] This also led in time to the development of potential ghettos in which unemployment was high and Swedish was not an everyday language for many of those living there.

Thus in spite of good intentions, strains began to appear in applying the normal policy and instances of racist violence were reported in areas with a high concentration of asylum-seekers. A backlog of asylum applications built up, mainly from the former Yugoslavia; many had been shelved on the assumption that the war would soon be over. When it became clear that this was unlikely, a decision was taken in 1993 to consider for permanent residence some 40,000 Bosnians. At the same time, however, a visa requirement was imposed to limit future arrivals.[92] In 1994 a similar offer of residence on humanitarian grounds was made to 20,000 long-standing asylum-seekers with families, most of whom were ethnic Albanians from Kosovo.[93]

This contrasted with a previous programme of deporting most Kosovo Albanians on the grounds that they were not in danger,[94] a policy which brought protests from UNHCR and Swedish NGOs. Church-based NGOs had also complained about the rejection of Bosnians with Croatian passports, producing evidence that some of them were returned to Bosnia against their will.[95] Deportation of rejected asylum-seekers had generally become more common, including some disturbing cases where a whole family was deported because one member of it committed a minor crime;[96] even worse were some cases where child abuse and other crimes committed by a man led to his family being deported along with him.[97] After public protests a more humane approach was, however, adopted.

The liberal nature of the two decisions offering residence to certain large groups of people was also at odds with a general tightening up of asylum policy in which appeals were treated more stringently, as established by a commission of inquiry in 1994.[98] All this generated some confusion in public opinion, which after swinging against refugees in 1992 returned to a greater tolerance two years later.[99] There had previously been a proposal to revise the law to give the parliament more control and establish a more consistent policy,[100] but this was dropped with a change of government in 1991. Instead a special commission of inquiry was set up to advise on policy (not, as in some countries, an excuse for postponing action); after the 1994 election this was replaced by two commissions to consider asylum and immigration separately.[101] Human rights activists currently feel that there is an urgent need to articulate clearer policies that the public can understand, while reaffirming the humanitarian principles on which questions of asylum, immigration and integration have previously been decided. If this can be achieved for Sweden, it will form a major contribution to the debate on such issues throughout the Union.

THE UNITED KINGDOM

For many people in the UK, not least among politicians, 'Europe' starts
on the other side of the Channel; their citizenship of the Union means
nothing to them. The country's name implies another basic assumption
that periodically generates heated debate: that its component regions
will never be part of a federal structure because they are united under
a single monarchy and a central government. Disaffected Scots and others
living far from London see it more as an English oligarchy. These factors
help to explain why the notion of an increasingly federal European Union
is one that many English politicians, in particular, find hard to accept
or justify in public. For those who do not actively reject the whole idea
– a very vocal minority – the advantages of the Union are studiously
described in terms of the economic benefits alone. There is usually a
proviso that this need not involve anything as threatening to the idea
of national sovereignty as a common currency.

At the same time national pride, allied with an imperial habit of mind
from previous generations, leads government ministers to insist that
on all issues the UK must play a leading role in the Union. If all the
other members disagree on an issue of principle, it is assumed that in
due course they will see sense and follow the British line. This has been
particularly marked in the negotiations undertaken by the present and
previous Conservative governments. It has led to protracted and acrimonious disputes, some of which have been described in previous
chapters, over such matters as social policy, labour relations and the
powers of the institutions of the Union. Perhaps surprisingly, the end
result has often been a compromise in which the UK is allowed to stay
outside an arrangement accepted by the other Member States – most
noticeably in the case of the Social Protocol to the TEU. There are signs,
however, of growing impatience with these concessions; although the
UK may claim tacit support for its position over the future evolution
of the Union, the idea that it can continue to opt out of features with
which it disagrees may have run its course.

Repelling the Invader

The UK can claim with some justification to have long led the way (to
the despair of human rights campaigners) in one key area of Union policy:
the development of strict and discriminatory rules on asylum and
immigration. The pattern was set as long ago as 1905, when an Aliens
Act was brought in to satisfy agitation against the immigration of

'undesirable and destitute aliens' from Eastern Europe. The Act and its successors in 1914 and later years introduced all the features of immigration control that are familiar today: immigration officers with extensive powers to refuse entry, compulsory return by shipping companies of those rejected, deportation of aliens whose presence is 'not conducive to the public good', and *ad hoc* visa requirements (first aimed at Jewish refugees in the 1930s). Asylum from persecution was only granted as an exception to the rule. Then, as now, the popular press kept up the pressure with a rhetoric that has not changed at all: from the start there were dire warnings against 'opening the floodgates' and predictions that allowing more immigrants to arrive would stir up prejudice against those already admitted.

The policy became more explicitly racist (though this was denied by ministers) with the passage of the Commonwealth Immigrants Acts in 1962 and 1968. The first was intended to restrict the entry of black citizens of former colonies who had previously been welcomed as a source of labour, and the second to block the free entry of passport-holding members of the Asian communities of Kenya and Uganda. Later Acts restricted family reunification and introduced the 'primary purpose rule' for intending spouses (Chapter 5); British citizenship was also redefined as an instrument of immigration policy in which there were no less than six categories of 'citizen', only one of which had a right of abode in the UK.[102]

In the 1990s asylum policy, already criticised as arbitrary and inhumane,[103] was also made more restrictive in a way that roused unprecedented protests from the House of Lords, UNHCR, church leaders, lawyers' associations, local authorities, Amnesty International and many other NGOs. An Asylum Bill was first published in 1991 after an apparently orchestrated series of stories in the press, some of them from official sources, on alleged abuses of the asylum procedure by 'bogus refugees'. It became law in 1993 (after an intervening general election) as the Asylum and Immigration Appeals Act.[104] The main features were an accelerated appeals procedure and wide-ranging rules (issued along with the Act) listing reasons for refusal. Deportation to 'safe third countries' was expected to increase as a result.[105] The Carriers' Liability Act, already criticised as contravening the Geneva Convention,[106] was extended and the fingerprinting of asylum-seekers introduced. As a concession to popular resentment whipped up by the press, the possibility of asylum-seekers being housed by local authorities under homelessness legislation was curtailed.

Detention of asylum-seekers and subsequent deportation were both facilitated by the Act, and led to further protests when they were put into effect with particular harshness. Conditions in the prisons and detention centres in which asylum-seekers were held led in 1994 to a wave of hunger strikes[107] and a riot in one centre.[108] It was pointed out that the rights of detained asylum-seekers were in many respects inferior to those of prisoners on remand or even convicted criminals.[109] Government ministers were unrepentant, even when held to be in contempt of court after defying an order banning the deportation of an asylum-seeker.[110] Deportations were sometimes executed by using violent methods of restraint such as gagging with adhesive tape, leading in one case to the death of a woman after arrest.[111] In another case an asylum-seeker died in prison after being forcibly restrained.[112]

This institutionalised violence, although it appalled those concerned with the welfare of asylum-seekers and led to localised public protests, took place against a background of general public indifference. It was a sobering reminder that even a democratically elected government, when supported by a compliant press and a docile governing party, can authorise what in other systems would be condemned as deliberate denials of human rights.

An Uncertain Faith

The UK's position as an 'odd man out' in so many areas of Union policy has meant that changes in UK law have generally been either a continuation of existing trends (as in asylum and immigration) or minimalist concessions to Directives voted in against UK opposition. It is remarkable how little has changed since the predecessor to this book was written in 1990;[113] some of the measures successfully blocked by the UK at that time are only now going through under the new rules of the TEU. Margaret Thatcher set an example of combative nationalism that her political heirs, along with disciples from the time of her ascendancy, have attempted (with rather less panache) to emulate ever since.

It used to be said that things would be very different for the UK (better or worse, according to one's views on European Union) under a government of the main opposition Labour Party. Its earlier conversion from doubt to enthusiasm over Europe arose at a time when it was dawning on the trade union movement that social and labour policies were advancing a great deal faster in the rest of the EC than they were at home. The Social Charter and the later Protocol to the TEU exemplified this reforming drive. Things have, however, changed in many ways since then. Jacques Delors, who articulated the twin goals of social reform and federal development, will no longer be there to give a lead as he did in an inspirational address to the UK Trades Union Congress in 1988.[114] The Labour Party has changed itself into a social-democratic party of the centre, reducing its dependence on the unions and marginalising its left wing. The party's main preoccupation is to regain power after a long period out of office.

There is certainly a commitment to abandoning the UK's isolation on social policy. However, promises made in opposition do not always survive the transition to government. If public opinion showed itself hostile to closer union in general, perhaps in a referendum on an issue like the common currency, party policy might change in a way that disappointed those who were hoping for an end to the long years of insularity. Campaigners on all the issues discussed here will need to keep their concerns well to the fore in the prelude to any general election. The UK can in fact offer a useful lead to other Member States in certain areas: for example its Race Relations Act (Chapter 6), though criticised at home as inadequate, is widely admired elsewhere. The rancorous disputes of earlier years could yet be forgotten in a climate of more cooperative policy development at Union level.

NOTES

1. *Le Monde*, 30 November 1994; translated for the *Guardian*, 1 December 1994.
2. *Libertés et droits de l'homme: les textes fondamentaux* (Paris: Ligue des Droits de l'Homme, 1992). Published as a supplement to *Hommes & Libertés*, no. 64 (1992).
3. See for example Commission nationale consultative des Droits de l'Homme, *1992. La lutte contre le racisme et la xénophobie: exclusion et droits de l'homme* (Paris: La Documentation française, 1993).
4. Jean-Claude Bernheim and Giovana Borgese, *Racisme et police en France* (Paris: Fédération internationale des Ligues des Droits de l'Homme, 1991); Michel Wieworka, *Sociologie du racisme: police et racisme* (Paris: Institut des Hautes Écoles de la Securité Intérieure, 1991); 'Racism: torture and ill-treatment in Western Europe', *AI Newsletter* (London: Amnesty International) February 1993, pp. 3–6; *France: shootings, killings and alleged ill-treatment by law enforcement officers*, AI Index EUR 21/02/94 (London: Amnesty International, 1994).
5. *Migration News Sheet*, December 1993; July, October, November and December 1994.
6. *Le Monde*, 17 June 1993.
7. *Migration News Sheet*, June, July and August 1993.
8. *Ibid.*, June, July and September 1993.

9. *Ibid.*, June, July, August, September, October and December 1993; *Platform Fortress Europe?*, July–August and September 1993; *Dossiers et Documents* no. 12 (Paris: Ligue des Droits de l'Homme, 1993); *Migration News Sheet*, December 1994 (on family reunification).

10. See for instance *Légiférer pour mieux tuer des droits* (Paris: Groupe d'Information et de Soutien des Travailleurs Immigrés, 1993).

11. *Migration News Sheet*, September, October, November and December 1993.

12. *Ibid.*, April 1994.

13. *Ibid.*

14. *Ibid.*, February 1994; *Statewatch*, January–February 1994.

15. *Migration News Sheet*, November 1994 and January 1995.

16. *Ibid.*, September 1994; *Statewatch*, November–December 1994.

17. See for instance *Flüchtlingspolitik und Asylrecht* (Düsseldorf: DGB–Bundesvorstand, 1992); also (from the same source, undated) the multi-part series *Rechtsextremismus* and *Einwanderungsland Deutschland: Fremd in eigenen Land?*

18. *Unbequᵉm* (Hamburg: Bundesarbeitsgemeinschaft Kritischer Polizisten und Politzistinnen) June 1993, pp. 7–8.

19. *Migration News Sheet*, November 1994.

20. See also *Immigration, minorities, foreigners: problem-solving in Britain and Germany* (Warwick: University of Warwick Centre for Research in Ethnic Relations/University of East Anglia, 1995).

21. *Statewatch*, November–December 1994.

22. For a full account of German asylum law and procedures see *Asylum in Europe, vol. II: review of refugee and asylum laws and procedures in selected European countries* (London: European Council on Refugees and Exiles, 1994) pp. 147–213.

23. *Migration News Sheet*, February and June 1993; *Neues Asylrecht: Abschied vom Schutz für politisch Verfolgte?* (Bonn: Amnesty International, 1993).

24. *Migration News Sheet*, August 1993.

25. *Ibid.*, October 1994.

26. *Ibid.*, August 1994.

27. *Platform Fortress Europe?*, February 1994.

28. *Migration News Sheet*, September 1993.

29. *Migration News Sheet*, January 1995.

30. *Guardian*, 27 March 1991.

31. *Ibid.*, 13 July 1991.

32. *Migration News Sheet*, December 1991.

33. *Ibid.*, September 1993.

34. *Ibid.*, January 1993.

35. *Ibid.*, July 1993.

36. *Guardian*, 14 September 1993.
37. *Migration News Sheet*, June 1994.
38. For example Otto Diederichs, 'Das Polizei von Rostock', *Bürgerrechte & Polizei* (Free University, Berlin: CILIP) no. 1/1993, pp. 6–15; *Tageszeitung*, 18 March/1 April/15 April 1993.
39. Albrecht Funk, 'Rassismus: Kein Thema für die deutsche Polizei?', *ibid.*, pp. 34–40; *Platform Fortress Europe?*, December 1993–January 1994; *Statewatch*, October 1994.
40. Luigi Barzini, *The Italians* (London: Penguin, 1968) p. 14.
41. Massimo Pastore, 'Italy: migration policies and border controls in the European context', published in German as 'Italien als Einwanderungsland–Migrationspolitik und Grenzkontrollen im europäischen Kontext', *Bürgerrechte & Polizei* (Free University, Berlin: CILIP) no. 3/1993, p. 62.
42. *Ibid.*, May and June 1993.
43. *Ibid.*, October 1994.
44. *Ibid.*, November 1994.
45. *Ibid.*, September 1993.
46. 'Rom e Sinti: popoli senza diritti', *Senza Confine* (Rome) May 1993, pp. 39–40.
47. *Migration News Sheet*, June and September 1994.
48. *Ibid.*, July 1993.
49. 'Immigrati, cosa propone la CGIL', *Senza Confine* (Rome) October 1993, pp. 19–21.
50. Bruno Nascimbene, 'Law of asylum in Italy', in Kay Heilbronner (ed.), *Asyl- und Einwanderungsrecht im europäische Vergleich* (Köln: Bundesanzeiger, 1992) pp. 55–62.
51. Bruno Nascimbene, 'The Albanians in Italy: the right of asylum under attack', *International Journal of Refugee Law*, vol. 3 (1991) pp. 714–20.
52. Information from Consiglio Italiano per i Refugiati, Rome.
53. *Bozza per una Legge attuativa dell'articolo 10 Comma 3 Costituzione* (Rome: Consiglio Italiano per i Refugiati, 1994).
54. Used here in preference to 'Holland', which strictly speaking is only one of its twelve provinces.
55. *Migration News Sheet*, January 1994.
56. Aldo Kuijer, 'The reflection of changing attitudes: recent changes in Dutch immigration, nationality and anti-discrimintation law', in Philip G. Muus (ed.) *Migration, immigration and policy in the Netherlands: report for OECD* (Amsterdam: University of Amsterdam, Institute of Social Geography, 1993) pp. 37–55.
57. *Ibid.*, April and November 1994.
58. *Ibid*, December 1994.

59. *Ibid.*, April and June 1994.
60. *Ibid.*, November 1994; *Statewatch*, November–December 1994.
61. *Migration News Sheet*, January 1994; Jan Holvast and André Mosshammer (eds), *Identificatieplicht* (Utrecht: Van Arkel, 1993); *Privacy en Registratie* (Amsterdam), September 1993, pp. 5–22.
62. Kuijer, 'The reflection of changing attitudes' (note 56).
63. Sharda Kartaram, *Final report on legislation against racism and xenophobia in the Netherlands* (Utrecht: Landelijk Bureau Racismebestrijding, 1992) p. 23.
64. *Migration News Sheet*, December 1994.
65. *Ibid.*
66. *Ibid.*, October 1994.
67. Kartaram, *Final report* (note 63) p. 22.
68. Kuijer, 'The reflection of changing attitudes' (note 56); G.-R. de Groot, 'Een wetsontwerp ter wijziging van de Rijkswet op het Nederlanderschap', *Migrantenrecht* (1993) no. 5/6, pp. 91–104.
69. *Migration News Sheet*, November 1993.
70. Organic Law 7/1985 (1 July 1985).
71. *Migration News Sheet*, February 1992.
72. *Ibid.*, October 1991.
73. *Platform Fortress Europe?*, June 1994.
74. *Migration News Sheet*, March 1994.
75. *Ibid.*, June 1994.
76. *Ibid.*, April 1994.
77. *Ibid.*, January 1994.
78. Law 5/1984 (26 March 1984). For the text and full discussion see Diego López Garrido, *El derecho de asilo* (Madrid: Trotta, 1991).
79. Law 9/1994 (19 May 1994).
80. *Migration News Sheet*, April and June 1994.
81. *Ibid.*, September 1994.
82. *Ibid.*, September and November 1994.
83. *Organic Act concerning the Ombudsman* (in Spanish and English) (Madrid: Defensor del Pueblo, 1988).
84. *Situación jurídica y asistencial de los extranjeros en España* (Madrid: Defensor del Pueblo, 1994).
85. *The Constitution of Sweden 1989* (Stockholm: Swedish Riksdag, 1990); *Constitutional protection of rights and freedoms* (Stockholm: Swedish Institute, 1993).
86. For more on the history and implications of the Act see *Platform Fortress Europe?*, May 1993.
87. *The Swedish Secrecy Act* (Stockholm: Ministry of Justice, 1986).

88. *Guardian*, 9 November 1994; Brigitta Kruse, 'Open up, the Swedes are here', *European Brief* (December 1994) pp. 27–8; Rutger Lindahl, 'Bringing the EU up, not Sweden down', *ibid*. pp. 73–4.

89. *Aliens Act (1989:529) and Aliens Ordinance (1989:547) with amendments 19th January 1989* (Stockholm: Ministry of Culture, 1993); *Immigrant and refugee policy* (Stockholm: Ministry of Culture, 1993). The second of these sets out Swedish policy in an EU and global context.

90. *Immigrant and refugee policy* (note 89) p. 35.

91. *Migration News Sheet*, June 1994.

92. *Platform Fortress Europe?*, July–August 1993.

93. *Ibid.*, May 1994; *Migration News Sheet*, May 1994.

94. *Migration News Sheet*, February and March 1994.

95. *Ibid.*, December 1994.

96. *Ibid.*, November 1994.

97. *Statewatch*, September–October 1994.

98. 'Utvärdering av praxis i asylärenden' (with English summary), *Statens offentliga utredningar*, 1994:54.

99. *Migration News Sheet*, July 1994.

100. 'Aktiv flykting- och immigrationspolitik', *Regeringens proposition* 1990/91:195.

101. *Migration News Sheet*, December 1994.

102. Laurie Fransman, 'Future citizenship policy', in Sarah Spencer (ed.), *Strangers and citizens: a positive approach to migrants and refugees* (London: Rivers Oram/Institute for Public Policy Research, 1994) pp. 282–306.

103. *United Kingdom: deficient policy and practice for the protection of asylum-seekers*, AIBS/RO/2/91 (London: Amnesty International British Section, 1991).

104. *Migration News Sheet*, August 1993; Chris Randall, 'An asylum policy for the UK', in Sarah Spencer (ed.), *Strangers and citizens: a positive approach to migrants and refugees* (London: Rivers Oram/Institute for Public Policy Research, 1994) pp. 202–31.

105. *Passing the buck: deficient Home Office practice in 'safe third country' asylum cases*, AIBS/RO/1/93 (London: Amnesty International British Section, 1993).

106. *United Kingdom. A duty dodged: the government's evasion of its obligations under the 1951 UN Convention on Refugees*, AIBS/RO/4/91 (London: Amnesty International British Section, 1991).

107. *Statewatch*, March–April 1994; *Migration News Sheet*, April and July 1994.

108. *Migration News Sheet*, July 1994.

109. *Prisoners without a voice: asylum-seekers detained in the United Kingdom* (London: Amnesty International British Section, 1994); *Migration News Sheet*, November 1994.

110. *Guardian*, 28 February 1993; *Migration News Sheet*, September 1993.

111. *Migration News Sheet*, September 1993; *United Kingdom: cruel, inhuman or degrading treatment during forcible deportation*, AI Index EUR 45/05/94 (London: Amnesty International, 1994).

112. *Migration News Sheet*, September 1993; *Charter for immigration detainees* (London: Inquest/Joint Council for the Welfare of Immigrants, 1994).

113. Michael Spencer, *1992 And All That: civil liberties in the balance* (London: Civil Liberties Trust, 1990).

114. Jacques Delors, *Europe 1992: the social dimension* (London: Commission of the European Communities, 1988); Spencer, *1992 And All That* (note 113) p. 103.

Conclusion

We have examined in turn the nuts and bolts of the European Union's law-making process, the framework of international human rights law to which it owes allegiance, and the problems in that field which the Union and its Member States have so far failed to address. There is no shortage of suggestions for reform, but they have had little impact on government decisions. A lightning tour of seven Member States of the Union has shown that the issues causing concern vary in relative urgency in different states, but the general trend of official policy is similar in all of them: a steady erosion of basic rights and freedoms for many individuals, to an extent that ought to be quite unacceptable in a Union of democratic nations.

This process has not developed in a random manner but as a deliberate response to perceived problems by the governments of the Member States, now (since Maastricht) making joint decisions in the Justice and Home Affairs Council. Anyone not familiar with the system might well ask how this could come about without action to halt it from the Union's other institutions: the Commission, the Court of Justice and the democratically elected European Parliament. The sad fact emerging here has been their total inability to tackle most of the issues relevant to human rights and civil liberties, because the Treaty on European Union specifically excludes such matters from their legal competence (Chapter 1). Title VI of the treaty (the 'third pillar') allows intergovernmental agreements to be made without involving the other institutions in most areas of policy covering asylum, immigration and police cooperation. It merely gives a spurious legitimacy to what the governments would have decided anyway.

It has also become clear that national parliaments have in most cases no control over what their governments agree within the Council. This 'democratic deficit' is most acute for Title VI matters, since no elected body is directly involved in decision-making. It poses a real threat to individual rights. It has been said with some justice that if the Union

213

was a nation state applying for membership, it would be rejected on the grounds that it was not a democracy.

Without implying a conscious conspiracy to undermine human rights, we can discern a pattern at the national level that helps to explain what has happened. The abolition of internal frontiers, seen by many as a holy grail worth sacrifices in other areas, has raised real but so far unsubstantiated fears of a Europe at the mercy of criminal organisations, unhindered by border controls and operating on a Union-wide basis. Each government dreads the infiltration of criminals from its neighbours, and suspects the latter of being less than vigilant in controlling crime. How much the activities of professional criminals were ever hampered by border checks is rarely discussed. Instead, comprehensive schemes for police cooperation, backed by vast computer networks for exchanging information, have gone ahead: first the Schengen Information System, now at last ready to become operational (Chapter 3), and most recently Europol (see below). In parallel with this, new technologies will give the police and security forces ever more powerful ways of conducting surveillance of the population (Chapter 7). Little thought seems to have been given to where this could lead if it is not strictly controlled.

The Schengen Convention, contracted in secrecy among a central core of Member States, embraces much more than police cooperation and has as its other main purpose the exclusion from the entire territory of anyone placed on a list of 'undesirables' by any of the signatories. The Schengen model has been adopted for the draft of a Union-wide Convention on controlling the crossing of its external frontiers, coupled with an extensive common list of mainly Third World countries whose citizens will require a visa in order to enter (Chapter 3). Although signing has been held up on account of a recondite quarrel between Spain and the UK, planning has gone ahead for this and another Convention defining a European Information System for exchanging personal data and other information. All these Conventions are seriously lacking in parliamentary and judicial control.

The draft Convention for Europol (Chapter 7) goes well beyond the police aspects of the Schengen model and is highly significant for several reasons. It will embody not only a computerised system for exchanges of factual information between police forces, but also a central organisation to collect and analyse intelligence and other 'soft' data. Subject to token safeguards on data protection, it may exchange information with states and organisations outside the Union. It could in the future be assigned an operational role as a 'European FBI', and will in practice be at the bidding of the Council to work on whatever crimes the assembled ministers consider to be the most serious, drawn from a comprehensive list of possibilities.

Europol exemplifies everything that is wrong with the procedure for setting up an agreement under Title VI: although posing unknown dangers to the rights of individuals through potential mistakes or misuses of personal data, the Convention bringing Europol into existence has been negotiated in a total secrecy more appropriate to a diplomatic treaty between nation states on a matter of war and peace. Nothing like it has been attempted before, yet the remedies open to the individual for any abuses are poorly defined and quite untested. It relies on every national police force following strict principles of data protection that may be quite novel to them. Europol has, however, moved inexorably forward amid exhortations that time is short and action must be taken. It has acquired a momentum of its own, and all those involved in it now have a vested interest in giving it ever-widening powers.

While Europol is designed to allay fears about a coming upsurge in international crime, other measures have been pushed through in response to claims that too many people are being allowed to enter the Union as refugees (Chapter 4) or as immigrants seeking work (Chapter 5). The excuse for clamping down on refugees has been that many of them are alleged to be 'bogus' asylum-seekers whose real motive is to benefit from the higher standard of living and social benefits offered within the Union. Again the hard evidence is largely lacking, since the only firm fact is that many more people sought asylum in the 1980s than in previous decades. There are other more plausible explanations for the change in view of the increasingly turbulent and dangerous state of many parts of the world, not to mention the famine and desperate poverty that are just as life-threatening as political persecution. The outcome, however, has been a set of draconian restrictions on the acceptance of refugees, agreed between Member States and again transacted outside the reach of Community law.

The first barrier to be surmounted by would-be refugees is the refusal of airlines to transport anyone not holding valid documents for entering the Member State concerned. If the airlines do accept such people, they stand to suffer heavy financial penalties imposed by their governments under an agreed policy of 'carrier sanctions'. Obtaining proper documents may be impossible for a person who is in fear of the authorities; and since refugees can only (under the Geneva Convention) apply for asylum after leaving their own country, this prevents an unknown number from ever submitting their claims. Governments have thus turned the airlines into reluctant agents of their immigration departments, and in so doing have clearly breached the spirit if not the letter of both the Geneva Convention and the Chicago Convention on civil aviation.

The second new measure affecting refugees is the uniform application of a 'host third country' (or 'safe third country') rule, under which anyone who *could* have claimed asylum in another country at an earlier stage of their journey to the Union may be promptly sent there, without any further examination of their claim. They do not even need to have set foot in that country, so long as it is believed to adhere to the Geneva Convention's rule prohibiting *refoulement* (return to a country where there is a risk of persecution).

Refugees surviving this test then face the edicts of an earlier intergovernmental agreement, the Dublin Convention. Although still not legally in force, it has been enthusiastically applied in practice. Following the precedent of the Schengen Convention, it lays down a 'one chance only' rule under which an asylum seeker can only submit an application to one Member State. This is purported to aim at ending the scandal of the 'refugee in orbit', shuttled from one state to another, by laying down strict rules defining which state must examine the application. The basic injustice of the system is that there is still no uniform interpretation of the narrow and increasingly outdated criteria of the Geneva Convention, so there is no guarantee that a person rejected by one state would fail to be accepted elsewhere. When it comes to *de facto* refugees allowed to stay on humanitarian or other special grounds (a dwindling proportion in some countries), then the variation in national practice is even wider.

Coupled with all this there are new measures to enable the rapid expulsion of those not accepted as 'genuine' refugees. New 'accelerated procedures' with minimal or non-existent rights of appeal are being brought in to ensure the prompt removal of those whose applications for asylum are deemed 'manifestly unfounded'. To enable such deportations to proceed smoothly, Member States have negotiated a growing array of bilateral 'readmission agreements' with states bordering the Union. These states in turn have started to negotiate similar agreements with countries lying even further from the Union.

Immigration of workers to the Union has been drastically cut back since the days when many from poorer countries were welcomed in order to fill temporary shortages of labour. In addition, stricter rules have been agreed to make the employment of those who do arrive more insecure, so that their chances of staying on are reduced. A remaining major source of immigration has been family reunification with those already established as residents. This could not be stopped without blatantly contravening the international Conventions asserting the importance of family life. Undeterred by this, the Member States have agreed on rules for immigrants that are far less generous than those applied to citizens moving from one Member State to another, by restricting as much as possible the categories of relative who have a right to be admitted. Wives are offered no independent right to stay in the event of a separation. Finally, Member States may reject anyone suspected of marrying a legal resident for the purpose of staying in the Union.

All this has helped to sour relations between the Union's native citizens and its many established immigrants, of whom some 10 million lack the nationality of a Member State. The second-class status of people without citizenship rights is a severe handicap, in some cases affecting even the children or grandchildren of the original immigrant, and no measures of 'harmonisation' or equalisation of rights have been forthcoming. Vicious press campaigns against illegal immigrants and 'bogus' asylum-seekers have fostered suspicion of anyone whose appearance denotes an origin from outside the Union. Racism (Chapter 6) has emerged in countries where it was virtually unknown before, and grown stronger in others where a colonial past left an inheritance of racist attitudes. Too many politicians in government have been woefully weak in failing to take a public stand against these developments, for fear of alienating a section of their electorates. At the Union level, action has been avoided on the dubious grounds that the treaties do not provide for Union legislation to deal with racism.

HOPE FOR THE FUTURE

The catalogue of negative developments outlined above might lead one to despair of ever reversing the trend and giving the Union a more humane motivation, more in keeping with the high ideals of those who founded the European Community. Certain facts do nevertheless encourage a guarded optimism. The first is that the Treaty on European Union is not cast in stone and has built into it a mechanism for periodic revision. The next opportunity for this arises in 1996, though discussions will have started well before that. Despite the declared intention of some Member States to change nothing or even to roll back the powers of the Union's institutions, others regard the present arrangement as inadequate and would welcome an enlargement of the scope of Community law to cover Title VI.

This would need to be coupled with a real law-making function for the democratically elected European Parliament, whose powers are currently weaker than those of any Member State parliament. As in other areas of Community law, the Court of Justice would be there to ensure a uniform interpretation of Union decisions by national governments.

In this connection, a written Constitution or Bill of Rights for the Union would make it easier for the Court to monitor new legislation for its adherence to the principles of human rights. At the very least, a reformed treaty should specifically condemn all forms of discrimination in addition to that affecting women. It should also lay down the principle that long-term residents lacking nationality of a Member State should have all the rights assigned to nationals as full citizens of the Union.

Even before revision of the treaty, new Member States like Sweden are likely to press for an end to the secrecy that surrounds Council decision-making, particularly where Title VI matters affecting the individual are concerned. With the possible advent of other new members, the Union is bound to overhaul its institutional structure and legislative procedures in some way to make them less unwieldy and slow to achieve agreement. There will be an opportunity for all non-governmental organisations to press for solutions that enhance democracy and guarantee equal rights for all, including a firm commitment to apply the same standards to those wishing to enter the Union from outside.

There is a chance in all this for the Union to embrace a less inward-looking philosophy and one not solely devoted to economic progress. This could involve a far-reaching overhaul of the policies followed on foreign trade in particular, so as to alleviate the dire conditions of life in the Third World that generate so many asylum-seekers and would-be immigrants to the Union. Such changes will take a long time to achieve and be slow to show an effect, but setting an example in this field could be the Union's most rewarding and lasting legacy to the world as a whole.

Finally, this book has highlighted some areas in which particular Member States can offer a better model for the Union to adopt (Chapter 8). France's Constitution, despite coming under political pressure, remains a reassuring reminder that the same principles of human rights remain valid over the centuries. They have been invoked in France as a fundamental basis for legislation covering even a technically complex matter like data protection. Germany, which also sets a high standard in that area, shows that it is possible (albeit with some strains) to accept refugees in far greater numbers than the limits insisted upon by many of its partners in the Union. Italy's parliament, in the midst of a long-running saga of political uncertainty, can still be persuaded to consider a model refugee law that would be more just than those being rushed through the legislatures of other states.

The Netherlands offers a strong lead to the parliamentarians of all other Member States, having showed that against all the odds, government ministers can indeed be held to account in a meaningful way for the positions they adopt in the Council. The Dutch government cannot (as in most other countries) present its parliament with an unexpected *fait accompli*, because a degree of prior consultation is guaranteed. The Danish parliament has similar powers where Union legislation is concerned. However, in the highly sensitive area of intergovernmental agreements where the European Parliament is excluded, the Dutch parliament is unique in being able to forbid its ministers to sign such an instrument unless the parliament has considered the full text and approved it. In the absence of a reform of the Union treaties to eliminate the democratic deficit in this area, all national governments should insist on adopting the Dutch model of parliamentary scrutiny.

Spain offers a little-known but highly successful model for the internal protection of human rights and civil liberties against any agency of the state. The *Defensor del Pueblo* has a virtually unrestricted power to investigate individual complaints of almost every kind and from any person whatever, using as a mandatory standard a modern and comprehensive Constitution. The *Defensor* can also be petitioned to challenge any new law that may be unconstitutional, so that the matter is taken up by the Constitutional Court. The powers of ombudsmen in other Member States, even in Sweden where the idea originated, are relatively more circumscribed. The restricted role assigned to the Community Ombudsman, only recently created by the Treaty on European Union, is feeble by comparison. The Spanish model could be usefully be copied at both national and Union levels.

Sweden's tradition of open government illustrates a truth that has yet to dawn on most of its new partners in the Union. With 'transparency' legally guaranteed in most activities of government and watched over by a vigilant press, Swedish citizens actually trust their rulers to an extent that astonishes observers from other cultures. The listing of everyone on a government database does not evoke the same suspicions about what might be done with the information; it is seen simply as a means of running the system more efficiently, rather than a tool of 'Big Brother'. When social problems arise and the government sets up an investigating commission, there is more confidence than elsewhere that this will lead to action rather than a shelving of the issue. It takes time to build up such trust, and other governments would do well to make the effort before their ministers sink even lower in public esteem.

Finally the UK, despite its capacity to pick a quarrel with every other Member State and its enthusiasm for the more repressive intergovernmental agreements, offers one example of a firm approach to a problem in human rights. Its Race Relations Act, despite its defects, is unique in Europe in having legal enforcement built into it. Though it has failed to banish racism from the UK, the Act shows that this is an area (like equal pay for equal work by women and men) where enforceable legislation is both feasible and effective when properly applied. The model could be followed at Union level in order to protect all other disadvantaged or minority groups whose interests have so far been neglected.

The view is not all bleak, then; but there are enough warning signs to indicate that the Union is in danger of losing the support of its peoples if the present repressive trend cannot be reversed. The Union needs to be seen more as a supranational authority on the side of the ordinary person, rather than an impersonal bureaucracy which 'harmonises' national laws to the detriment of individual rights. Government ministers need to stand back from their attempts to manipulate the system in a constant quest for national advantage, and ask themselves whether they could do more to make the Union an institution to be admired and supported both inside and outside its boundaries. Last but not least, all those outside government who care about the issues need to continually point out ways in which such a change could be brought about.

Appendix: Sources of Information

In the telephone and fax numbers given below, the country and area codes for international dialling are shown in square brackets.

The *Commission of the European Communities* has its headquarters in Brussels with the postal address rue de la Loi 200, B-1049 Brussels, Belgium (tel. [32 2] 299 1111). National offices of the Commission can provide the direct-line numbers of individuals or their departments.

The *European Parliament* is at rue Belliard 97-113, B-1047 Brussels, Belgium (tel. [32 2] 284 2111); Palais de l'Europe, F-67075 Strasbourg Cedex, France (tel. [33 88] 174 001); and L-2929 Luxembourg (tel. [352] 430 01). MEPs have offices in both Brussels and Strasbourg, while the Directorate-General for Research is based in Luxembourg. A list of all MEPs with their national office addresses and telephone/fax numbers is given in publications such as *Vacher's European Companion*, 113 High Street, Berkhamsted HP4 2DJ, UK (tel. [44 1442] 876 135, fax 870 148).

The headquarters of the *United Nations High Commissioner for Refugees* is at CP 2500, CH-1211 Geneva, Switzerland (tel. [41 22] 739 8111, fax 731 8546) and there are also offices in Member States; these are listed in the ELENA handbook (see below) along with offices in some non-EU states. The office at rue van Eyck 11a, B-1050 Brussels, Belgium (tel. [32 2] 649 0153/8119, fax 641 9005) deals particularly with European Union matters.

Documentation Centres and Databases

The Commission has offices and information points in every Member State and a number of other countries as well, and these may incorporate a small library. However, detailed enquiries about documents are increasingly referred to the European Documentation Centres (EDCs) attached to academic institutions across the Union. All of these have the daily *Official Journal of the European Communities*; they also hold copies of Commission policy papers and proposals for legislation (the 'COM documents') and other official material, but a proportion of the EDCs hold only those relating to a restricted range of policy areas. There are moves to involve public libraries in the information network, so that copies of documents may be requested through a local branch library. The more important ones may also be sold through state publishing agencies. Material from Eurostat is held comprehensively by only one central library in each Member State.

The European Parliament has offices in every Member State, again with libraries in some cases. The reports of committees of the Parliament are held there, together with the *Official Journal* but not most of the Commission documents. EDCs also hold the Parliament's committee reports, but only on microfiche.

On-line databases covering all aspects of Union activity are accessible through a computer modem and telephone line, on paying a sub-scription to a public packet-switched data network (PSDN). There are further charges for access to the more useful databases. Some of them are also available as CD-ROMs. For information contact *Eurobases*, c/o Commission of the European Communities, rue de la Loi 200, B-1049 Brussels, Belgium (tel. [32 2] 295 0001/0003, fax 296 0624).

As explained in Chapter 2, Council of Europe documents may have to be obtained from the headquarters at Palais de l'Europe, 67075 Strasbourg Cedex, France (switchboard tel. [33 88] 41 2000; general infor-mation 41 2560, fax 41 2790; main publications 41 2033, fax 41 2780; human rights 41 2024, fax 41 2704/2825; legal affairs 41 2202, fax 41 2764/2794; migration 41 2166, fax 41 2785). A telephone call is the best way of ensuring a response.

Regular Publications

Commercial periodicals giving details of recent developments include the daily *Agence Europe* and other regular journals covering the whole range of Union activity, but some of these are voluminous and expensive. A comprehensive bimonthly digest of information is provided by *European Access*, published in the UK (Chadwick-Healey, Cambridge) and held by libraries. Readers of this book will have noticed, however, that the chapter notes most often refer to specialist news bulletins. These are produced by NGOs at a much smaller subscription cost, and include critical comments by experts in the field. The three bulletins most often cited here are as follows:

- *Migration News Sheet,* rue Joseph II 172, B-1040 Brussels, Belgium (tel. [32 2] 230 3750, fax 231 1413). Published in French as *Migrations Europe.* Subscribers also receive free copies of new CCME Briefing Papers (see below). For a higher cost, 'corresponding subscribers' can ask for copies from a list of the more important recent documents issued by the Commission, the European Parliament, the Council of Europe and other sources.
- *Fortress Europe?,* (formerly *Platform Fortress Europe?*) Blomstervägen 7, S-9133 Falun, Sweden (tel./fax [46 23] 267 77).
- *Statewatch,* PO Box 1516, London N16 0EW, UK (tel. [44 181] 802 1882, fax 880 1727). Also offers other publications and floppy disks containing past and current material.

Occasional mention has also been made of *ESMV List of Events,* a bulletin issued by the Netherlands Centre for Immigrants, Kanaalweg 84b, Postbus 638, 3500 AP Utrecht, The Netherlands (tel. [31 30] 963 084, fax 944 410 or 941 410); *JCWI Bulletin* from the Joint Council for the Welfare of Immigrants (JCWI), 115 Old Street, London EC1V 9JR, UK (tel. [44 171] 251 8708, fax 251 5100); and *Privacy Laws & Business,* Roxeth House, Shaftesbury Avenue, Harrow HA2 0PZ, UK (tel. [44 181] 423 1300, fax 423 4536). The last organisation also hosts an annual conference on data protection with a strong emphasis on Union legislation. Another source of information on questions of asylum, immigration, policing and especially racism is the bimonthly *European Race Audit,* a digest of country reports published by the Institute of Race Relations, 2–6 Leeke Street, London WC1X 9HS, UK (tel. [44 171] 837 0041, fax 278 0623). For Italian readers there is *Aspemigrazioni,* via Giolitti 21, 10123 Turin, Italy (tel. [39 11] 839 5443, fax 839 5577).

Non-governmental Organisations

Only NGOs with a transnational scope or a broad interest in Union affairs will be listed here. A directory of national organisations active in many of the areas covered here is published by *United for Intercultural Action,* Postbus 413, 1000 AK Amsterdam, The Netherlands. (tel. [31 20] 623 4902, fax 623 4902 or 636 7270).

NGOs concerned with the whole range of human rights are not numerous and some are much more active than others. Many of them are linked by the *Fédération Internationale des Ligues des Droits de l'Homme*

(FIDH), 40 Passage Dubail, F-75010 Paris, France (tel. [33 1] 4037 5426, fax 4472 0586). An FIDH project on human rights in the European Union is hosted by the Ligue des Droits de l'Homme at rue Watteau 6, B-1000 Brussels, Belgium (tel. [33 2] 502 1426, fax 502 1819). The *Quaker Council for European Affairs* is at square Ambiorix 50, B-1040 Brussels, Belgium (tel. [32 2] 230 4935, fax 230 6370).

Lawyers, advice agencies and documentation centres relating to asylum seekers and refugees are linked by the *European Legal Network on Asylum* (ELENA) and listed in an annual handbook published by the *European Council for Refugees and Exiles* (ECRE) from 3 Bondway, London SW8 1SJ, UK (tel. [44 171] 820 1156 for ELENA or 582 9928 for ECRE, fax 820 9725). Each country has an ELENA coordinator.

Amnesty International has an International Secretariat at 1 Easton Street, London WC1X 8DJ, UK (tel. [44 171] 413 5500, fax 956 1157); its reports are distributed by national offices in each country (including the UK). National sections are not authorised to work on abuses of human rights in their own countries, with the important exception of the mal-treatment of asylum-seekers; they may therefore issue their own reports on that topic.

The *Churches' Commission for Migrants in Europe* (CCME) is at rue Joseph II 174, B-1040 Brussels, Belgium (tel. [33 2] 230 2011, fax 231 1413). The *Migrants' Forum* is at rue de Trèves 33, B-1040 Brussels, Belgium (tel. [32 2] 230 1414/2412, fax 230 1461). A European Directory of Ethnic Minority and Migrant Organisations is published by JCWI (see previous section). Lawyers and NGOs working in different European countries for both immigrants and asylum-seekers are listed by the *Immigration Law Practitioners' Association*, 115 Old Street, London EC1V 9JR, UK (tel. [44 171] 250 1671, fax 253 3832).

The *Standing Committee of Experts on International Immigration, Refugee and Criminal Law* (the 'Meijers committee') has its secretariat at Postbus 638, 3500 AP Utrecht, The Netherlands (tel. [31 30] 963 900, fax 944 410).

Anti-racist groups tend to be organised on a fairly localised basis, though some of them share titles similar to *SOS Racism*. The few police monitoring groups are also largely national in scope.

The *Minority Rights Group* is at 379 Brixton Road, London SW9 7DE, UK (tel. [44 171] 978 9498, fax 738 6265). The *Roma National Council*, which publishes a regular *Rom News*, is at Simon von Utrecht Str., D-20359 Hamburg, Germany (tel. [49 40] 319 4249, fax 310 475).

Women's organisations in different countries send delegates to meetings of the *European Women's Lobby*, rue de Meridien 22, B-1030 Brussels, Belgium (tel. [32 2] 217 9020, fax 219 8451).

Workers' rights and general matters of social policy are covered by the *European Trade Union Confederation*, rue Montagne aux Herbes Potagères 37, B-1000 Brussels, Belgium (tel. [32 2] 209 2411, fax 218 3566).

The *International Lesbian and Gay Association* is at rue du Marché au Charbon 81, B-1000 Brussels, Belgium (tel./fax [32 2] 502 2471).

The *European Forum for Child Welfare* is at rue Defacqz 1, B-1050 Brussels, Belgium (tel. [32 2] 534 5547, fax 534 5275).

NGOs in the areas of civil liberty, health, social welfare and culture subscribe to *Euro Citizen Action Service* (ECAS), rue Defacqz 1, B-1050 Brussels, Belgium (tel. [32 2] 534 5166, fax 534 5275). Discrimination of any kind is a special ECAS concern.

The problems arising when citizens of one Member State are arrested and imprisoned in another (a topic not covered here, but one where injustices continue to arise) are the concern of *Fair Trials International*, Bench House, Ham Street, Richmond TW10 7HR, UK (tel./fax [44 181] 332 2800).

This is, of course, a far from exhaustive list but workers in any organisation are generally happy to help with details of other groups in their field and the names of particular experts. Writing a letter to a busy NGO does not guarantee a reply, and the best course for a seeker after information is to obtain the name of a person who can be contacted by fax or preferably by telephone.

Index

Main or defining entries are shown in bold type